RESEARCH TO PRACTICE?

IMPLICATIONS OF RESEARCH ON THE CHALLENGING BEHAVIOUR OF PEOPLE WITH LEARNING DISABILITY

Edited by Chris Kiernan

PUBLICATIONS
bild

Library of Congress Cataloging in Publications Data

Research to Practice? Implications of research on the challenging behaviour of people with learning disability/ edited by Chris Kiernan.
p. cm.
Includes bibliographical references and index.
ISBN 1 873791 25 9 (pbk.): £19.95 ($42.00 U.S.)
1. Mentally handicapped – Mental Health – Congresses. 2. Mentally handicapped – Behavior modification – Congresses. 3. Behavior disorders in children – Congresses. 4. Mentally handicapped – Services for – Great Britain. 5. Learning disabled – Services for – Great Britain. I. Kiernan, Chris.
(DNLM: 1. Learning Disorders – therapy – congresses. 2. Self-Injurious Behaviour – therapy – congresses. 3. Behavior Therapy – congresses. WS 110 R4325 1993)
RC451.4.M47R47 1993
362.1'968588 – dc20
DNLM/DLC
for Library of Congress
93-8150
CIP

British Library Cataloguing in Publication Data

A CIP catalogue record for this book is available from the British Library.

ISBN 1 873791 25 9

First Published 1993

© **Copyright 1993 BILD Publications**

BILD Publications is the publishing office of the
British Institute of Learning Disabilities (Registered Charity No. 1019663)

Published and distributed by:
BILD Publications, Frankfurt Lodge, Clevedon Hall,
Victoria Road, Clevedon Avon BS21 7SJ England

*Printed & bound by the Cookley Printers Limited,
Baskerville House, 56 Bridge Road, Cookley, Kidderminster,
Worcs, England DY10 3SB.*

*Cover design by Hothouse Image,
26 Lower Wood, The Rock, Telford TF3 5DN*

CONTENTS

                                                                    Page

Foreword iv

Acknowledgement vi

Affiliations and Funders vii

PART 1 - EPIDEMIOLOGY   Page

1. **EPIDEMIOLOGY OF SELF-INJURY, CHARACTERISTICS OF
   PEOPLE WITH SEVERE SELF-INJURY AND INITIAL
   TREATMENT OUTCOME**
   Glynis H Murphy, Chris Oliver, John Corbett, Lissa Crayton,
   Jackie Hales, Donna Head and Scott Hall 1

2. **ASSESSING THE PREVALENCE OF AGGRESSIVE
   BEHAVIOUR AND THE EFFECTIVENESS OF
   INTERVENTIONS**
   Oliver Russell and Phil Harris... 37

3. **CHALLENGING BEHAVIOUR**
   Chris Kiernan and Hazel Qureshi 53

PART 2 - FAMILY RESPONSES   Page

4. **FAMILY FACTORS AND PARENTS' REPORT OF
   BEHAVIOUR PROBLEMS IN 6-14 YEAR OLD CHILDREN
   WITH DOWN'S SYNDROME**
   Tricia Sloper and Steve Turner 69

5. **IMPACT ON FAMILIES: YOUNG ADULTS WITH LEARNING
   DISABILITY WHO SHOW CHALLENGING BEHAVIOUR**
   Hazel Qureshi 89

PART 3 - ANALYSIS AND MANAGEMENT
Page

6. **CHALLENGING BEHAVIOUR IN PEOPLE WITH SEVERE LEARNING DISABILITIES BEHAVIOUR MODIFICATION OR BEHAVIOUR ANALYSIS?**
Bob Remington 119

7. **SELF-INJURIOUS BEHAVIOUR: FROM RESPONSE TO STRATEGY**
Chris Oliver 135

PART 4 - SERVICE ORGANISATION
Page

8. **SUPPORTING PEOPLE WITH SEVERE LEARNING DISABILITIES AND CHALLENGING BEHAVIOURS IN ORDINARY HOUSING**
David Felce and Kathy Lowe 191

9. **THE SPECIAL DEVELOPMENT TEAM**
Peter McGill and Jim Mansell 209

10. **COMMUNITY SUPPORT TEAMS FOR PEOPLE WITH LEARNING DISABILITIES AND CHALLENGING BEHAVIOURS**
Eric Emerson, Paul Cambridge, Jane Forrest and
Jim Mansell 229

11. **SERVICE PROVISION FOR PEOPLE WITH MILD LEARNING DISABILITY AND CHALLENGING BEHAVIOURS: THE MIETS EVALUATION**
Julie Dockrell, George Gaskell, Hamid Rehman and
Charles Normand 245

PART 5 - STAFF TRAINING   Page

12. **WORKING WITH PARENTS: THE MANAGEMENT OF SLEEP DISTURBANCE IN CHILDREN WITH LEARNING DISABILITIES**
    Lyn Quine 273

13. **TRAINING CLINICAL PRACTITIONERS**
    Peter McGill and E Veronica Bliss 305

14. **SOME DETERMINANTS OF STAFF FUNCTIONING IN RELATION TO BEHAVIOURAL CHALLENGES FROM PEOPLE WITH LEARNING DISABILITIES (A view from a national training and consultancy service)**
    John Clements 321

PART 6 - NATIONAL GUIDANCE   Page

15. **SERVICES FOR PEOPLE WITH LEARNING DISABILITIES AND CHALLENGING BEHAVIOUR OR MENTAL HEALTH NEEDS: THE PROJECT GROUP REPORT**
    Jim Mansell 333

PART 7 - RESEARCH TO PRACTICE?   Page

16. **FUTURE DIRECTIONS FOR RESEARCH AND SERVICE DEVELOPMENT FOR PEOPLE WITH LEARNING DISABILITIES AND CHALLENGING BEHAVIOUR**
    Chris Kiernan 351

INDEX 366

FOREWORD

People with learning disabilities and challenging behaviour represent one of the most important and demanding sections of the learning disabilities population. In particular, with the moves to community care for all people with learning disability, they present a significant challenge to that initiative.

The needs of people with challenging behaviour have long been recognised by Department of Health policy makers as well as field agencies. This recognition has led to substantial attention being paid to the group on the policy side culminating in the setting up of a Project Group the remit of which was to provide specific guidance concerning needs and services to health and social services authorities. The outcome of the work of this Group was published in February 1993 as the Mansell Report (see Mansell, Chapter 15, this volume).

During the last two decades the Department of Health have also funded a substantial amount of research concerning challenging behaviour.

In 1990 Eleanor Grey from the Research and Development Division of the UK Department of Health obtained funds to mount a conference centering on research on the challenging behaviour of people with learning disabilities funded by the Department. The Learning Disabilities Client Group felt that the papers in the conference should try to draw out the implications of research for policy and practice.

The Hester Adrian Research Centre, as one of the main recipients of Department of Health funding for research on challenging behaviour, offered to organise the conference and to edit the proceedings. The Department agreed that, rather than restricting coverage solely to Department of Health research, projects funded by other agencies in the UK should also be included. In addition to research projects it also seemed essential to include papers on dissemination of research and "good practice".

The participants in the conference were invited as representatives of key organisations which had an influence on national and regional policies, on service provision, training, and research. The response to our invitations was excellent. It was generally agreed that the conference was successful in providing an atmosphere of open discussion of key issues of concern to policy workers, service providers, and researchers.

Jackie Hales from the Hester Adrian Research Centre undertook the task of organising the practical arrangements for the conference with great ability and enthusiasm. She also successfully organised all the presenters into providing extended abstracts of their presentations prior to the conference and prepared this manuscript for publication. I would like to thank her on my own behalf, and on behalf of the other presenters and the participants, for her tremendous contribution. I would also like to offer thanks to my colleague Eric Emerson whose help in constructing the programme was invaluable. Thanks should also go to the presenters who invested a great deal of work in preparing and presenting their papers and who (in the main!) kept to publication deadlines.

Finally, special thanks should go to Eleanor Grey without whose resolve and continued support the conference could never have taken place.

ACKNOWLEDGEMENT

Figures 2 and 3 in Chapter 1 are reprinted with the kind permission of the Editor of the Journal of Intellectual Disability Research (formerly Journal of Mental Deficiency Research).

AFFILIATIONS AND FUNDERS

E Veronica Bliss, Honorary Lecturer,
Hester Adrian Research Centre, University of Manchester. The Manchester Diploma is supported by Burnley, Pendle, and Rossendale District Health Authority.

Paul Cambridge, Lecturer in Applied Psychology of Mental Handicap,
Centre for Applied Psychology of Social Care, University of Kent at Canterbury.
Research funded by the Joseph Rowntree Foundation and the Mental Health Foundation.

John Clements
Applied Psychology Services, Warlingham, Surrey

John Corbett, Professor of Developmental Psychiatry,
Department of Psychiatry, University of Birmingham.
Formerly Clinical Teacher, Institute of Psychiatry, London.
Research funded by a Department of Health grant to the Institute of Psychiatry, London.

Lissa Crayton, Research Worker,
Psychology Department, Institute of Psychiatry, London.
Research funded by the Department of Health.

Julie Dockrell, Lecturer in Psychology,
Department of Social Psychology, London School of Economics, London.
Research funded by the Nuffield Foundation and South East Thames Regional Health Authority.

Eric Emerson, Senior Research Fellow, Deputy Director,
Hester Adrian Research Centre, University of Manchester.
Research funded by the Jospeh Rowntree Foundation and the Mental Health Foundation.

David Felce, Director,
Mental Handicap in Wales: Applied Research Unit, Department of Psychological Medicine, University of Wales College of Medicine, Cardiff.
Research funded by a Department of Health grant to Health Care Evaluation Research Team, University of Southampton and the Department of Health/Welsh Office.

Jane Forrest, Research Fellow,
Centre for Applied Psychology of Social Care, University of Kent at Canterbury.
Research funded by the Joseph Rowntree Foundation and the Mental Health Foundation.

George Gaskell, Senior Lecturer in Social Psychology,
Department of Social Psychology, London School of Economics, London.
Research funded by the Nuffield Foundation and South East Thames Regional Health Authority.

Jackie Hales, Research Worker,
Psychology Department, Institute of Psychiatry, London.
Research funded by the Department of Health.

Scott Hall, Research Worker,
Psychology Department, Institute of Psychiatry, London.
Research funded by the Department of Health.

Phil Harris, Lecturer,
Cardiff Institute of Higher Education, Cardiff.
Formerly Research Fellow, Norah Fry Research Centre, University of Bristol.
Research funded by the Department of Health.

Donna Head, Principal Clinical Psychologist,
Leicestershire Health Authority.
Formerly Research Worker, Psychology Department, Institute of Psychiatry, London.
Research funded by a Department of Health grant to the Institute of Psychiatry, London.

Chris Kiernan, Professor of Behavioural Studies in Mental Handicap,
Hester Adrian Research Centre, University of Manchester.
Research funded by the Department of Health.

Kathy Lowe, Research Fellow,
Mental Handicap in Wales: Applied Research Unit, Department of
Psychological Medicine, University of Wales College of Medicine, Cardiff.
Research funded by the Department of Health/Welsh Office.

Peter McGill, Senior Lecturer in Applied Psychology of Mental Handicap,
Centre for Applied Psychology of Social Care, University of Kent at
Canterbury.
Funding from the South East Thames Regional Health Authority for the
Special Development Team, its evaluation and the Kent Diploma.

Jim Mansell, Professor of Applied Psychology of Mental Handicap, Director,
Centre for Applied Psychology of Social Care, University of Kent at
Canterbury.
Research funded by the Joseph Rowntree Foundation, the Mental Health
Foundation, and the South East Thames Regional Health Authority.

Glynis H Murphy, Senior Lecturer in Psychology,
Psychology Department, Institute of Psychiatry, London.
Research funded by the Department of Health.

Charles Normand, Professor of Health Policy,
Department of Public Health and Policy Health Services Research Unit,
London School of Hygiene and Tropical Medicine, London.
Research funded by Nuffield Foundation and South East Thames Regional
Health Authority grants to the Department of Social Psychology, London
School of Economics.

Chris Oliver, Senior Lecturer in Psychology,
Psychology Department, Institute of Psychiatry, London.
Research funded by the Department of Health and the Mental Health
Foundation. Computer equipment donated by Viglen Limited.

Lyn Quine, Senior Research Fellow,
Centre for Research in Health Behaviour, Institute of Social and Applied Psychology, University of Kent at Canterbury.
Research funded by the Department of Health, the Joseph Rowntree Foundation, and the Mental Health Foundation.

Hazel Qureshi, Senior Researcher,
National Institute for Social Work, London. Formerly Research Fellow, Hester Adrian Research Centre, University of Manchester.
Research funded by a Department of Health Grant to Hester Adrian Research Centre, University of Manchester.

Hamid Rehman, Research Officer,
Department of Social Psychology, London School of Economics, London.
Research funded by the Nuffied Foundation and South East Thames Regional Health Authority.

Bob Remington, Reader in Psychology,
Department of Psychology, University of Southampton.

Oliver Russell, Reader in Mental Health, University of Bristol; Honorary Consultant Psychiatrist to the Phoenix NHS Trust; Director, Norah Fry Research Centre, University of Bristol.
Research funded by the Department of Health.

Tricia Sloper, Deputy Director,
Cancer Research Campaign Education and Child Studies Research Group, Department of Public Health and Epidemiology, University of Manchester. Formerly Research Fellow, Hester Adrian Research Centre.
Research funded by a Department of Health grant to Hester Adrian Research Centre, University of Manchester.

Steve Turner, Research Fellow,
Hester Adrian Research Centre, University of Manchester.
Research funded by the Department of Health.

PART 1

EPIDEMIOLOGY

CHAPTER 1

EPIDEMIOLOGY OF SELF-INJURY, CHARACTERISTICS OF PEOPLE WITH SEVERE SELF-INJURY AND INITIAL TREATMENT OUTCOME.

*Glynis H Murphy, Chris Oliver, John Corbett,
Lissa Crayton, Jackie Hales, Donna Head and Scott Hall*

Self-injurious behaviour has long been recognised as a puzzling and sometimes life-threatening phenomenon which occurs quite commonly amongst people with severe learning disabilities in institutions. A series of studies of people resident in mental handicap hospitals in the UK, USA, and Europe have suggested that between eight and fifteen per cent show such behaviour (Ballinger, 1971, Maisto et al, 1978, Schroeder et al, 1978, Maurice and Trudel, 1982, Griffin et al, 1984). Until the late 1980s, however, there were no studies of self-injurious behaviour amongst children and adults living in the community. Moreover, although there were numerous single case studies of the treatment of people with learning disabilities and severe self-injury (Murphy and Wilson, 1985), there were no examinations of the characteristics of total populations of people with such behaviour and no large treatment trials, providing constructional behavioural treatment. Service planning for children and adults with severe self-injury was therefore extremely difficult. All that service planners could be certain of was that, within a large area of several million population, it was likely that one or two people with learning disabilities would require heroic efforts from treatment teams to prevent serious and permanent tissue damage (eg Jones et al 1974, Romanczyk and Goren 1975, Spain et al, 1985).

Here we report on research funded by the UK Department of Health over a period of nearly ten years from 1983. The objectives of the research were:

a) To establish the prevalence of self-injurious behaviour amongst all children and adults in touch with learning disability services in a defined area of the UK.

b) To examine the characteristics of those with the most severe self-injury.

c) To provide treatment for a small number of the most severely injurious people.

The research team has included a number of psychologists, a nurse, and a psychiatrist over the ten years at different stages of the study and has benefited from excellent co-operation from staff, clients and residents within the region studied. Some of the data reported here have been presented elsewhere (Oliver et al, 1987, Murphy et al, 1988) but there are no other comprehensive accounts of all three parts of the project.

THE SURVEY STAGE

Method

Contact was made with all learning disability service providers in a single Health Region in the UK (total population 3.5 million). The initial contacts with psychiatrists, psychologists, paediatricians and community physicians in the Region were followed by contacts with head teachers of special schools, managers of Social Education Centres, officers-in-charge of hostels and homes (run by Social Services or by the private and voluntary sectors) and Community Mental Handicap Teams. All these service providers were asked if anyone in their care had shown self-injurious behaviour of sufficient severity to have caused tissue damage (eg bruising, bleeding) in the last four months (see Oliver et al, 1987 for details). When replies to the initial contact letters were positive, team members visited the relevant facility and interviewed the appropriate member(s) of staff (or parents if appropriate), to obtain basic demographic information, an estimate of degree of disability, current medication, type and frequency of SIB (once per hour or more; once per week or more but less than once per hour; less than once per week but more than once per four months), treatment of SIB and extent of outside help. The reliability of the data are described in Oliver et al (1987); essentially, the inter-informant reliability levels were high on caseness and on other indices but were less good on number of topographies and level of handicap.

Results

Of the 870 people referred to the project 251 had not caused themselves tissue damage by SIB in the previous four months and three had an IQ over 70, leaving 616 people meeting the study criteria (see Figure 1). For 20 of these parental permission for further data collection was not given, therefore the following data refers to the remaining 596 people.

Figure 1   Diagram showing numbers of people referred to the project at the survey stage with numbers screened, places of residence, and rates of SIB.

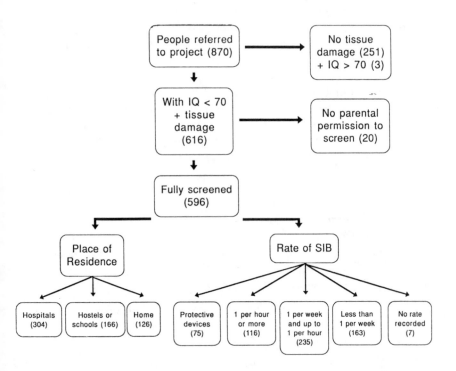

For these 596 individuals, the average age was 24.8 years and the range was two years to 88 years. The majority of people lived in mental handicap hospitals (51 per cent) whilst 21 per cent lived with their parents and 28 per cent were resident in hostels, staffed homes, or residential schools (see Figure 1). The younger people were mostly living at home, though there were some children below 10 years living in hospital (see Figure 2). Almost a quarter had no formal day activity and this was far more common amongst those living in hospital. Only 12 per cent were thought to have a mild learning disability.

Figure 2   Numbers of people showing SIB of criterion level in 5 year age bands living in different residential settings.

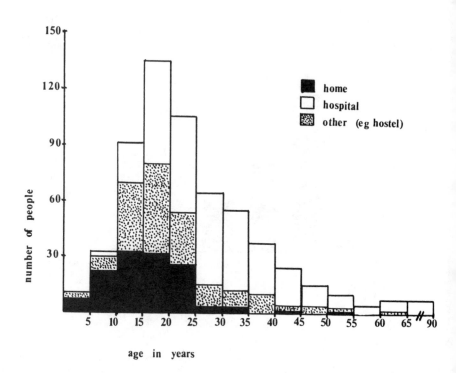

The prevalence of self-injurious behaviour amongst those living in mental handicap hospitals was 12 per cent overall but it varied considerably with age: it was under five per cent for the older groups and nearly 40 per cent for those between 10 and 20 years (see Figure 3). For those living outside hospitals the prevalence of self-injury was lower. For adults attending community based Social Education Centres in the largest county in the Region the prevalence figure was three per cent. In schools for children with severe learning difficulties, the prevalence was three per cent for under fives, four per cent for five to ten years old, eight per cent for 10-15 years old and 12 per cent for those over 15 years.

Figure 3   Prevalence of SIB by age in the hospital resident population (people in hospital = 2532); of those, 304 showed SIB of the criterion level.

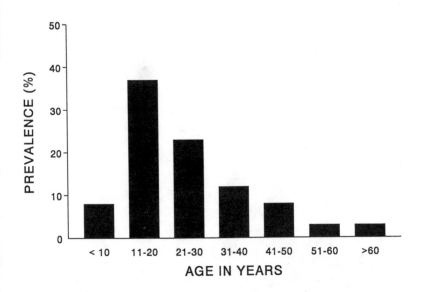

The most common topographies of self-injurious behaviour were skin picking (39 per cent of all individuals), self-biting (38 per cent), head punching and slapping (36 per cent) and head-to-object banging (28 per cent). Other topographies occurred in 10 per cent or fewer individuals, with certain topographies, such as cutting with tools, occurring rarely (two per cent of individuals). Over half of the people surveyed engaged in more than one topography, 20 people engaging in five or more types of self-injury.

There were 77 people whose self-injurious behaviour was so severe and so damaging that they wore protective devices for all or part of the day and/or night and often these devices were extremely restrictive (eg straight-arm splints). The topographies in which these people engaged more often included head banging and were often multiple (see Oliver et al, 1987). Meanwhile another 116 people were estimated by their staff to be self-injuring once per hour or more but were not wearing protective devices.

ostensibly for their behaviour (anti-convulsants, prescribed for 32 per cent, have been excluded) and this was more common for older individuals and those living in hospital. In the majority of cases the medication prescribed was anti-psychotic (36 per cent) while for a few it was anxiolytic (10 per cent), anti-depressant or hypnotic/sedative in type. Very few people were enrolled on written, psychological treatment programmes (11 had such programmes currently in place and one person was receiving psychoanalytical therapy).

Discussion

The overall estimate of the prevalence of self-injury within institutions for people with "mental handicap" was commensurate with figures from previous studies (see Ballinger, 1971, Maisto et al, 1978, Schroeder et al, 1978, Maurice and Trudel, 1982), although the very high rate of nearly 40 per cent prevalence for the 10-20 years old was startling and probably reflected the recent policy of not admitting children to hospital unless it was absolutely unavoidable. The prevalence rates of SIB amongst adults with learning disabilities in the community appeared comparable to those of two studies which were completed at almost the same time in other countries: Kebbon and Windahl (1985) reported a prevalence of four per cent from a postal survey of hospital and non-hospital residents in Sweden and Rojahn (1986) found a prevalence of two per cent amongst those living in non-hospital facilities in Germany, also by postal survey. The topographies of self-injury and the association with severe and profound levels of disablity were confirmed by other studies (see Johnson and Day, 1992, Emerson, 1992, for reviews).

An alarming number of individuals in the survey were receiving psychotropic medication, even though there is little evidence of its efficacy (eg Williams et al, 1984). Very few were enrolled on any kinds of psychological intervention programmes, although these are well-established as effective in reducing SIB, at least in the short-term (AABT Task Force Report, 1982, Murphy and Wilson, 1985). Such treatment is far more commonly available in some parts of the world than in others (eg Griffin et al, 1984, reported that 40 per cent of people with severe self-injury in Texas were on formal psychological programmes, although Maurice and Trudel, 1982, in Montreal reported only six per cent on programmes). Finally, an alarming number of children and adults with severe self-injury, seen during the survey, were subjected to "management of SIB by use of protective devices" and this mirrored the situation in Montreal where 31 per cent of people were wearing "restraint equipment" (Maurice and Trudel, 1982).

Many staff seemed to have turned to protective devices in desperation but, nevertheless, the individuals who wore the devices were often experiencing a very poor quality of life and the devices were not often applied in the manner recommended by Spain and colleagues (ie as part of a general programme of skill-building, with a built-in plan for fading and consideration of the appearance and long-term effects) (Spain et al, 1985).

Figure 4

Example of protective device (straight arm splints).

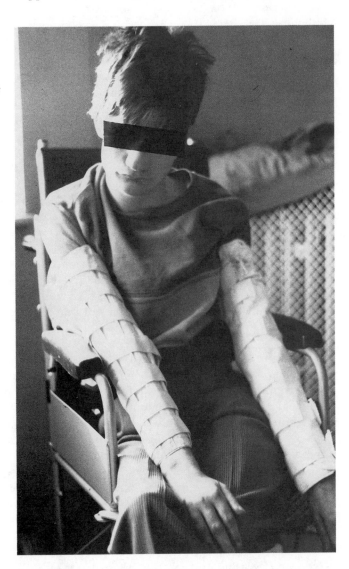

CHARACTERISTICS OF PEOPLE WITH SEVERE SELF-INJURY

In surveying people with learning disabilities and self-injurious behaviour, it was clear that the individuals with the poorest quality of life were those who wore protective devices. These devices were often highly restrictive (see example in Figure 4) and yet did not always prevent the individual from self-injury, though they usually minimised the tissue damage. People wearing devices for all or part of the time were, on average, younger and more cognitively disabled than the remainder of the group (see Oliver et al, 1987). They were also more likely to engage in multiple topographies and in particularly dangerous topographies (ie head-to-object banging, head punching, and teeth banging) than were the others. It was apparent, therefore, that this group of people evidenced a major service need and their characteristics were subsequently studied in more detail.

In this second stage of the study, a variety of information was collected:

(i)   Demographic and historical information.

(ii)   Staff estimates of the form and frequency of self-injury (as for the survey stage) and details of how the self-injury was managed.

(iii)   Neuropsychiatric data, using ICD 10 criteria (collected by Professor John Corbett).

(iv)   Details of people's skills, using the Vineland Adaptive Behaviour Scales, survey form (Sparrow et al, 1984).

(v)   Details of people's other challenging behaviours, using a shortened version of the AAMD Adaptive Behaviour Scale, part II (Nihira et al, 1974).

(vi)   Information on people's responses to the removal of their protective devices.

(vii)   Direct observations and questionnaire data on the function of people's self-injury.

(viii) Questionnaire data on the frequency and forms of people's self-restraint.

Some of this information was collected by staff interview (ie the demographic and historical data, the Vineland and ABS part II, staff estimates of SIB, and details of management), some was collected by staff questionnaire (ie self-restraint data and some of the details on the function of SIB), some from case notes (ie some of the demographic and historical information, some neuropsychiatric data) and some was collected by directly observing the individual with learning disabilities (ie some of the neuropsychiatric data, analogue data on the function of SIB, and data on people's responses to the removal of restraints). The information arising from (vii) and (viii) above will not be discussed here (for details see Oliver, 1991).

Of the 77 people who wore protective devices at the time of the survey, five had died by the time of this second stage of the study. Two of these five had suffered from Lesch-Nyhan syndrome. None of the five had died of causes directly relating to their self-injury. A further two had moved away and the staff and/or parents of another 14 declined to take part. Full data were collected for 54 of the remaining 56 people and all of the findings described below refer to these 54. They did not appear to be significantly different from the total group of 77.

Demographic and Neuropsychiatric Data

Table 1 shows details of the group of 54 people who wore protective devices at the survey stage and were seen in the second stage. About half were female and the average age of the group was 25 years (range 3-45 years). Slightly over half were living in hospital, about a quarter were living at home and the remainder were resident in group homes, hostels or residential schools.

In terms of the cause of learning disabilities, only six per cent had Down's syndrome and eight per cent had other genetic conditions, whilst for 65 per cent of cases the cause of disability was unknown (see Table 1). Atypical autism was diagnosed (by Corbett) in 23 per cent of cases and over half of the 54 cases had a history of epilepsy (see Table 1).

Table 1 Demographic and neuropsychiatric data for the 54 people seen in the second stage of the study.

Demographic Data		
Sex	48%	female
Age		Mean 25.2 years
		(range 3 - 45 years)
Residence	56%	in hospital
	15%	in hostels/group homes
	27%	in parents' homes
Neuropsychiatric data		
Cause of LD	6%	Down's syndrome
	8%	other genetic causes
	4%	postnatal injury or infection
	17%	birth or perinatal problem
	65%	unknown cause
Psychiatric	69%	none
diagnoses	23%	atypical autism
(ICD 10)	8%	childhood disintegrative disorder
Epilepsy	43%	none
	51%	lifetime epilepsy
	6%	last year only

Self-injurious Behaviour

At the time of the survey all 54 people were wearing protective devices (20 of them wore their devices all day, 34 wore them for part of the day). The forms of the devices are shown in Table 2. The most common form was a rigid arm splint (usually these were made of cloth and Velcro with inflexible plastic sticks inserted lengthways to prevent elbow flexion). These were usually worn on both arms (see Figure 4), sometimes for the whole day. They were highly restrictive, as were the gloves which were employed for a further 11 per cent of cases and the straps used to restrain some people (coded under "other" protective devices). By the time of the second stage of the study quite a number of people were no longer wearing protective devices (see Table 2) although their self-injury did not appear to have improved in a major way (see next page).

Table 2   Data on self-injurious behaviour and protective devices for the 54 people at the time of the survey and the second stage.

	Survey Stage (n = 54)	Second Stage (n = 54)
1. Type of protective devices		
None	0%	44%
Splints	44%	33%
Gloves	11%	2%
Helmet	9%	4%
Other	20%	6%
Multiple	15%	11%
2. Number of topographies of SIB		
Up to 2	72%	59%
3 or 4	20%	30%
5 or more	7%	11%
3. Severity index		
Mean	5.23	5.11
sd	3.01	3.45

Staff were interviewed about the topographies and frequencies of each person's SIB, as for the survey stage. At the time of the survey, the most common topographies amongst the 54 people were head punching (54 per cent), head-to-object banging (43 per cent), digit chewing (33 per cent) and skin picking and scratching (30 per cent). Fourteen of the 54 people (25 per cent) engaged in one topography only, while the remainder engaged in two or more. It can be seen from Table 2 that 27 per cent of people at the survey stage and 41 per cent at this second stage showed three or more topographies. Each person's SIB was also rated on a severity index which took into account both numbers of topographies and frequencies of each topography: any rare topography (estimated by staff as occurring less than once per week) was scored as 1, any medium rate topography (estimated by staff as occurring once or more per week but less than once per hour) was scored as 2 and frequent topographies (estimated by staff as occurring once per hour or more) were scored as 3. These scores were then summed across a person's topographies to give an overall severity index. It can be seen from Table 2 that, for the 54 cases seen at the time of the survey, the mean severity index was 5.23 (standard deviation 3.01) while at the second stage (two years later) the mean severity index was 5.11 (standard deviation 3.45).

Skills and Behavioural Difficulties

The most reliable information on people's skills was probably that obtained from staff interviews, using the Vineland Adaptive Behavior Scales (formal psychometric assessments were remarkably unproductive with many people and will not be reported here). The mean overall adaptive behaviour age equivalent was 11.5 months (range 1-36 months) and the mean standard score was 19.2 (sd 0.58). Figure 5 shows the mean age equivalents (and standard errors) for daily living skills, motor skills, receptive and expressive language and socialisation skills. People's daily living skills were significantly better than their other skills while expressive language and socialisation skills were significantly poorer than other skills. Only 16 per cent of people were thought by their staff to be under-using their skills because of their self-injury.

Figure 5   Mean Vineland Adaptive Behavior Scale age equivalents for five domains (and standard errors).

VINELAND ADAPTIVE BEHAVIOR SCALE

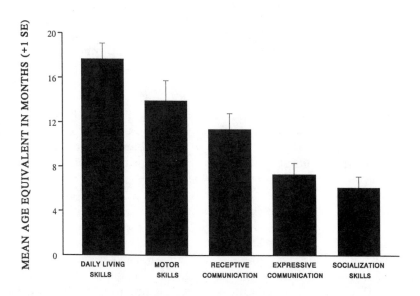

There were high rates of physical disability and sensory impairments as well as learning disabilities. Only 30 per cent of the 54 people could walk without assistance, 26 per cent could walk with assistance and 43 per cent were non-ambulant. Medical examination of individuals (by Corbett), and data from case notes, indicated that 27 per cent of people were blind and a further nine per cent had some visual impairment; seven per cent had a profound hearing loss and seven per cent some hearing impairment.

Self-injurious behaviour was not the only challenging behaviour shown by individuals. According to staff, interviewed with the shortened version of the ABS part II, 89 per cent of the people engaged in stereotyped behaviour, 66 per cent in temper tantrums, 40 per cent were physically aggressive and 36 per cent showed destruction of property (see Table 3).

Changes to the self-injury over time

For most of the 54 people, self-injurious behaviour was a chronic problem. Where it was possible to establish when the behaviour began, from case notes and interviews with parents/staff who had known the person from their early years, it transpired that the SIB was of extremely long duration. The mean age at which SIB began was seven years (sd 5.2 yrs) and the mean duration of SIB was 14 years (sd seven yrs) in the 26 people for whom these figures could be established with any confidence. Many people had also worn a variety of protective devices over the years: 65 per cent had worn splints, 28 per cent a helmet, 17 per cent gloves, four per cent a collar. Of the 54 people, 48 had worn other devices such as padding or strapping. One person had worn seven different devices in the past, two others had worn four and five had worn three different devices (the remainder had worn two or fewer).

For many staff and parents it was difficult to recall precisely what had happened to people's self-injury over time. The most reliable information about changes over time came therefore from a comparison of data from the staff interviews at the survey and second stages of the study, which were separated by a period of two years.

Two of the 54 people were reported by staff to have ceased their self-injury by the time of the second stage of the study. One of these was a boy who had removed very large portions of his own hair and who had worn socks or gloves over his hands at the time of the survey. He had been treated by a behavioural programme designed by a clinical psychologist while he was resident in a children's hostel and had stopped removing his hair by the

Table 3   Other challenging behaviours shown by individuals (as measured by the shortened ABS, part II).

	Percentage of cases showing the behaviour(s) (occasional and/or frequent)
1. Aggressive behaviour	40%
2. Damage to property	36%
3. Screaming and temper tantrums	66%
4. Running away	6%
5. Stereotyped behaviour	89%
6. Social withdrawal	38%
7. Postures and mannerisms	30%
8. Odd vocal habits	66%
9. Oral habits	81%
10. Stripping	28%
11. Hyperactive behaviour	28%
12. Sexual problems	34%
13. Sleep problems	29%
14. Other unacceptable behaviours	25%

time of the second stage of the study. The other person who was reputed to have stopped his self-injury was a young man who had shown severe eye-poking at the survey stage but was said by staff at the second stage interview to have ceased eye-poking (in fact some eye-poking was seen on direct observation, suggesting that, while the rate may have reduced, the self-injury did still occur at times).

The remaining 52 people were said by the staff interviewed to be continuing to self-injure. The lower half of Figure 6 shows the change, for each individual, in the number of topographies reported by staff at the first (survey stage) and second interview, two years later. Seventy-eight per cent of people had changed their number of topographies by one or fewer, while seven per cent had decreased by two or more topographies and four per cent had increased by two or more topographies. Such changes, however, need to be viewed against the background of the reliability of the data collected. It might be, for example, that apparent decreases and increases in people's topographies merely reflect the difficulty of obtaining such

Figure 6   Differences in number of topographies across time and
across informants.

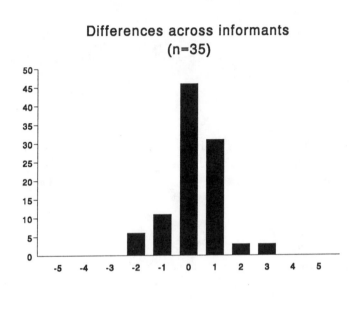

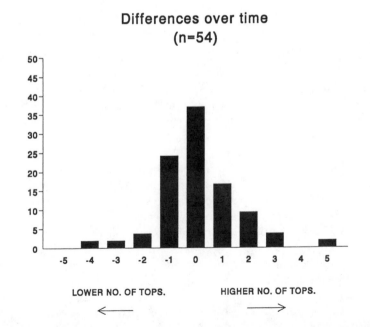

information in a reliable way from informants. For most people, the member of staff interviewed about the topographies and frequencies of self-injury in the survey stage was not the same member of staff interviewed at the second stage (due to staff turnover, shift working, classroom changes, etc). Consequently, it seems appropriate to compare the apparent changes in numbers of topographies over time for the 54 people seen at the second stage to the differences between two informant's estimates of a person's topographies in the survey stage (two informants were interviewed on the same day in the same day placement for 35 people in the survey stage, to provide inter-informant reliability levels, see Oliver et al, 1987). It is important to note that this is by no means a perfect comparison, since the clients for whom two informants were available at the survey stage were not necessarily severely injurious nor were they wearing protective devices. The top half of Figure 6 shows the percentage of cases for whom two informants differed in their estimates of numbers of topographies in the survey stage, for comparison with the lower half of the Figure showing the percentage of cases apparently changing their numbers of topographies over time. The variances of the two distributions were compared, using the F ratio and they were not significantly different (F 2.2, df 53, 34). The mean change in number of topographies over time (0.111 for n=54) was also compared to the mean difference between informant's estimates of a person's topographies (0.229 for n=35), using a t test and the means proved to be not significantly different (t=0.445, p=0.331).

The other measure of the severity of people's self-injury was the severity index (see above). Figure 7 shows the apparent changes in the 54 people's severity indices over time (lower half of the Figure) and the differences in severity indices resulting from the interviews with two informants at the survey stage for 35 people (just as for numbers of topographies above). The variance of the two distributions was compared, using the F ratio and it appeared that the variances were significantly different (F 2.75, df 53, 32). The mean change in severity index over time (-0.120 for n=54) was not statistically different, however, from the mean difference in severity index across informants (0.394 for n=33) according to a t test (t=0.804, p=0.215). It appeared therefore that neither the number of topographies nor the severity of the SIB in the 54 people seen in the second stage of the study had significantly changed over the two year period.

Figure 7 Differences in severity index across time and across informants.

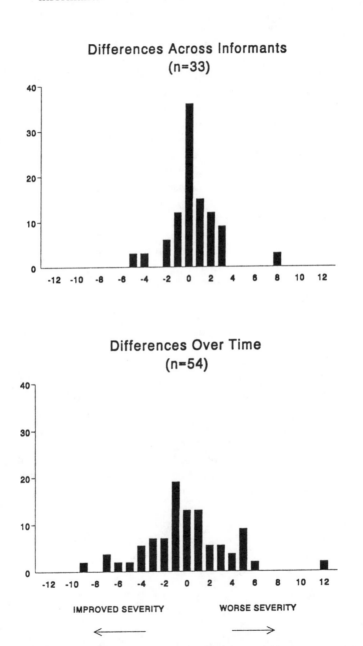

Management of self-injurious behaviour

For the sample selected for closer study in this second stage of the project, the most common form of management at the time of the initial survey had been, by definition, the use of protective devices. Two years later, at the time of the second stage of the project, 42 per cent of the sample were still wearing the same protective devices, a further 16 per cent were wearing different devices and 42 per cent had ceased to wear any protective equipment, even though as a group it appeared that their self-injury had not substantially improved (see above). The most common form of device at the time of the second stage remained the straight arm splint (see Table 2 and Figure 4).

Even where protective devices were necessary for all of a person's waking hours, there were times when they needed to be removed (eg for bathing). Frequently staff found such times extremely difficult to manage and it was decided to examine the effect of brief removal of devices for all those people (n=17) for whom staff estimated that this would not provide any immediate danger of major tissue damage. Fourteen of these people wore splints, one wore a helmet and two carried objects and/or wrapped themselves in clothing as a form of protection.

The devices were removed in a systematic way, as follows:

Start :	Baseline for 1 minute
1 min.00 secs:	Verbal warning of removal of device(s)
1 min.15 secs:	Verbal and gestural warning of removal of device(s)
1 min.30 secs:	Warnings repeated and device(s) removed
+30 secs later:	Devices verbally and gesturally offered
+30 secs later:	Devices replaced
+1 min.00 secs:	Repeat baseline

The responses of people to the verbal and gestural warnings and to the removal and replacement of devices were videotaped for analysis (for details see Oliver, 1991). None of the people made a negative response (ie crying, moaning, pulling away, moving away, hitting the researcher) to a verbal warning of device removal but three responded negatively to gestural warnings, four to the actual removal and five attempted to retrieve the devices (which were left within reach when removed). Eleven people either began to self-injure or cried or moaned or self restrained during the 30 seconds when their devices were off and nine people actively or passively assisted in the replacement of their devices. Only one person resisted the replacement of his protective equipment.

At the time of the first survey, medication was commonly prescribed, particularly for those living in hospital. It was impossible to be certain, for most people, that their medication had been prescribed to control their self-injury (or even other challenging behaviour) as often the prescriptions were of long standing. Frequently there appeared to be no formal monitoring of changes in behaviour and no scheduled "drug holidays" by which to assess the effects of medication. Nevertheless, about a third of the sample were receiving anti-psychotic medication at the time of the survey and 73 per cent were still receiving it at the second stage. Only small numbers of people were receiving other medication, such as hypnotics, anxiolytics or lithium and none were prescribed stimulants or anti-depressants (about a third were on anti-convulsants at the survey and at the second stage of the project).

The high rates of SIB amongst the sample and the frequent use of protective devices to prevent severe injury, suggested that many people posed difficult day-to-day management problems for staff. It transpired, however, on staff interview, that while most facilities (77 per cent) reported that they had an agreed policy for managing a person's SIB, only a few (12 per cent) had a written policy and 23 per cent of facilities reported having no particular management policy for the person's SIB. Moreover, where people had separate day and residential facilities, the day facility staff were unaware of what the residential SIB management policy was in 67 per cent of cases (amongst the remainder, the policies were the same in residential and day facilities in 22 per cent and different in 11 per cent of cases).

Conclusions

It appeared from this second stage of the project that people who wore protective devices to prevent serious injury from SIB tended to have had long histories of self-injury and had often worn previous types of protective devices. They were frequently profoundly disabled, often non-ambulant and often had sensory impairments and other challenging behaviours as well as SIB. They seemed to show little improvement in self-injury over a two year period and frequently remained on medication for years. Few facilities had written policies for managing the person's SIB and often people showed an apparent liking for their protective devices, though in many cases it did appear that staff tried not to use devices unless it was necessary (as many people did stop wearing devices over the two year period).

It is difficult to compare these findings to those of other studies, as there are few other investigations of whole populations of individuals with severe self-injury and certainly no other reports of a group who all wore protective devices. From comparison to the figures given by Ballinger (1971) and Schroeder et al (1978), it appears that the current group are particularly disabled, with even fewer having any expressive language and far more having a profound level of intellectual disability, as far as this can be gauged. It may be that the individuals who end up wearing protective devices are the least able of all those who show severe self-injury: perhaps it is the difficulty that staff and/or parents have in communicating with them or in promoting skill building and other alternative behaviours that leads carers to resort to protective devices.

Schroeder et al (1978) reported a higher prevalence of visual impairment amongst those in his hospital sample with SIB than amongst those in the same hospital without SIB (22 per cent vs seven per cent) and the high rate of visual impairment in this study suggests that it is possible that such children and/or adults are more at risk of developing SIB, although a prospective study would be needed to confirm this. A similar argument may hold for those with physical disabilities (Ballinger, 1971, also found high rates of non-ambulation, significantly more of those who could not walk showing self-injury) and for hearing impairments (though Schroeder et al, 1978, reported no differential in rates of hearing loss it is likely that the base rate was under-estimated).

Other challenging behaviours have also appeared to be common in those who self-injure in other investigations. Maisto et al (1978) and Maurice and Trudel (1982) found an association with aggressive behaviour while Maisto et al (1978) and Schroeder et al (1978) recorded high rates of stereotyped and other "misbehaviours". In terms of self-injury, the topographies described in other studies are not always identical, as some investigators have been more inclusive than we were in their definition of SIB (including, for example, pica and self-induced vomiting). The current finding of high rates of multiple topographies has been confirmed by others, however: Maurice and Trudel, (1982), for instance, reported that more than half of the adults in their three hospital study showed more than one topography of self-injury.

Findings on the chronicity of self-injury have been very variable. Schroeder et al, (1978), asked staff in their state facility to refer all those who self-injured, at three separate points in time, each a year and a half apart. Comparisons of the three surveys indicated that only 31 clients were referred on all three occasions and only 70 were referred on two occasions (out of 208 clients ever referred on any occasion). It might appear from this that the individuals were not showing chronic SIB and yet data presented on chronicity by Schroeder et al (1978) indicated a mean duration of seven years of SIB for those with less severe SIB and 12 years of SIB for more severe SIB. Schroeder and colleagues investigated those who were initially referred but not re-referred and concluded that the result had been due to successful behavioural treatment for many of the individuals, though it was not clear whether they had ceased self-injury entirely or simply improved enough not to be re-referred (data on staff reliability as regards "caseness" was not reported). Schroeder later reported that 52 of the 208 individuals had only temporary improvements in their SIB and were still requiring high level interventions eight years later (Schroeder et al, 1986). This kind of extreme chronicity fits better with our data on the duration of SIB for the individuals in this second stage of the study and the apparent lack of change over a two-year period. It is also confirmed by Windahl's findings in Sweden (Windahl, 1988) and Griffin's in Texas. Griffin (1984) showed in a follow-up of individuals receiving behavioural programmes with aversive components that 69 per cent were still on such programmes seven years later. The wisdom of continuing this kind of treatment over this length of time is of course debatable as the data does not indicate whether the SIB simply continues regardless of the programmes in place or whether the SIB disappears but re-develops with the same (or different) functions. Either way, it seems likely that for people with very severe SIB the behaviour is commonly chronic and may require high level interventions over a long period of time.

THE TREATMENT OF SEVERE SELF-INJURY

It was clear from the survey stage of the study that there were large numbers of adults and children engaging in self-injury living in the Region and that very few were receiving any active form of treatment for their self-injury, apart from psychotropic medication. It appeared from the second study, which examined those whose self-injury had been severe enough to require protective devices, that on the whole these people were very disabled, both intellectually and physically, that they frequently had a history of chronic self-injury and that their protective devices were often very restrictive. They appeared to be the most in need of treatment, since the quality of their life was often very poor, typically involving restriction to a wheelchair, in straight arm splints for much of the day, often with no written programme describing how their self-injury should be dealt with.

Psychotropic medication was commonly employed as a treatment measure for those with severe self-injury, according to the survey data. It appeared from the second stage of the project that individuals often remained on medication for considerable periods of time. There is remarkably little evidence, however, of treatment effectiveness for traditional psychotropic medication in people with severe self-injury (Williams et al, 1984). Rather, the published literature suggests that the most successful form of treatment for children and adults with severe self-injury is behavioural (Murphy and Wilson, 1985, Oliver and Head,1990).

It was therefore decided that, in the third stage of the project, a selected group of the 20 most severely self-injurious individuals would receive behavioural treatment. The clear importance of functional analyis to treatment design (Iwata et al, 1982, Carr and Durand, 1985, Oliver and Head, in press) meant that all treatment plans would need to be based on a thorough functional analysis. The ethical issues surrounding the use of aversive stimuli in treatment (Murphy, in press) led to a decision that no aversive stimuli (defined as in Horner, 1990) would be employed in the treatment plans (cf. Bruhl et al, 1982, Linscheid et al, 1990) and it was agreed that treatment would be delivered in the individual's usual place of daytime residence or provision, because of the criticisms that have been made of special units (Newman and Emerson, 1991).

It was also decided that the common reporting of unexplained cycles of increases and decreases in the frequency and intensity of self-injury in those severely afflicted (eg Jones et al, 1974, Romanczyck and Goren, 1975) meant that a control group would be necessary, to ensure that any reductions in self-injury in the treatment group would be of clinical significance and could be attributed to the treatment with some confidence. Initially, it had been hoped that a comparison group who would receive non-specific support but no behavioural treatment could also be included. However, the ethical committees approached considered that this was not ethical, since behavioural treatments were established as more effective and should therefore be used, if there was treatment available.

It was finally agreed that there would be a single "no treatment" control group, which would be comprised of individuals who lived too far from the project to receive treatment. They (or their staff or parents) were to be free to seek treatment through their local team at any time but this was to be logged by the research team to assist them when interpreting outcome.

Two examples of individuals treated in this third stage of the project will be given here, together with discussion of some general issues which arose from the project. A full report of the project will appear at a later date (see also Oliver and colleagues' Final Report to the Department of Health, 1993).

Case example: Dawn

Dawn was a 23 year old woman, who had been included in both the initial survey and the second stage of the study, as a result of her severe self-injury. Her mother had suffered from rubella during pregnancy and Dawn had subsequently been born with a profound hearing loss and only partial sight. At the time of the third stage of the project, Dawn was living in a hostel and attending a local authority special needs day service, on a daily basis. The intervention project began in the day service.

Dawn had very limited skills and was assessed on the Vineland Adaptive Behavior Scales as having an overall adaptive age equivalent of 11 months. When her hands were unrestricted, Dawn engaged in frequent hand-to-head and hand-to-body hitting. She had chosen some very unusual protective devices for herself while at the day centre: two large coloured filters with wooden handles. Dawn chose to wear these over her hands at the day centre and became upset and self-injurious when they were removed (see Figure 8). The staff therefore allowed her to wear the devices, even though they restricted her use of her hands for other activities. When these filters were not available, Dawn tended to find other restrictive devices (such as large rolls of sellotape) or she would wrap her hands in her clothing.

Functional analysis showed that the current function of Dawn's self-injury was to obtain the return of her filters, since her self-injury increased immediately they were removed (from zero per minute to an average of eight hits per minute). Her SIB varied very little from that high rate thereafter and reduced again only when the devices were returned, even though it was not impossible for her to engage in self-injury when wearing the filters (see Figure 4 in Oliver and Head, in press). It was hypothesised that the filters had become reinforcing (Favell et al, 1981) and that her self-injury was being reinforced repeatedly by the return of the filters following high rate bursts of self-injury.

The intervention programme consisted of two main strategies: the filters were gradually cut down in size over a period of a year and the filters were used as part of a DRO programme (ie they were only returned to Dawn following periods with no self-injury). The intention was that the period for which Dawn was required not to self-injure prior to receiving her filters back would be gradually increased and the size of the filters would be gradually decreased until they could be replaced by a cosmetically acceptable alternative, such as bracelets.

Figure 8   Dawn wearing her filters.

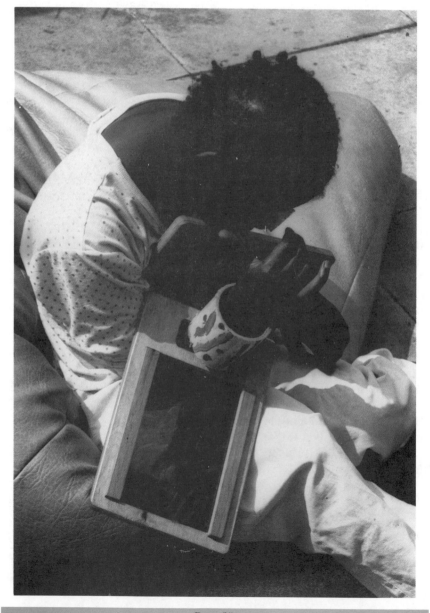

The filters were cut down in six stages. Initially, they measured 33cms in length. By the end of a year they had been reduced by about half to 16cms in length. The altered contingencies for returning Dawn's devices at the end of a "filters off" period continued throughout the cutting down of the filters. It appeared to be less successful than the fading of devices, in that it was not possible to increase the period for which Dawn was required not to self-injure from its initial level of 20 seconds over the 13 months intervention. Moreover, it appeared that despite much training and demonstration, the staff were providing relatively few opportunities (about eight a week, at best) for Dawn to learn about the new contingency for the return of her filters. This may have been because the staff found this procedure aversive, since it involved refusing Dawn the two items she clearly "wanted" until such a time as she stopped self-injuring for at least 20 seconds. This usually meant waiting for less than a minute but could sometimes mean waiting for 10 minutes, during which time Dawn would self-injure and show signs of distress. Nevertheless, there was evidence that Dawn was self-injuring somewhat less when she was without her filters since the rate of SIB reduced from an average of eight per minute to just over four per minute during "filters off" time over the year of treatment.

All the intervention occurred at Dawn's day placement, with the intention of transferring successful procedures to her hostel in due course. At the hostel, Dawn's method of self-restraint was different from that at her day placement: the absence of the coloured filters meant that she always wrapped herself in her clothes in the hostel. When the filters were at stage 5, the hostel staff asked for the filters to be sent home with Dawn at the end of each day because she had started to wrap herself so tightly that she was causing her arms to swell. Shortly after the filters were cut down again (stage 6), Dawn began to wrap excessively at her day placement, despite the fact she was already wearing the filters. It was uncertain whether the sudden difficulties were caused by the filters reaching a "critical" size or whether Dawn's SIB had suddenly become worse for other reasons (eg she had a mild infection; her key worker was on holiday; the filters were perhaps being misused at the hostel). In any case, it was decided to retreat several stages in the procedure and return to the larger filters.

By the end of a year's intervention, Dawn's self-injury, when not wearing the filters, had reduced by about half (see Figure 5 in Oliver and Head, in press). However, Figure 9 shows the percentage of time Dawn spent wrapping her hands and arms at the day placement, with a clear increase in wrapping in the spring of 1990, a return to the larger filters in the summer of 1990 and a subsequent reduction in wrapping.

Shortly after this point (summer 1990), the formal intervention had to cease. The staff at the day centre had every intention to repeat the process of the intervention once Dawn's SIB had settled again but follow-up (winter 1992) indicated that they had not done so.

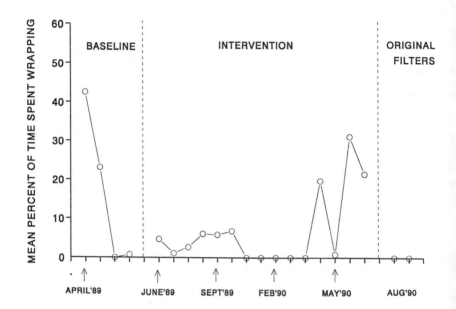

Figure 9   Mean percentage of time Dawn spent wrapping her arms in her clothes.

Case example: Keith

Keith was a 28 year old man who was living in a residential unit for people with challenging behaviour in the grounds of a large hospital, at the time of the intervention project. On the Vineland Adaptive Behavior Scales, he attained an overall age equivalent of one year eleven months. He had no spoken language but was ambulant and had some basic self-care skills. His self-injurious behaviour was chronic, having been part of his repertoire for at least 18 years, and Keith had been included in both the survey stage and the second stage of the studies described above. When the intervention began his SIB consisted of hand-to-head slapping, body slapping, head-to-object banging and body-to-object banging. Keith had a helmet to prevent major tissue damage, but he did not wear this all day.

Functional analysis of Keith's self-injury by direct observation indicated that it had the function of gaining staff attention and it was hypothesised that staff responded to Keith's SIB because they found it aversive, particularly when it occurred in long bursts. It seemed likely that they were then reinforced for responding by the subsequent reduction in SIB and that Keith's SIB was maintained on a variable ratio schedule (Hall and Oliver, 1992).

The intervention consisted of the following strategies: firstly, a DRO schedule provided reinforcement for periods of three minutes without SIB (this period was set by reference to his average rate of SIB); secondly, self-injurious behaviour, when it did occur, was followed by what is probably best described as a brief period of required relaxation (Keith was sat on the nearest chair, with a member of staff behind him holding his arms, to prevent self-injury). This latter strategy was chosen in preference to extinction because of the dangers of extinction with self-injurious behaviour.

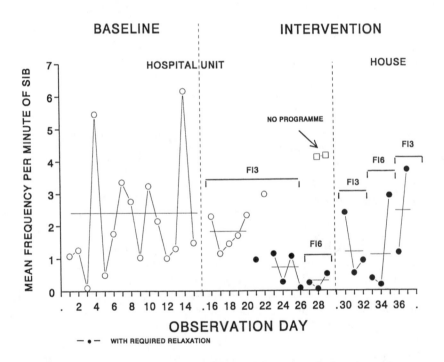

Figure 10 Frequency of Keith's SIB in baseline, hospital unit, and home. Square boxes indicate the mean per 20 minute session.

Figure 10 shows the frequency of SIB (summing all topographies) during the baseline and the intervention period. It can be seen that the rate of self-injury reduced considerably over the first few months, even though the programme was only operating for part of the day (ie between about 9am and 5pm, signalled to Keith by visible presence of edible reinforcers). Moreover it was possible to move to a longer fixed interval (of six minutes) for the DRO schedule, something which had not been possible for Dawn.

Keith was subsequently moved from the hospital-based residential unit to a community-based house (see Figure 10). Staff at the house were provided with the same training that had been given to the residential unit staff (see Oliver et al, 1993, Final Report to the Department of Health for details) and they began to operate the same programme. Keith's rate of SIB began to escalate, however, returning to baseline levels, despite a return from the six minute to a three minute DRO schedule. A visit to the new home by the research staff, with an intensive all-day re-institution of the programme suggested that it was still effective. Staff at the facility were reluctant to adopt it however and shortly after this the intervention had to cease. The responsibility for continuing and monitoring the programme passed to a local community-based team and it was thought likely that the programme would not continue to be effective because of the staff views about its necessity and form. At follow-up, about nine months later, however, it transpired that Keith was progressing well and was showing only low rates of SIB. Worryingly, the required relaxation part of the programme had been continued, in a slightly altered form (Keith was required to relax full length on a bean bag for one minute in a quiet room following bursts of SIB) but there was no formal DRO programme. The staff had, however, taught Keith to ask for drinks, which he very much liked, by using a Makaton sign and it appeared that this was acting as a natural form of DRO, Keith requesting drinks frequently throughout the day. Interestingly, when interviewed at follow-up, staff reported disliking the formal DRO part of the previous programme for ideological reasons but felt comfortable with the naturalistic DRO. A local psychologist had helped them to assess the effectiveness of the required relaxation part of the programme (by dropping this facet of the intervention for a period of days and logging the effect on Keith's SIB) and it became clear that this was an important part of the programme because Keith's SIB escalated rapidly without it (from one burst a day to over 300 a day within a period of 18 days).

Discussion

Initially, it had been intended that 20 individuals would be offered behavioural treatment through the three year period of the research programme. To enrol a new client on to the project every six weeks had seemed feasible in the planning stage but turned out to be completely impossible in practice. The functional analysis alone could sometimes take nearly six weeks, given that for this group of severely injurious young adults the function was rarely easy to determine. Thereafter, trials of interventions, usually in the form of brief repeated sessions, had to take place before it was possible to train staff to take over effective procedures. The intention then was for research staff to withdraw and visit on an intermittent basis to collect data on progress or to advise when programmes needed adjusting. The reality was, however, that research staff put in hundreds of hours (and in some cases nearly a thousand hours), only to find that as soon as they withdrew progress would begin to decline. The result was that only five people were treated over the three years (and control data collected). It may have been that the central problem was one of maintaining staff commitment. In some cases (eg Keith, described above) staff were able to be candid about the difficulties they had with the programmes, at least at follow-up. Certainly it did appear that most staff teams found that direct treatment, involving technical aspects (such as schedules of reinforcement), were difficult to sustain and this seemed to be more a function of their ideology than of the task difficulty. Nevertheless, in some cases it was almost impossible to discern any progress, even when researchers were operating programmes, and it may be, for this particular group of clients with relatively limited abilities, few other skills, few alternative reinforcers, very chronic and high rate self-injury, that the success rate of behavioural programmes is going to be relatively low. Moreover, the enormous time commitment for clinical psychologists in providing such high level treatment programmes makes them almost prohibitive as part of ordinary CMHT work, even though the data requirements for ordinary clinical practice would of course be very different from that in a research project.

Few other projects of any size have attempted to treat such severe self-injury in individuals with such limited skills, using non-aversive methods. Bruhl et al, (1982), for example, in treating 18 individuals resorted to aversive methods for seven of the 18, reported negative results for another three of the 18 and complete success with non-aversive methods for only five of the 18 (and partial success for the remainder). Nolley et al, (1982), on the other hand, employed wholly positive methods and claimed success for 12 of the 16 clients treated over a four-year period. A close examination of their data, however, shows that for several of those for whom success is claimed, the reduction in rates of SIB could only have been considered a reduction compared to the levels in a previous treatment and there was no true reduction compared to the original baseline (see, for example, Joe and Cheryl in Figure 4 and Sam in Figure 5 of Nolley et al). A more recent project employing positive behavioural methods found much the same level of success and difficulty (Paisley et al, 1990).

We conclude that effective treatment programmes are certainly possible for young adults with chronic and very severe self-injury but that they are not infallible, even with our current new technology (functional analysis, constructional approaches and functional communication training). Moreover, in terms of services, the programmes need almost prohibitively high inputs of psychologist's time, are extremely stressful to run and the programmes themselves are very fragile. Whilst we hestitate to end on such a depressing note, we are considering whether it would not be a better investment of staff time and a more effective use of highly specialist expertise to examine the feasibility of early intervention for those beginning to show SIB in childhood. We have been fortunate enough to be funded by the Mental Health Foundation to investigate the early development of self-injury in children with learning disabilities, under five years old, with the eventual aim of developing programmes of early intervention for this most debilitating of difficulties.

REFERENCES

AABT TASK FORCE REPORT (1982). The treatment of self-injurious behaviour. *Behaviour Therapy, 13,* 529-554.

BALLINGER B R (1971). Minor self-injury. *British Journal of Psychiatry, 118,* 535-538.

BRUHL H H, FIELDING L, JOYCE M, PETERS W AND WEISLER N (1982). Thirty-month demonstration project for treatment of self-injurious behavior in severely retarded individuals. IN J H Hollis and C E Meyers (Eds) *Life-threatening Behavior.* Washington: American Association on Mental Deficiency.

CARR E G AND DURAND V M (1985). Reducing behavior problems through functional communication training. *Journal of Applied Behavior Analysis, 18,* 111-126.

EMERSON E (1992). Self-injurious behaviour: an overview of recent trends in epidemiological and behavioural research. *Mental Handicap Research, 5,* 49-81.

FAVELL J E, McGIMSEY J F, JONES M L AND CANNON P R (1981). Physical restraint as positive reinforcement. *American Journal of Mental Deficiency, 85,* 425-432.

GRIFFIN J C, WILLIAMS D E, STARK M T, ALTMEYER B K AND MASON M (1984). Self-injurious behavior: a state-wide prevalence survey, assessment of severe cases and follow-up of aversive programmes. IN J C Griffin, M T Stark, D E Williams, B K Altmeyer and H K Griffith (Eds) *Advances in the Treatment of Self-injurious Behavior.* Austin, Texas: Department of Health and Human Services, Texas Planning Council for Developmental Disabilities.

HALL S AND OLIVER C (1992). Differential effects of severe self-injurious behaviour on the behaviour of others. *Behavioural Psychotherapy, 20,* 355-365.

HORNER R (1990). Ideology, technology and typical community settings; use of severe stimuli. *American Journal on Mental Retardation, 95,* 166-168.

IWATA B A, DORSEY M F, SLIFER K J, BAUMAN K E AND RICHMAN G S (1982). Toward a functional analysis of self-injury. *Analysis and Intervention in Developmental Disabilities, 2,* 3-20.

JOHNSON W L AND DAY R M (1992). The incidence and prevalence of self-injurious behavior. IN J K Luiselli, J L Matson and N N Singh (Eds) *Self-injurious Behavior: Analysis, Assessment and Treatment.* New York: Springer-Verlag.

JONES F H, SIMMONS J Q AND FRANKEL F (1974). An extinction procedure for eliminating self-destructive behaviour in a 9-year old autistic girl. *Journal of Autism and Childhood Schizophrenia, 4,* 241-250.

KEBBON L AND WINDAHL S (1985). Self-injurious behaviour: results of a nation-wide survey among mentally retarded in Sweden. Paper read at the 7th World Congress of the IASSMD, New Delhi, India.

LINSCHEID T R, IWATA B A, RICKETTS R W, WILLIAMS D E AND GRIFFIN J C (1990). Clinical evaluation of the self-injurious behavior inhibiting system (SIBIS). *Journal of Applied Behavior Analysis, 23,* 53-78.

MAISTO C R, BAUMEISTER A A AND MAISTO A A (1978). An analysis of variables related to self-injurious behavior among institutionalised retarded persons. *Journal of Mental Deficiency Research, 22,* 27-36.

MAURICE P AND TRUDEL G (1982). Self-injurious behavior prevalence and relationships to environmental events. IN J H Hollis and C E Meyers (Eds) *Life-threatening Behavior.* Washington: American Association on Mental Deficiency.

MURPHY G, OLIVER C, CRAYTON L AND CORBETT J A (1988). The chronicity of self-injurious behaviour. Paper read at the 8th IASSMD Congress, Dublin.

MURPHY G AND WILSON B (1985). *Self-injurious Behaviour.* Kidderminster, BIMH Publications.

MURPHY G (in press). The use of aversive stimuli in treatment: the issue of consent. *Journal of Intellectual Disability Research.*

NEWMAN I AND EMERSON E (1991). Specialised treatment units for people with challenging behaviour. *Mental Handicap, 19,* 113-119.

NIHIRA K, FOSTER R, SHELLHAAS M AND LELAND H (1974). *AAMD Adaptive Behavior Scale,* 1974 revision. Washington: American Association on Mental Deficiency.

NOLLEY D, BUTTERFIELD B, FLEMING A AND MULLER P (1982). Non-aversive treatment of severe self-injurious behavior: multiple replications with DRO and DRI. IN J H Hollis and C E Meyers (Eds) *Life-threatening Behavior.* Washington: American Association on Mental Deficiency.

OLIVER C (1991). Self-injurious behaviour in people with mental handicap: prevalence, individual characteristics and functional analysis. Unpublished PhD Thesis, London University.

OLIVER C AND HEAD D (1990). Self-injurious behaviour in people with learning disabilities: determinants and interventions. *International Review of Psychiatry, 2,* 101-116.

OLIVER C AND HEAD D (in press). Self-injurious behaviour: functional analysis and interventions. IN R S P Jones and C B Eayrs (Eds) *Challenging Behaviour and Intellectual Disability: A Psychological Perspective.* Clevedon, Avon: BILD Publications.

OLIVER C, MURPHY G AND CORBETT J A (1987). Self-injurious behaviour in people with mental handicap: a total population study. *Journal of Mental Deficiency Research, 31,* 147-162.

PAISLEY T J H, WHITWAY R B AND HISLOP P M (1990). Client characteristics and treatment selection: Legitimate influences and misleading inferences. IN A C Repp and N N Singh (Eds) *Perspectives on the use of Non-aversive and Aversive Interventions for Persons with Developmental Disabilities.* Sycamore, Illinois: Sycamore Publishing Company.

ROJAHN J (1986). Self-injurious and stereotypic behavior of non-institutionalised mentally retarded people: prevalence and classification. *American Journal of Mental Deficiency, 91,* 268-276.

ROMANCZYCK R G AND GOREN E R (1975). Severe self-injurious behaviour: the problem of clinical control. *Journal of Consulting and Clinical Psychology, 43,* 730-739.

SCHROEDER S R, SCHROEDER C S, SMITH B AND DALLDORF J (1978). Prevalence of self-injurious behaviors in a large state facility for the retarded: a three year follow-up study. *Journal of Autism and Childhood Schizophrenia, 8,* 261-269.

SCHROEDER S R, BICKEL W K AND RICHMOND G (1986). Primary and secondary prevention of self-injurious behaviors: a life-long problem. IN K D Gadow (Ed) *Advances in Learning and Behavioral Disabilities, 5.* Greenwich, CT: JAI Press.

SPAIN B, HART S A AND CORBETT J A (1985). The use of appliances in the treatment of severe self-injurious behaviour. IN G Murphy and B Wilson (Eds) *Self-injurious Behaviour.* Kidderminster, Worcs: BIMH Publications.

SPARROW S S, BALLA D AND CICCHETTI D V (1984). *Vineland Adaptive Behavior Scales.* Minnesota: American Guidance Service.

WILLIAMS D E, WEIR H F, HARGRAVE R L, PARKER C M AND MAREK K (1984). Effects of a facility-wide psychoactive drug evaluation/ behavior management system. IN J C Griffin, M T Stark, D E Williams, B K Altmeyer and H K Griffin (Eds) *Advances in the Treatment of Self-injurious Behaviour.* Texas: Texas Planning Council for Developmental Disabilities.

WINDAHL S I (1988). SIB in a time perspective: A follow-up of SIB prevalence and frequency after 10-13 years. Paper read at the 8th IASSMD Conference, Dublin.

CHAPTER 2

ASSESSING THE PREVALENCE OF AGGRESSIVE BEHAVIOUR AND THE EFFECTIVENESS OF INTERVENTIONS

Oliver Russell and Phil Harris

INTRODUCTION

No human behaviour arouses more social concern than that of aggression. The treatments provided by therapists and professional carers in response to aggressive behaviour continue to be a major source of controversy. The use of punitive procedures has a long history, despite strong ethical objections and dubious evidence as to their effectiveness (Horner et al 1990, Mulick 1990). Alternatives to punishment have received far less attention, although the lobby for positive interventions to build skills, teach concepts, solve problems, repair relationships and aid personal growth and development is rapidly gaining ground (La Vigna and Donellan, 1986, McGee et al, 1987, Lovett, 1985).

At the present time there is little doubt that aggressive behaviour can, and does, present a serious challenge to carers and to service providers. Such behaviour often has the effect of disrupting normal life and individuals with learning disabilities may be taken out of the mainstream of society and placed in institutions. Policies for the resettlement of institutional populations into community settings have stimulated the creation of new services for people with challenging behaviour (Blunden and Allen 1987). These new services have been shaped by the beliefs, attitudes and values which we attribute to people with the double handicap of a learning disability and challenging behaviour and by our knowledge of the nature, extent and circumstances of the problems or challenges which they present.

THE RESEARCH BRIEF

This study was funded by the Department of Health and was conducted in two stages; the aim of the first stage was to document the nature, extent and circumstances of aggressive behaviour among people with learning disabilities; the second stage explored the effectiveness of services and of the interventions which took place. This paper provides an overview of the research. The first part of the paper reviews our studies of prevalence. The second part outlines our approach to the assessment of the effectiveness of interventions. More details are available in other reports (Harris, in press, Harris and Russell 1989a, b, 1990a,b, 1992).

ASSESSING THE SIZE OF THE PROBLEM

Estimating prevalence

In the first stage of the project we studied the prevalence of aggressive behaviour among people with learning disabilities living in one health district in the South of England. The survey was conducted in a health district which had a total population of 370,000 and which comprised a mix of urban and rural communities. At the time of the survey a well established Mental Handicap Register for the district recorded 1,362 people as having a learning disability. According to the register 352 people (25.8 per cent) were living in one or other of the long-stay hospitals managed by the National Health Service. The rest were either living in their family homes or in residential facilities in the community.

True prevalence can only be established by screening whole populations. Administrative prevalence may be estimated by identification of cases through the records of service agencies. An administrative prevalence approximates to a true prevalence only in a comprehensive and well co-ordinated service (Fryers 1984). In the health district which we studied there were many services provided by the health authority, the social services department and the voluntary and private sector. Although there was less co-operation than might have been desirable there had nevertheless been a good degree of co-ordination in providing information for the register. We were satisfied that the information available provided a reasonably comprehensive record of most people with a learning disability living in that health district.

Prevalence estimates may be further confounded by two additional factors. Firstly, it may be difficult to arrive at a generally agreed definition. We found that this was particularly true when trying to define aggression. The term aggressive behaviour is used in so many different ways that no single definition can possibly cover all meanings. In this study an operational definition was chosen.

Secondly, behaviour is often specific to a particular setting. Aggressive behaviour, for example, can vary considerably according to the context in which it occurs. Influential factors within the setting will include the opportunity to engage in meaningful activities, the quality of the social environment, and the degree to which personal choice and preferences are both possible and encouraged (for details see Harris and Russell, 1989a).

Defining aggressive behaviour

In order to identify the target group it was necessary to develop an operational definition of aggression. A number of definitions of aggression and related concepts such as violence, dangerousness and self-injury were reviewed. All the definitions of aggression which we examined included some notion of doing harm or the threat of injury to others. Eventually a definition of aggressive behaviour was developed with the help of service providers and incorporated into the following sentence which appeared in the initial letters sent to all the facilities contacted.

'While we are primarily interested in identifying people who present serious problems such as biting, kicking, scratching etc which result in injury to others, for example bruising, bleeding, or other tissue damage, we would also like to include all individuals whose actions such as shouting/screaming at others, or violence towards objects may not necessarily result in injury but do present serious management difficulties because of the threat or risk of injury to others.'

The Survey

Many service providers were contacted, including all head teachers of schools for children with severe learning difficulties in the county, managers of local authority day centres, community mental handicap teams, hospital managers (including the Special Hospitals), psychiatrists, psychologists, and residential service managers of private, local authority and voluntary homes and hostels. (Children who were under school age and the prison population were, however, not included in the survey).

Most service providers were initially contacted by telephone and the aims and objectives of the research were discussed with them. This initial approach was followed by a letter asking the recipient to identify all children and adults with learning disabilities who displayed aggressive behaviour. They were asked to use the above definition to decide whether or not to include a person in their return.

Seventy eight facilities responded and 200 people were reported to present aggressive behaviour of whom 26 were pupils attending school. All of the service providers whom we approached agreed to co-operate.

Screening the target group

The screening stage involved following up all those who were initially identified and conducting interviews with service providers. Detailed information was collected using a structured interview schedule. Items included in the schedule were drawn from a literature review, from existing interview schedules, and from information given by service providers.

The schedule contained three sections:

1. Personal characteristics
2. The Check-list of Challenging Behaviours
3. Setting characteristics

Seven interviewers were recruited and trained to use the structured interview schedule. Interviews were completed for all those referred. The data was collected and analysed and reliability checks were carried out. In all, 168 interviews were included in the analysis.

The Check-list of Challenging Behaviours (CCB) was used as a screening device. The CCB consists of two sections. The check-list of aggressive behaviour included behaviours involving physical harm to others. A self-injury item was included in this list as it could be rated on the same severity scale. Each item in the aggressive behaviour check-list was rated for **frequency, severity** and **management difficulty** using five-point rating scales. The second check-list consisted of other types of challenging behaviour which may be associated with aggression. Items in the second check-list were rated for frequency and management difficulty only. The CCB was used to collect data on all 168 people referred. A principal component analysis of the data supported the internal validity of the CCB since the majority of items in the first principal component were aggressive behaviours. Inter-rater, test-retest and between interviewer reliabilities achieved acceptable levels for a survey instrument although the samples were small. The content validity was high but some omissions were identified (for details of the Challenging Behaviour Check-list see Harris, Thomson and Russell 1992, Harris, Humphreys and Thomson under revision).

The overall prevalence rate of aggressive behaviour among the 159 people with learning disabilities from this health district for whom we had adequate base population data was 17.6 per cent. The lowest rate of aggressive behaviour was identified in the day services (9.7 per cent) and the highest in hospitals within the health district (38.2 per cent). The prevalence rate among those attending schools for children with severe learning difficulties was 12.6 per cent. (Harris and Russell 1989a).

The results of this study relate to administrative prevalence but the extent to which this reflects the true prevalence of aggressive behaviour among people with learning disabilities depends on the reliability and validity of case identification and whether or not cases were known to service providers. Although no formal external validity checks were obtained at this stage of the data collection we believe that the survey identified the vast majority of those with learning disabilities who would fall into the category of severe aggressive behaviour.

Living accommodation

Over half of the people identified as showing aggressive behaviour were living in hospital wards (55.4 per cent). Two were resident in a special hospital; four were in private or voluntary homes. About a quarter of the group were living in the family home and these were mainly children and teenagers. Most of the others (17.3 per cent) were living in staffed housing or hostels.

Patterns of aggressive behaviour

As already discussed, the prevalence of aggressive behaviour is partly a reflection of the way in which it is defined. In this research the definition which we used led to the identification of three groups of people with aggressive behaviour: in the first group, 21 people were reported to engage in verbally aggressive and threatening behaviour. The second group consisted of 37 people who were said to be physically aggressive but who caused no injury to others. In the third group, 108 individuals were reportedly involved in incidents which resulted in some degree of injury to another person.

Setting variables

Behaviour may also vary considerably according to the social context in which it occurs. As indicated earlier, previous studies have suggested that environmental variables are better predictors of how people will behave than are individual characteristics or traits. The data were examined for differences in the **frequency, severity** and **management difficulty** of aggressive behaviour between schools, day facilities and hospitals. A comparison of frequency ratings in each setting showed that aggressive behaviour was reported to occur most **frequently** among those in the school population. Similarly on the severity ratings the school group was highest and significantly higher than for day facilities. No two groups were rated significantly differently in respect to **management difficulty**.

Some characteristics of the group

Contrary to expectations there was not a strong association between the person's sex and the presence of aggressive behaviour. Sixty nine per cent of the group were male but, given that there were more males (59 per cent) than females among the population of people with learning disabilities on the register in the health district, this difference only just reached statistical significance. There was no significant evidence of an association between the person's sex and the presence of aggressive behaviour within those at schools or in a mental handicap hospital.

The average age of the group was 34 years. Ages ranged from 8 to 85 years. Thirty four per cent of the group were between the ages of 15 and 29 and six people were over 70 years of age. The age of the person did emerge as a significant variable in the relationship between severity of outcome and perceived management difficulty. Children whose actions resulted in severe injury were less likely than adults to be seen as presenting extreme management problems. Furthermore when comparing frequency of aggression in schools, day facilities and hospitals it was found that aggressive behaviour occurred most frequently in the schools sample.

Aggressive behaviour over the life span.

Results from the study suggested that in terms of the development of aggressive behaviour over the life span, the general picture is that the behaviour often starts early in life, although serious difficulties may not have become apparent at this stage. Aggressive and other distressing behaviours tend to become more unmanageable during the teenage years and often continue into adulthood. In the past, people with severely aggressive behaviour have usually been referred to secure accommodation in hospital settings. In this way difficulties were contained but with little evidence of effective development for the individuals concerned.

Range and frequency of aggressive behaviour

Sixty nine per cent of the 168 people identified were said to have engaged in at least one act of physically aggressive behaviour during the previous month. Hitting out at others (ie punching/slapping/pushing/pulling people) was the most frequently reported type of behaviour and involved 50.6 per cent of the sample. There was a much lower incidence of other behaviours such as kicking (23.4 per cent), pinching (21.4 per cent), scratching (20.2 per cent), biting (12.6 per cent), headbutting (7.1 per cent) and using weapons (6.5 per cent). Details of other types of challenging behaviour were collected and it was found that self-injury, withdrawn, stereotypical and ritualistic behaviours were also common (Harris and Russell 1989b).

Injury to others

Although the number of people who were reported as presenting aggressive behaviour was quite high, the risk of a serious injury to others was low. About 40 per cent of the group never injured anyone. On the other hand, serious injuries (requiring medical attention) and very serious injuries (resulting in stays in hospital or certified absences from work) were accounted for by eight people. It was clear that two of these people no longer presented problems of aggression. The six remaining people were reported to have been involved in recent incidents resulting in severe injury to another person. They represented less than 0.5 per cent of the total population of people with learning disabilities from the district.

Extreme management problems

Extreme management problems were also limited to a small minority. Eighteen people were said to present extreme problems of management (defined as needing the help of at least one other member of staff). They represented 1.3 per cent of people with learning disabilities from the district. Thirteen of these people lived on hospital wards and in seven of these cases the people concerned were considered to be inappropriately placed. It was noticeable that in most cases the informants suggested a need for smaller living groups, higher staffing ratios and more appropriate staff skills. There was very little evidence of an expressed need for more secure accommodation.

Among the 18 who were the more difficult to manage physical restraint was the most common form of crisis intervention. Over half the group had been restrained in the previous month, while less than half the informants reported that they had received training in restraint. The use of drugs was the single most frequently reported treatment used to prevent or reduce aggressive behaviour in this group. Over half the group were said to be on drug treatments, the most common being anti-psychotic drugs, especially chlorpromazine. Seven people in this group regularly took three or more different types of medication. Agreed written behaviour modification programmes were only evident in three cases. There was little evidence of alternative strategies for this group. Despite the lack of treatment procedures, and the lack of evidence as to their effectiveness, the majority of the carers reported that they were satisfied with the present methods of managing the individual's behaviour.

EVALUATING SERVICE INTERVENTIONS

The original aim of the research was to evaluate selected interventions for people who present aggressive behaviour and to explain the efficacy of these interventions. However, the difficulty of identifying well-defined treatments and interventions in practice prompted a move away from these ambitions.

Methods

We adopted the perspective that the main issue for research was the progress of individual service users within the context of a particular service. We decided that the most useful approach, at this stage, was to examine the lives of a small number of individuals in detail. Four people with learning disabilities were chosen to participate in the research. The sample consisted of three women and one man and their ages ranged from 19 to 31 years with a mean age of 23.3 years. They were chosen primarily for the challenges they presented to service providers and because they lived in different types of residential settings. One of the women lived in a private residential home in the community with two other people with challenging behaviour. A second woman had a shared care arrangement, spending some time living with her parents and some time in a mental handicap hospital. In the hospital she shared a ward with 23 highly dependent people with learning disabilities. The third woman lived in a voluntary trust home which she shared with four other people who also had challenging behaviour. The man lived in a Social Services community home at the beginning of the study with five other people some of whom had challenging behaviour. During the study he was transferred to a mental handicap hospital where he lived on a ward with nine other people all of whom were considered to have some form of challenging behaviour.

Criteria for evaluation

Two sets of criteria were established for the evaluation. The first set of criteria was concerned with the progress of service users:

* quality of life
* adaptive skills
* aggressive behaviour

The second set of criteria focused on the organisation and support of staff in service settings:

* staff ratios and turnover
* staff support and stress

Quality of life

In order to assess the quality of life we used the Life Experiences Check-list (LEC) which was developed by Ager (1990) as a means of gauging the extent to which individuals enjoy experiences common to other members of the general population. The LEC was chosen for use in this research because it has the advantage of being accessible to service users and yielding scores which can be compared with a general population sample.

The LEC is concerned with the activities and experiences of service users. It is a measure of experience rather than competence and only items requiring little in the way of skill for them to be accessible are included. The scale consists of 50 items centred around five domains - Home, Leisure, Relationships, Freedom and Opportunities - with 10 items in each domain. The LEC can be completed by a service user with reading ability or by an informant on the person's behalf. It is also possible for an informant to complete an LEC with a service user. Completion of the check-list yields a global score indicating the range of life experiences and a profile showing scores for each of the five domains. In our research, we found that the LEC showed a high degree of face validity. The resultant information was used to compare service users across settings, over time in the same setting and with the general population sample.

Adaptive skills

Information on adaptive skills was collected by interviewing staff and parents, through informal and structured observations and by assessment using the Vineland Adaptive Behaviour Scales (Sparrow et al, 1984). In some cases records were also used to provide additional information or to corroborate existing data. The main focus was on social and communication skills, as the first phase of the research had suggested that these skills were inversely related to the frequency of aggressive behaviour. The Survey Form of the Vineland Adaptive Behaviour Scales (VABS) was chosen for use in the research because the main domains for adults - Communication, Daily Living Skills and Socialization - closely reflected the areas of interest.

Aggressive behaviour

In the first phase of the research we found that defining and measuring aggressive behaviour were complex processes. As well as having a wide range of forms and functions, aggressive behaviour can be assessed in different ways, eg frequency of occurrence, severity of outcome and management difficulty to others. High frequency behaviour can be observed directly, while incidents resulting in serious injuries are uncommon and, therefore, more difficult to observe. Management difficulty can be assessed simply by asking staff, however, their perceptions are subjective and there may be considerable variation between staff. It was evident from the prevalence study that both the frequency and severity of aggressive behaviour were positively correlated with perceived management difficulty. The stronger correlation was between management difficulty and the severity of aggressive behaviour (Harris and Russell, 1989b). Perceived management difficulty appeared to be the best predictor of the level of challenge presented to a service.

In this evaluation, qualitative data were collected from interviews with staff and parents and this was an important source of information about perceptions of management difficulty. Existing records were sometimes useful sources of serious incidents of aggressive behaviour as injuries to others were often recorded under health and safety regulations. Finally, the Check-list of Challenging Behaviour (CCB) was used to indicate the type and range of aggressive behaviour and to rate each behaviour for frequency, severity and management difficulty. Other types of challenging behaviour were also recorded using the CCB since the prevalence survey revealed that although physical and verbal aggression were the most frequently reported behaviours, many people were said to present additional challenging behaviour, especially ritualistic, stereotypical and withdrawn behaviour (Harris and Russell, 1989b). Using the CCB to collect data on aggressive and other types of challenging behaviour allowed comparisons to be made between service users in different settings and over time for the same service user in the same setting.

Staff ratios and turnover

Staff-to-client ratios were examined in two ways: first, the total number of staff and total number of clients in any one setting was noted; second, the average (mode) number of staff working with the average (mode) number of clients at any one time was noted for each setting. Staff turnover referred to the number of staff who had left their job (for whatever reason) and were not expected to return to that particular work setting. This was calculated as a percentage of the total staff number over a stated period of time.

Staff support and stress

In the absence of an existing means of evaluating staff support, a Staff Support Questionnaire (SSQ) was developed as part of the research. The SSQ is a self-report measure of support which takes between 10-20 minutes to complete. It is organised into four main sections. The first section is concerned with **role ambiguity** which results from a lack of clarity about the job. The second section includes questions about **personal support** at work. This included support in crisis situations, the availability of emotional support in the form of someone to talk to when experiencing difficulty and the opportunity for regular supervision or performance reviews. The identification of **risk situations** and the availability of clear guidelines if something goes wrong is the focus of the third section. The fourth section includes four questions about **job satisfaction**. In addition, there are a number of questions pertaining to staff attitudes towards clients and their situations (Harris and Thomson, in press). The General Health Questionnaire (GHQ-28) (Goldberg and Williams, 1988) was used in the evaluation as a measure of stress-related mental health. The SSQ and the GHQ-28 were administered concurrently to staff as part of the project. Since the GHQ-28 was a well validated measure of mental health it was used to validate the SSQ. A total of 41 staff were given an SSQ and GHQ-28 to complete.

RESULTS

The progress of the service users

The research found that two of the service users were making progress according to the criteria adopted. The evidence suggested that they were enjoying a wide range of experiences comparable to the average person in the general population. The findings indicated that given the appropriate support they were able to make use of the opportunities that living in the community provided. Both users were encouraged and supported in developing their communication, socialisation and daily living skills and were performing at a high level compared to other people with learning disabilities living in residential facilities. For one user the incidence of aggressive behaviour had clearly decreased. Neither user was considered to present major management difficulties due to aggressive or other types of challenging behaviour.

The other two service users were not making progress. The quality of their life experiences was poor compared to the general population. Neither user had sufficient opportunity to develop their adaptive skills. One service user showed an increase followed by a decrease in the incidence of aggressive behaviour. The other appeared to show a decrease in aggressive behaviour although the reliability of the data was uncertain in this case. In both cases, the management difficulty of aggressive and other types of challenging behaviour was low towards the end of the study.

The findings suggested that change in aggressive behaviour alone is not sufficient for evaluating the progress of service users. Using this single criterion, all four service users in the study appeared to be making similar progress especially in terms of the management difficulty of aggressive behaviour. An evaluation of services needs to take into account the extent to which individuals enjoy experiences common to other members of the general population as well as opportunities for personal development and changes in adaptive skills. Change in aggressive behaviour alone is not sufficient for evaluating the progress of service users. There appears to be a high degree of interdependence between challenging behaviour, adaptive skills and quality of life.

Service users were more likely to make progress if they were well supported by staff, involved in decision-making about what they did and where they lived and helped to take advantage of opportunities for personal development. The findings suggested that progress can be made on the basis of ordinary life principles.

The impact on staff support and stress

Staffing was identified as the most important resource in a service. A systematic and flexible means of calculating staff-to-user ratios was called for which takes into account the needs and wants of service users, the aims and objectives of the service and how staff are deployed to work with service users. The findings suggested that staff support and stress are relatively independent of staff-to-user ratios, low support and high stress can occur where staff-to-user ratios are adequate, but it is less likely that high support and low stress will be present when the ratios are inadequate.

Staff were more likely to feel supported when role ambiguity at work is low, that is when staff are clear about their objectives and responsibilities, know what their superior expects from them and thinks about the quality of their work. Personal support was important including access to someone who will listen in times of difficulty, practical help during crisis situations and regular supervision or performance reviews. Risk situations need to be identified for each individual with challenging behaviour as well as guide lines about what to do if something goes wrong.

The nature of interventions

The research indicated that it is essential to distinguish clearly between crisis interventions such as the use of seclusion, physical and chemical restraint and therapeutic interventions which are designed to bring about beneficial change for the person concerned. The more successful therapeutic interventions appeared to focus on developing social relationships and communication skills rather than attempting to reduce aggressive behaviour directly. The degree to which individuals are empowered to take control over their own lives may be an important consideration.

CONCLUSIONS

The study highlighted the difficulty of research in this area. Interventions tended to be multi-component rather than single; this usually involves the simultaneous manipulation of many variables making it extremely difficult to determine what is bringing about change. Outcome measures are poorly developed; it is difficult, for example, to obtain reliable and valid information on the frequency, severity and management difficulties of aggressive behaviour. Future research may do better to concentrate on the nature and quality of social interactions between service users and service providers.

REFERENCES

AGER A (1990). *The Life Experience Check-list Manual.* Windsor: NFER Nelson.

BLUNDEN R AND ALLEN D (Eds) (1987). *Facing the Challenge: an ordinary life for people with learning difficulties and challenging behaviour.* London : King's Fund Centre.

FRYERS T (1984). *The epidemiology of severe intellectual impairment: The dynamics of prevalence.* London: Academic Press.

GOLDBERG D AND WILLIAMS P (1988). *A user's guide to the General Health Questionnaire.* Windsor: NFER Nelson.

HARRIS P (in press). The nature and extent of aggressive behaviour amongst people with learning difficulties (mental handicap) in a single health district. *Journal of Intellectual Disability Research.*

HARRIS P AND RUSSELL O (1989a). The prevalence of aggressive behaviour among people with learning difficulties (mental handicap); Interim Report. University of Bristol: Norah Fry Research Centre.

HARRIS P AND RUSSELL O (1989b). The nature of aggressive behaviour among people with learning difficulties (mental handicap); Second Report. University of Bristol: Norah Fry Research Centre.

HARRIS P AND RUSSELL O (1990a). Rising to the challenge? The lives of five people with very challenging behaviour; Third Report. University of Bristol: Norah Fry Research Centre.

HARRIS P AND RUSSELL O (1990b). Aggressive behaviour among people with learning difficulties - the nature of the problem. IN A Dosen, A Van Gennep and G J Zwanikken (Eds) *Treatment of Mental Illness and Behavioural Disorder in the Mentally Retarded.* Leiden, the Netherlands: Logon Publications.

HARRIS P AND RUSSELL O (1992). How to meet the challenge. *Health Service Journal,* October 8, 28-29.

HARRIS P, HUMPHREYS J AND THOMSON G (under revision). A Checklist of Challenging Behaviours: assessing aggressive behaviour attributed to people with learning difficulties.

HARRIS P AND THOMSON G (in press). The Staff Support Questionnaire: a means of measuring support among staff working with people with challenging behaviour. *Mental Handicap.*

HARRIS P, THOMSON G AND RUSSELL O (1992). An evaluation of services for four people with learning difficulties and aggressive behaviour; Final Report. University of Bristol: Norah Fry Research Centre.

HORNER R H, DUNLAP G, KOEGEL R L, CARR E G, SAILOR W, ANDERSON J, ALBIN R W AND O'NEILL R E (1990). Toward a technology of "non-aversive" behavioural support. *Journal of the Association for Persons with Severe Handicaps, 15,* 125-132

LA VIGNA G W AND DONELLAN A M (1986). *Alternatives to punishment: solving behaviour problems with non-aversive settings.* New York: Irvington Publications Inc.

LOVETT H (1985). *Cognitive Counselling and Persons with Special Needs: adapting behavioural approaches to the social context.* New York: Praeger.

McGEE J J, MENOLASCINO F J, HOBBS D C AND MENOUSEK P E (1987). *Gentle Teaching: a non-aversive approach to helping persons with mental retardation.* New York: Human Sciences Press.

MULICK J A (1990). The ideology and science of punishment in mental retardation. *American Journal on Mental Retardation, 95,* 142-156

SPARROW S S, BALLA D A, CICCHETTI D V (1984). *Vineland Adaptive Behaviour Scales: Interview Edition-Survey Manual.* Minnesota: American Guidance Service.

CHAPTER 3

CHALLENGING BEHAVIOUR

Chris Kiernan and Hazel Qureshi

INTRODUCTION

In the development of policy, service planning, and clinical practice for people with learning disability and challenging behaviour data concerned with the numbers, location, characteristics of individuals, and on current management issues can highlight a range of factors which require attention. The data described in this chapter were derived from a large-scale study of children, young people, and adults known to or within services for people with learning disability in the North Western Regional Health Authority. The data presented were derived from a survey of the populations in seven districts (Health Authorities and corresponding Local Authorities) (Kiernan, Qureshi and Alborz, 1989) and an interview-based study of the perspectives of managers in education, social services, and health departments in these districts (Routledge, 1990). Other publications based on these data include Kiernan (1992), Qureshi (1991), (in press), and Qureshi and Alborz (1992). A third component of the study is decribed by Qureshi (this volume and Qureshi, 1991-2, 1992).

METHODS

The survey covered seven District Health Authorities (DHAs) and corresponding Local Authorities (LAs) in the North Western Regional Health Authority. The districts approached were selected to provide examples of differing types of authorities on the Craig (1985) classification. They included inner city areas, metropolitan districts, traditional manufacturing and high status growth area County Council districts. There was no representative of Craig's rural area in the Region.

All day and residential facilities for children and adults with learning disability were covered in the survey. People from the districts covered who were in long-stay hospitals in and outside the Region and other out-district placements were screened.

An operational definition of challenging behaviour was developed in the context of a pilot project. This identified people through the consequences of their behaviour in terms of injury to themselves or others, damage to or destruction of their environment, or severe social disruption which affected the quality of the lives of other people. Individuals were also included in the survey if their challenging behaviour was controlled through some feature of the service setting. This aspect of the definition was intended to apply, for example, to people whose self-injury was controlled through restraints or to people whose offending was controlled through Secure Provision.

The definition was operationalised in a Setting Interview and, for out-Region placements, a screening letter. These instruments allowed identification of people to be included in the survey but were cast more broadly in terms of criteria for inclusion than the subsequent Individual Schedule. This instrument asked for details of the characteristics of individuals in terms of abilities and challenging behaviour, current impact on the environment and management strategies. Challenging behaviours were rated by respondents as "one of this person's most serious management problems", "present, but a lesser problem", "previously, or potentially a serious problem but controlled in this setting", or "not a problem for this person". On the basis of this Schedule a number of individuals identified through the Setting Interview were eliminated as not reaching the criteria adopted by the Individual Schedule.

The Setting Interview was conducted with a senior member of staff in Regional settings. A single Individual Schedule was also completed with the staff member if individuals were identified through the Setting Interviews. Other Individual Schedules were then completed by staff within the setting and returned by post to the research team. Individual Schedules were sent to out-Region placements where relevant individuals were identified.

A further study within the programme involved interviews with managers of services for people with learning disability on services for people with challenging behaviour (Routledge, 1990). These interviews were completed in all districts with education, social services and health managers. The interviews covered existing services, the managers' perception of the issues surrounding challenging behaviour, their views on the effectiveness of their current services including issues of cross-agency working, and their views of future development of services for people with challenging behaviour.

RESULTS

The reliability of the Setting Interview varied from 0.62 to 0.71 depending on settings; the reliability of items used from the Individual Schedule were all over 0.70. The survey achieved a response rate of 100 per cent from settings within districts and 80 per cent from out-district settings. Around 4,200 people were screened including 896 in long-stay hospitals and 164 in other out-district placements.

The survey identified 16.7 per cent of the population of people with learning disabilities known to or in contact with services for people with learning disability. This administrative definition of learning disability excluded people who would be defined psychometrically as learning disabled but who were not known to specialist services. This group would substantially comprise people with mild learning disability including an unknown number of offenders.

The survey identified 734 individuals, 30 per cent of the long-stay learning disability hospital population and 13 per cent of the community population. However, because of the greater size of the community population, adults living in hospitals and the community were equally represented in the population identified as showing challenging behaviour (community 37.7 per cent; hospital 37.4 per cent). The majority of the 175 children and young people (19 or under) in the population identified lived in the community (97.1 per cent), the remaining children and young people living in hospital.

The age distribution of people within the population showed a peak prevalence in the 20 to 29 age group with a fall in the numbers of people identified with age. Comparison with the age distribution of people on the Salford Case Register suggested that people in the 20 to 39 age groups were over-represented in the population of people with challenging behaviour. Comparison of the hospital and community groups in the population indicated that people identified in hospitals were older (Kiernan, Qureshi and Alborz, 1989).

The abilities of the population of people with challenging behaviour were highly variable. Ninety per cent of the population were fully mobile. The 625 people in the mobile group were variable in terms of communication, self-care and domestic skills. For example, around 22 per cent of the adult mobile group had no speech or other means of formal expressive communication. However 47 per cent were able to speak in phrases and had moderate to good receptive abilities. In the 70 strong non-mobile group 38 per cent of adults were reported as having no speech and little or no understanding of speech. On the other hand 23.8 per cent of non-mobile adults were able to speak in phrases and had moderate to good receptive abilities. Sixty per cent of the mobile group were rated as having severe learning disability as opposed to 80 per cent of the non-mobile group.

Around one-third of the population identified were reported as suffering from epilepsy, the proportion being higher in the non-mobile group. Around 12 per cent overall were said to have a recorded psychiatric diagnosis, eight of whom were suffering from depressive illnesses, eight, other affective disorders, 27 schizophrenia and ten an unclassified psychotic condition. The majority of people in this group were mobile.

The mobile and non-mobile groups differed in terms of the frequency with which differing types of challenging behaviour were reported (Table 1). In terms of **serious** management problems **only** the Table shows that, for mobile adults, physical attacks were the most commonly reported challenging behaviour, with destructiveness and self-injury being ranked fifth and sixth. For the adult non-mobile group self-injury was reported as a serious management problem for over forty per cent of the group. Nonetheless, one in five people in the non-mobile group showed physical attacks as a serious management problem. Hospital and community comparisons suggested that, in terms of ratings by respondents, the two groups were broadly comparable. Table 2 shows the serious problems reported for the adult mobile and non-mobile groups in the two settings. Comparisons of the mobile groups suggests that non-compliance and temper tantrums are much more prevalent in the community groups but that self-injury is more prevalent in the hospital group. In the small non-mobile groups self-injury appears again to be more prevalent in the hospital group.

Table 1   Percentage of the adult mobile and non-mobile people reported as showing different serious challenging behaviours (Kiernan, Qureshi and Alborz, 1989).

Mobile N = 478		Non-Mobile N = 42	
	Per cent		Per cent
Physical attacks	23.3	Self-injury	40.5
Non-compliance	21.3	Physical attacks	21.4
Temper tantrums	20.7	Temper tantrums	16.7
Anti-social behaviour	18.4	Non-compliance	9.5
Destructiveness	17.2	Unpleasant habits	9.5
Self-injury	14.9	Destructiveness	7.1

The majority of people identified in the survey showed more than one challenging behaviour. Amongst serious challenging behaviours, 26.3 per cent of people showing destructive behaviour were also reported as making

Table 2 Percentage of adults in hospital and community populations identified showing different challenging behaviours. Challenging behaviours shown by more than one person. Numbers in parentheses represent individuals showing the behaviour.

MOBILE

Hospital N = 235	Per cent	**Community** N = 242	Per cent
Physical attacks	22.1	Non-compliance	28.9
Self-injury	18.7	Temper tantrums	24.4
Destructiveness	17.4	Physical attacks	24.4
Temper tantrums	16.6	Anti-social	21.1
Anti-social	15.7	Verbal abuse	19.8
Non-compliance	13.6	Destructiveness	16.9
		Self-injury (rank 10)	11.2

NON-MOBILE

Hospital N = 19	Per cent	**Community** N = 23	Per cent
Self-injury	52.6 (10)	Self-injury	30.4 (7)
Physical attacks	21.1	Physical attacks	21.7
Temper tantrums	15.8	Temper tantrums	17.4
Unpleasant habits	15.8	Verbal abuse	8.7 (2)
Destructiveness	10.5 (2)		

serious physical attacks and 25.4 per cent self-injured. Over all levels of challenging behaviour 50 per cent of those reported as making physical attacks were also reported as showing destructive behaviour and 57.3 per cent of people showing destructive behaviour as making physical attacks (Kiernan, Qureshi and Alborz, 1989). These data indicate the degree to which challenging behaviours need to be considered as parts of an overall pattern of behaviour rather than as single phenomena.

The impact of challenging behaviour on their carers and other people with a learning disability is indicated by the finding that in 46 per cent of instances some staff members were said to be frightened by people making physical attacks and some staff members were angry or annoyed in 57.3 per cent of cases. Some other people with learning disability were said to be frightened by people making physical attacks in 76.5 per cent of cases and 76.5 per cent became angry or annoyed. Of people who made physical attacks on others 51.2 per cent were reported as usually causing at least minor injuries to staff and 64.3 per cent at least minor injuries to others.

Of the 291 people where physical attacks on staff or other people was a serious management problem, 16.2 per cent (47 people) were said to have caused between minor and serious injuries to staff at some time and a slightly higher percentage had caused this level of injury to other people (18.6 per cent, 54 people). Serious levels of injury, ones which required hospital treatment for broken bones, stab wounds or the like, had been inflicted at some time on staff by 26 people (8.9 per cent) and on others by 30 people (10.3 per cent).

The level of intervention required to control challenging behaviour was rated on a scale from no intervention to physical intervention by more than one member of staff. A verbal response was said to be usually required in the case of 38.8 per cent of people showing physical attacks and physical intervention by more than one member of staff for 33 per cent of people. The maximum level of response required was physical intervention by one member of staff for 33.4 per cent of people showing physical attacks and intervention by more than one member of staff in 44.5 per cent of cases. Physical intervention by one member of staff was said to be required as a maximum level of intervention for 50.3 per cent of people showing self-injury and 41.3 per cent of people showing destructive behaviour (Kiernan, Qureshi and Alborz, 1989).

Respondents were asked to indicate whether behaviour modification programmes had been developed to manage challenging behaviour. Twenty per cent of people making physical attacks, 27 per cent of people showing self-injury and 28 per cent of people showing destructive behaviour were said to have such programmes in place. Respondents were also asked to indicate whether drugs were prescribed to control challenging behaviour. Fifty three per cent of people making physical attacks, 73 per cent of people who were reported as showing self-injury and 51 per cent of people showing destructive behaviour were reported as being given drugs to control the behaviours.

Further analyses of the findings concerning use of anti-psychotic drugs showed that 24.5 per cent of people given anti-psychotic medications were prescribed chlorpramazine, 18.9 per cent thioridazine and 14.1 per cent haloperidol (Kiernan, Reeves and Alborz, in preparation). There were frequent reports of combinations of anti-psychotic medications with other anti-psychotic medications, anti-psychotic depot injections or other psychoactive drugs.

Several multivariate analyses were undertaken to establish the influence of variables covered in the survey on the likelihood of prescription of anti-psychotic medications (Kiernan, Reeves and Alborz, in preparation). With all other variables controlled, a set of three core variables was isolated as primarily influential. These were psychiatric diagnosis; where the person was resident; and their district of origin. Of the 69 people reported as having a specified psychiatric disorder 67 per cent (48) were prescribed an anti-psychotic drug as opposed to 47 per cent (198) of the 421 people for whom there was no disorder specified. (These and other percentages in this and other analyses are adjusted for the influence of the other main variables). Consequently, although established psychiatric diagnosis was influential in prescription of anti-psychotic medication the majority of the 246 people prescribed anti-psychotics (80 per cent) did not have a reported psychiatric diagnosis.

A far higher percentage of people in hospital disturbed wards (68 per cent) and non-disturbed wards (63 per cent) were prescribed anti-psychotic medication than those living in hostels in the community (39 per cent) or in their family homes (28 per cent). It has to be borne in mind that these results control for such variables as the type and seriousness of challenging behaviour and the consequences of challenging behaviour.

The third major variable, district of origin, had comparable effects. The percentage of people prescribed anti-psychotic drugs varied from 61 per cent in one district to 38 per cent in two other districts when all other variables were taken into account. This district variation may, in part, be explained by responsibility being taken by individual psychiatrists for hospital and community populations of the different districts.

The three major variables isolated in this analysis were the major determinants of prescription of anti-psychotic drugs. They all suggest wide variations in prescription practice dependent on factors independent of levels of challenging behaviour.

In order to throw further light on the variables affecting prescription an analysis was undertaken which controlled for the effects of the three major determinants. This analysis revealed five variables, all related to the social impact of challenging behaviour, as significant determinants. They were: the level of physical intervention required to control behaviour; the number of factors rated by staff as causing stress; the number of behaviours rated as serious problems; the level of aggressive behaviour; and whether the person injured others.

It can be argued that, within the context of the three variables in the first analysis, these variables are those which affect the decision to request and to prescribe anti-psychotic medication. Given the relatively small number of people with a recorded psychiatric diagnosis who were prescribed anti-psychotic medication it seems clear from these analyses that anti-psychotic medication was being used mainly in an attempt to control behaviour which was socially disruptive.

The analyses presented so far relate to the total population identified in the survey. Managers of services identified two levels or types of challenging behaviour (Routledge, 1990). These were behaviours which they believed would be resistant to changes in the social and physical environment and behaviours which were created or maintained by service deficiencies. These included poor physical environments, a lack of stimulating activities and the unsuitable congregation of people with a wide range of special needs. Inadequate levels of staffing were also felt to be influential as well as low levels of staff tolerance. Lack of staff training and therefore poor skills, both in general and in relation to work with people with challenging behaviour, was also cited. Poor access to professional support for front-line staff in work with people with challenging behaviour was highlighted. Managers argued that "expert" support was inadequate and that people who did have expertise in this area had typically acquired such skills as a result of personal interest rather than professional training. Managers saw future development of quality services as being dependent on general service development and the development of community-based individualised services supported by adequate expertise (Kiernan, 1992, 1993).

A refinement of the definition of challenging behaviour adopted in the survey as a whole was developed to identify the smaller "core" of people with serious challenging behaviour indicated by managers (Qureshi and Alborz, 1992). Individuals were selected who had **at some time** caused more than minor injuries to themselves or others, or destroyed their immediate living or working environment; or, showed behaviour **at least weekly** which required intervention by more than one member of staff for control; or placed them in physical danger; or caused damage which could not be rectified by immediate care staff; or caused at least an hour's disruption; or caused more than a few minutes disruption **at least daily.**

Using this definition the profile of an "average" district with a 220,000 population was computed. This analysis suggests that, in the average district, ten children and young people would be identified, including six between the ages of 16 and 19, as well as 13 adults in community settings. A further 17 adults from the district would be living in hospitals and a further two people in other out-district placements. The six young people between the ages of 16 and 19 and the 19 people in out-district placements would all require adult community provision, probably of both residential and day care, in the forseeable future.

There were however variations in the numbers of people showing challenging behaviour related to the demographic characteristics of districts (Qureshi and Alborz, 1992). On a standardised comparison the two inner city areas showed higher numbers of people identified as opposed to the two metropolitan districts and the three County Council districts.

IMPLICATIONS

Studies of the type described in this chapter have strengths but also inherent limitations. The strengths of the study include the very substantial coverage provided which allows generalisations to be made on the representativeness of data and to characterise effectively the whole population covered. However, despite the extensive coverage of the study, the definition of learning disability adopted excluded people who may be so defined using a psychometric definition. As noted this strategy would probably exclude from consideration an unknown number of people with mild learning disability who show challenging behaviour, but who do not come in contact with learning disability services.

Other limitations apply, in particular, to the degree to which survey and interview research instruments can throw light on the reasons why challenging behaviour occurs and on quality of management. The current study could only hope to indicate areas where more detailed analyses should be directed.

Given these considerations the following implications for policy, service planning and clinical practice may be offered:

*   There is a clear need to plan adult services for people with challenging behaviour who are:-
    Currently in community settings
    Will be resettled from long-stay hospitals
    Moving to adult services from services for children and young people

    The numbers of people with serious challenging behaviour currently in long-stay hospitals and moving to adult services from educational provision is likely to equal or exceed those currently in adult community services.

*   Planning of services for this group will therefore require a high level of co-ordination between Education, Health, and Social Services in order to ensure appropriate transfer of information and skills in the management of individuals.

*   There is a clear need to plan individualised services. This follows from:-
    The heterogeneity of the group
    The undesirability and unsuitability of congregate services
    The relatively small numbers of people with serious challenging behaviour

    Although individualised services may require a great deal of planning and monitoring, and be relatively expensive, several lines of evidence suggest that people with challenging behaviour are currently expensive both in service time and in financial terms. Improved training and organisation may offset the need for substantial additional resources.

*   There is an indicated need to review the quality of front-line management, staff training and support.

*   There is a need to develop expertise, both in terms of front-line staff and supporting professionals, in respect of methods of analysing and managing challenging behaviour.

*   There is a need to review the quality and effectiveness of current management strategies. This applies particularly to:-

    Restraint and control. Given the common finding that physical intervention by staff was required to control challenging behaviour it would seem desirable for agencies to review the types and desirability of the restraint and control techniques employed.

Behavioural programmes. Such programmes are accepted as probably the only effective approach currently available for the management of challenging behaviour. The survey suggested that such programmes were in place for less than one third of people identified as showing major challenging behaviours. In addition, given the limitations of the methodology, the quality and appropriateness of the programmes could not be assessed. Experience within the Region would cast serious doubt on the quality of such programmes. Evidence from other Regions would support this scepticism.

Drug interventions. The results of the current survey suggest that the use of anti-psychotic medication was widespread and determined mainly by prescription practices and an attempt to control challenging behaviour through such medication. Clearly extensive variation in prescription practice strongly suggests the need for medical audit in order to identify good practice and to harmonise overall practice. Given that there is little evidence to suggest that anti-psychotic medication has specific effects on individual challenging behaviours, and that the overall sedative effects which they produce frequently are accompanied by extra-pyramidal disorders, there appears to be a need for medical audit in order to reduce the overall frequency with which these drugs are prescribed. It should also be noted that the quality of research on the impact of psychoactive drugs on challenging behaviour is poor. The funding of further research in this area seems to be clearly indicated.

REFERENCES

CRAIG J (1985). *A 1981 Socio-economic Classification of Local and Health Authorities of Great Britain.* London: HMSO.

KIERNAN C (1992). Services for people with mental handicap and challenging behaviour in the North West. IN J Harris (Ed) *Service Responses to people with Learning Difficulties and Challenging Behaviour.* Kidderminster: BIMH.

KIERNAN C (1993). Future Directions. IN R S P Jones and C B Eayrs (Eds) *Challenging Behaviour and Intellectual Disability: A Psychological Perspective.* Clevedon, Avon: BILD Publications.

KIERNAN C, QURESHI H AND ALBORZ A (1989). Characteristics of People Showing Severe Problem Behaviour. Manchester: Hester Adrian Research Centre.

KIERNAN C, REEVES D AND ALBORZ A (in preparation). The use of anti-psychotic drugs with adults with learning disabilities and challenging behaviour.

QURESHI H (1990). "Facing the Challenge": How can parents deal with violent outbursts from their mentally handicapped children once they are grown up? Do they feel supported by community mental handicap nurses? *Nursing Times,* November 7, 46-48.

QURESHI H (1991). "He's mine ... I feel an utter failure": The views of parents caring for young adults with challenging behaviour. *Community Living,* July, 10-11.

QURESHI H (1991-2). Young adults with learning difficulties and challenging behaviour: Parents' views of services in the community. *Social Work and Social Sciences Review, 3,* 104-123.

QURESHI H (in press). Prevalence of challenging behaviour in adults. IN I Fleming and B Stenfert Kroese (Eds) *People with Severe Learning Difficulties and Challenging Behaviour: a source book.* Manchester: Manchester University Press.

QURESHI H AND ALBORZ A (1992). Epidemiology of challenging behaviour. *Mental Handicap Research, 5,* 130-145.

ROUTLEDGE M (1990). Services for People with a Mental Handicap whose Behaviour is a Challenge to Services: A review of the Policy and Service Context in the Seven Districts covered by the HARC Behaviour Problems Project. Hester Adrian Research Centre, University of Manchester.

PART 2

FAMILY RESPONSES

CHAPTER 4

FAMILY FACTORS AND PARENTS' REPORT OF BEHAVIOUR PROBLEMS IN 6-14 YEAR OLD CHILDREN WITH DOWN'S SYNDROME

Tricia Sloper and Steve Turner

INTRODUCTION

In the 1960's, the stereotype that people with Down's syndrome were sociable and good natured began to be challenged by evidence that behaviour problems among children with Down's syndrome were by no means uncommon, with reported prevalence rates of 20 to 50 per cent for institutionalised people (Menolascino, 1967, Moore et al, 1968). It is now clear that there is considerable variation within this population with regard to the incidence of problem behaviour (Byrne, Cunningham and Sloper, 1988) and a pertinent question for services concerned with children with Down's syndrome and their families is which particular child and family factors are associated with higher or lower rates of behaviour problems.

Existing literature provides a number of indications of possible associations. Studies of children with Down's syndrome reviewed by Gibson (1978) suggest that behaviour problems may be more prevalent among boys, older children, and those with a lower developmental level or with communication problems. Hart et al (1984) linked behaviour and management difficulties in non-handicapped children with upper respiratory tract and ear infections. Such health and communication problems are more prevalent among the Down's syndrome population (Cunningham et al, 1985, Turner et al, 1990). The high level of hospitalisation among children with Down's syndrome (Turner et al, 1990) may be expected to result in more behaviour problems, as found in studies of non-handicapped children (eg Quinton and Rutter, 1976).

Family factors such as the quality of mother-child interaction and parental adjustment have also been linked to behaviour problems in children with learning disability (Brooks-Gunn and Lewis, 1984, Crawley and Spiker, 1983, Emde and Brown, 1978).

However, many of these factors may be inter-related and it is of interest to investigate which factors show the strongest independent associations with problem behaviour.

The present study examined the prevalence of a range of behaviour problems among a representative sample of 7 to 14 year old children with Down's syndrome living at home in Greater Manchester, and went on to identify predictors of the variance in the prevalence level found. Earlier work with the same cohort of families, completed when the children were aged 5 to 10, confirmed the existence of serious behaviour problems for a minority of families (Cunningham et al, 1986), although overall prevalence appeared to be no higher than in children without disability of a similar developmental level (Richman et al, 1982). The current investigation took place within a wider study of adaptation of children with Down's syndrome and their families (Sloper et al, 1988). Data were obtained from interviews and self-completion questionnaires involving both mothers'and fathers' questionnaires completed by the teacher who best knew the child, and through assessment of the child's developmental level. The wide range of data collected enabled the use of techniques of multivariate analysis in order to identify the most significant correlates of selected outcome measures, including an index score of behaviour problems. Analysis of the Behaviour Problems Index was completed for 114 of the 123 children who took part in the study.

The Behaviour Problems Index used in the present study was based on one developed for the earlier study of the same cohort of families (Cunningham et al, 1986). This index in turn was based on the Behaviour Screening Questionnaire devised by Richman et al (1982) for use with young non-handicapped children, with additional items derived from studies of children with learning disability (Wing and Gould, 1978, Gath and Gumley, 1984). These latter items were included to reflect behaviours more common for children with learning disability, which are not included in scales for non-disabled children.

Whenever a behaviour was reported, parents were asked to assess how serious a problem it represented to them. The sum of these assessments was also used to construct an index score - the Appraisal Index. The use of two separate indices was designed to take account of the possibility that behaviour "problems" in the children were not necessarily viewed as such by parents, and that variations in appraisal may be related to factors such as the resources of the family, the gender of the parent or the age of the child. It was also felt that if parents were given the opportunity to rate their response to a behaviour separately from reporting its occurrence, this may help to reduce possible bias in the Behaviour Problem Index itself - for example through the under-reporting of behaviours that were not felt to be a problem. It was felt to be important to identify which factors were related to parental perceptions of the child's behaviour as problematic and therefore the Appraisal Index was used as a separate outcome measure for both mothers and fathers.

CHARACTERISTICS OF THE SAMPLE

Table 1 shows background information for the 114 children whose parents provided information on behaviour problems. The age range of the children (6-14) is wide, although in fact 84 per cent were aged between 7 and 11, with a mean of 9 years 3 months. Sixty one per cent were boys.

The children were assessed on the McCarthy Scales of Children's Abilities (McCarthy, 1972) and, for children whose developmental level fell below the limits of this test, the Bayley Scales of Infant Development (Bayley, 1969). IQ was calculated by computing MA/CA, as many of the children's scores fell outside the norms for the tests. Eighty three per cent of the children had IQ scores between 20 and 50, four per cent scored under 20 and 14 per cent scored over 50. The mean score was 39.7.

Table 1 Characteristics of the children for whom Behaviour Problems Index score was obtained (N = 114)

1. Age range	6-8 years	9-11 years	12-14 years
	35%	56%	9%
	(40)	(64)	(10)
(Mean = 9.3 years)			
2. Gender	Male	Female	
	61%	39%	
	(70)	(44)	
3. IQ	Up to 20	20.1 to 50	50.1 to 70
	4%	82%	14%
	(5)	(93)	(16)

THE BEHAVIOUR PROBLEMS QUESTIONNAIRE

Parents were asked a series of questions about their child's behaviour in the previous month. Fourteen categories of behaviour were used, mostly self-explanatory (see Table 2). Examples of disturbed behaviours are: shouting/screaming; running away; hoarding. Examples of habits are: rocking; biting nails; twiddling with objects. Response rates varied for individual questions, but 114 mothers and 82 fathers completed enough questions to enable an Index score to be assigned to that child. The low number of responding fathers was due to single parent families and higher non-response among fathers who were present in the family. The correlation between Index scores computed for mothers and for fathers was high (r = 0.77, n = 76). However, mothers tended to report more behaviours (mean Index score = 72.8) than fathers (mean = 70.4), which suggested that the mothers, as the main carers, may have been more accurate and comprehensive in the reporting of behaviours in a variety of settings and times of day. For this reason the analysis of the Behaviour Problem Index scores used mothers' responses.

The most frequently reported behaviour categories were: disturbed behaviours; habits; fears; sleeping; and management, all reported by more than 50 per cent of the mothers (Table 2).

Table 2   The Behaviour Problems Questionnaire 14 categories, covering 54 behaviours

Type of behaviour problem	% of mothers reporting
1. Disturbed behaviours	92%
2. Habits	86%
3. Fears	79%
4. Sleeping	63%
5. Management	56%
6. Eating	49%
7. Concentration/amusement	44%
8. Over/under activity	44%
9. School problems	43%
10. Attention-seeking	41%
11. Toileting	39%
12. Irritability	18%
13. Rituals	16%
14. Worries	10%
	(n = 116-118)

Table 3 Most serious problems - Parental appraisal

(A) MOTHERS Type of Behaviour Problem	Appraisal Score	N
1. Concentration/amusement	2.5	51
2. Management	2.5	63
3. Sleeping	2.4	76
4. Toileting	2.3	60
5. Disturbed behaviours	2.3	108
6. Over/under activity	2.2	50
7. Habits	2.1	99
8. Irritability	2.1	21
9. Attention-seeking	2.0	48
10. Fears	1.8	105
11. Eating	1.8	57
12. Rituals	1.7	17
13. School-related	1.5	50
14. Worries	1.3	12
Mean score	2.2	

(B) FATHERS Type of Behaviour Problem	Appraisal score	N
1. Management	2.7	54
2. Concentration/amusement	2.4	38
3. Toileting	2.3	40
4. Sleeping	2.3	61
5. Irritability	2.3	15
6. Disturbed behaviours	2.2	72
7. Over/under activity	2.2	34
8. Attention-seeking	2.0	34
9. Habits	2.0	54
10. Worries	1.8	6
11. Fears	1.8	69
12. Eating	1.6	46
13. Rituals	1.6	14
14. School-related	1.3	86
Mean score	2.1	

The mean scores for appraisal of problems indicate which areas of behaviour parents found most problematic. Table 3 shows mean scores for mothers and fathers for the 14 categories of behaviours, based on scores of: 1 for "not a problem"; 2 for "a nuisance only"; 3 for "a slight problem", and 4 for "a definite problem". The rankings are very similar for mothers and fathers, though with some differences to those shown in Table 2 based on reported incidence only. Rituals and worries are confirmed as both infrequent and relatively unimportant behaviour problems in this age group. On the other hand, management problems were encountered by most mothers and were given a high "problem rating" by both sets of parents. Within the 14 categories, four individual behaviour problems stood out as being both relatively common and problematic. In the "disturbed behaviour" category, "running away" was both commonly reported and highly rated as a problem - 19 mothers and 14 fathers said it was "a definite problem". "Inappropriate behaviour with people outside the family" was reported as "a definite problem" by 19 of the 55 mothers who mentioned it, and 6 of the 31 fathers. The two other individual behaviour problems judged to be "a definite problem" by more than 10 per cent of parents were: being wet at night; and waking at night. Behaviour problems were apparently serious for a relatively small number of parents however, and the value of asking parents to both report and rate behaviour problems is that it helps to avoid the assumption that certain behaviours necessarily mean problems for families, while highlighting those behaviours and those families where problems are perceived.

It will be noted that many of the behaviours included in the Behaviour Problems Index do not come within the usual definitions of 'challenging behaviour'. Indeed, other chapters in this volume point to the low incidence of such behaviour in this age group. However, we would argue that it is important to understand which behaviours do 'challenge' parents of children in this age group and also to acknowledge the challenge of a child who frequently exhibits a wide variety of difficult behaviours. Although a number of the behaviours measured are problems common to children without disability (eg sleeping problems; toileting problems; poor concentration), the implications for the family are different for a child whose development is slower, whose understanding is more limited, whose physical size is larger and who has exhibited the problem over a number of years. All these factors present a greater challenge to parents attempting to deal with the behaviour on a day to day basis.

Thus, in the analysis of scores on the Behaviour Problems Index and the appraisal scores, we wanted to answer two questions. Firstly, which child and/or family factors were significantly associated with higher behaviour problem scores and secondly, which factors, over and above the frequency of problem behaviours, related to parents perceiving behaviour as more problematic.

In earlier studies with the Down's syndrome cohort (Cunningham et al, 1986) we had identified two groups of families where the children showed the same range and frequency of problem behaviours, one group of mothers found considerable problems in management of their children, but the other group did not. The key to the differences between the two groups appeared to lie in the quality of the mother-child relationship and the ability of the mothers to view their children positively in spite of problems in their behaviour. In this study, we aimed to investigate this further using a broader range of measures of child and parent characteristics.

In addition, using longitudinal data on behaviour problems and child and family characteristics over a two year period for a sub-sample of 49 children, we wished to identify whether any factors could be shown which were predictive of increased or decreased problem behaviour over time.

The identification of both concurrent and predictive factors in relation to problem behaviour in children can provide useful information for services. It can suggest factors in early childhood which may be predictive of increasing risk and therefore indicate where services need to be targeted to try to prevent such risk. It can also indicate child and family factors outside the actual behaviour which need to be included in the focus of interventions.

Factors related to scores on the Behaviour Problems Index

In all the analyses reported here a similar method was adopted. Firstly, we investigated the statistical associations between the outcome scores (in this case total behaviour problems scores) and a wide range of measures of child and family characteristics. From this we identified those variables which showed significant univariate relationships with the outcome measure. We then entered these variables into a multiple regression analysis in order to determine which ones were most strongly and independently related to the outcome. In the longitudinal analysis, variables from time 1 were entered into an analysis of time 2 behaviour problems scores, to identify factors which were predictive over time.

Table 4 Factors relating to Behaviour Problems Index scores*

		% of BPI Score Explained
1.	Child self-sufficiency -	16.6%
2.	Child health index +	12.0%
3.	Poor parent-child relationship +	8.4%
4.	Housing inadequacy +	6.1%
5.	Family cohesion -	3.9%
	Total % variance explained	50.7%*

F = 13.53, p = 0.000, n = 86
(+/- indicate direction of relationship)
* with control for social desirability response bias

Table 4 shows the results of the cross sectional analysis of current scores. Table 5 shows the results of the longitudinal analysis. The two variables most strongly associated with Behaviour Problems Index scores in the cross sectional analysis related directly to the child: higher scores on behaviour

Table 5 Factors at Time 1 relating to change in Behaviour Problems Index scores from 1984-85 (Time 1) to 1986-87 (Time 2) (2 years span)

Predictor Variable at Time 1		% of Time 2 BPI Score Explained
1.	Total behaviour problems score +	38.4%
2.	Maternal adjustment to child (Judson Score) -	6.8%
3.	Chronological x developmental age -	6.0%
4.	Behaviour disturbances: screaming +	4.6%
	Total % variance explained	55.5%

F = 13.09, p = 0.000, n = 47
(+/- indicate direction of relationship)

problems were related to lower scores on self sufficiency and higher scores on health problems in the children. Two other significant variables measured aspects of family functioning: higher scores on behaviour problems were related to low family cohesion scores; and interviewers' assessments of a poor relationship between the child and one or both parents. The final significant variable, mothers' ratings of housing inadequacy, reflected socio-economic factors as it was also strongly related to measures of social class and financial problems.

The association between self-sufficiency and behaviour problems reflected strong associations between behaviour and a number of developmental measures. The analysis of relationships with individual behaviours showed that developmental ability was strongly related to problems in toileting, over- or under-activity, habits, concentration, amusing self, management and disturbed behaviour. These problems, to some extent, reflect physical and mental maturity.

This relationship was further illuminated in the longitudinal analysis as shown in Table 5, where children of lower chronological and mental age were more likely to have shown increases in behaviour problems over the two year period, whereas those of higher chronological and mental age were more likely to have shown decreases.

Given the chronological and developmental age range of the sample, this suggests a peak in problems coinciding with chronological ages of seven to nine years and mental ages of two to three years and under. The higher levels of problems for such children reflect a developmental age at which toileting problems are common, concentration span is limited, behaviour and activity level is volatile and less easily managed because the children are less responsive to reasoning. However, the physical size and chronological age of the children would make such behaviour less acceptable, less easy to handle and, therefore, more of a problem. In addition, the continuation of such problems over a period of years and the slower rate of development of these children may have compounded and accentuated the effects on the families and also made normal developmental problems more difficult to deal with as they became established patterns of behaviour. This underlines the importance of support to families of young children with learning disabilities in helping them to deal with early developmental problems of behaviour and try to avoid such patterns becoming established.

The association between health problems and behaviour difficulties had also been found in our earlier cohort studies (Cunningham et al, 1986) and in studies of non-handicapped children (Hart et al, 1984). Further analysis of the relationship in this study showed that the strongest associations were with frequent minor infections and illnesses in the last year, eg coughs and colds, ear infections, diarrhoea and vomiting, rather than longer term, chronic problems. An analysis of which particular behaviour difficulties related to health problems further illuminated this. The behaviours implicated were sleeping difficulties, irritability, disturbed behaviours and school-based problems. Recurrent illness, which affects a child's mood and routine may be expected to have effects on these types of behaviour. Parents are generally more likely to accept different standards of behaviour from children when they are ill. However, there may be a risk that if children have frequent periods of illness and, in addition, have learning disabilities, it is more difficult to re-establish routines and change habits, so that maladaptive behaviours become established and continue when the illness has passed. This points to the importance of early monitoring and treatment of health problems, support for parents in helping them to anticipate and cope with behaviour problems which may arise during illness and help in understanding why these problems occur. As expected, mothers of children with more health problems did have more contacts with health services, but this was not the case overall for children with higher levels of behaviour problems. It may be that such services focussed on the health problems themselves and did not address the wider implications of the relationship of recurrent health problems to behaviour.

The association of the two parent and family variables with behaviour problems scores does not clearly suggest the direction of these effects. The most likely relationship is spiral or transactional, with problems in family and child relationships exacerbating behaviour problems and vice versa. In the longitudinal analysis, maternal adjustment to the child, as measured on the Judson scale (Judson and Burden, 1980) was related to change in behaviour problems over two years, indicating that where mothers had poor adjustment to the child at the initial measurement point, behaviour problems scores were likely to increase over the two years, but where mothers showed good adjustment, problems were likely to decrease. The relationship was significant when controlling for the initial level of behaviour problems so was not a function of mothers of children having few problem behaviours showing better adjustment. This result points to the effect of parent factors over time. This effect seems to lie in the mothers' acceptance of and adaptation to the child's handicap. An additional clue to the effect lies in the evidence from the longitudinal data that children who showed disturbed, socially intrusive behaviours, as evidenced in this case by screaming, were likely to show increases in behaviour problems over time.

Further analysis indicated that maternal acceptance was more likely to deteriorate over time for children who showed disturbed, socially intrusive behaviour and for mothers where relationships within the family, particularly the marital relationship were poor. These results suggest a series of factors may impinge on maternal adaptation and child behaviour: if the child shows evidence of disturbed behaviours, the mother may find it more difficult to adapt to the child; if, in addition, there are problems in family relationships the mother's reaction is accentuated, it is more difficult for her to deal with the behaviour problems and as these increase, the relationship with the child worsens, as do problems within the family.

Although this explanation does not define causal factors related to the initial behaviour problems or maternal adaptation, it does indicate a probable cycle of increasing problems, and the urgent need for interventions with families experiencing these types of problems in order to prevent the predicted worsening situation. Some children and families may be able to respond to intensive help early in the development of such problems, particularly where such help focuses both on ways of dealing with the behaviour problems and on helping the parents to interpret the child's behaviour in a more positive way and maintain positive parent-child interaction. Individual examples of some families within the cohort who received such help and were able to deal with problems are encouraging but, on the other hand, there are also examples of families who have received such help and only shown minimal improvement. One of the factors which appears to distinguish the second group of families is related to the final variable of housing inadequacy, which entered the analysis of the Behaviour Problems Index, ie social disadvantage.

It seems that socio-economic factors, by placing extra demands and stresses on the family, may militate against their ability to carry out and benefit from such interventions. Thus, the combination of the family and parent related factors in these results begins to indicate families with multiple problems, both in relationships and in socio-economic circumstances, whose children are at risk for high levels of behaviour problems.

The data on service contacts in this study indicates that the provision of help to such families may have been lacking in some respects. Families of children with the highest levels of behaviour problems were likely to have more contacts with social workers but not with psychologists or teachers. It is possible, therefore, that interventions which may help parents to deal actively with such problems were not provided for these families.

FACTORS RELATED TO PARENTS' APPRAISAL OF BEHAVIOUR

As mentioned earlier, parents having children with similar levels of behaviour problems did not always find these problems equally difficult. The analyses of mothers' and fathers' appraisal of problems scores give some indications of factors over and above the level of behaviour problems which make it likely that parents will find it more difficult to cope with the child's behaviour. The results of these analyses are shown in Table 6.

Table 6 Factors relating to parental appraisal of behaviour problems*

A) MOTHERS	% of Appraisal Score Explained
1. Behaviour Problems Index +	28.3%
2. Child excitability +	6.0%
3. Maternal age +	4.1%
4. Child IQ -	3.0%

Total % variance explained 41.4%*
F = 11.98, p = 0.000, n = 91

B) FATHERS	% of Appraisal Score Explained
1. Behaviour Problems Index +	41.3%
2. Child distractability +	5.9%
3. Marital dissatisfaction +	3.7%

| Total % variance explained | 56.8%* |

F = 17.42, p = 0.000, n = 58
(+/- indicate direction of relationship)
* with control for social desirability response bias

For mothers, these factors were the child having a low IQ and high excitability and the mother being older. Thus the children showing the lowest levels of functioning in relation to their chronological age were perceived by mothers as presenting the most serious problems. If, in addition, they were particularly excitable, the problems were compounded.

Children of the lowest developmental ability would be more difficult to manage because of their lower levels of understanding, poorer communicative ability and shorter attention span. If they were also chronologically older (as indicated by IQ), thus past the stage at which the behaviours may be seen as acceptable, and if the behaviours had persisted over a number of years, the problems for parents would be increased.

The characteristic of excitability again relates to the management of the child. Excitable children are more unpredictable and less easily handled. Consequently behaviour is perceived as more problematic.

The influence of higher maternal age suggests that the older mothers may have had less resources of energy to deal with behaviour and/or they may have been less tolerant of behaviour. They may have had different expectations of behaviour and of the limitations that the child's behaviour imposed on their own lives. As parents get older and their contemporaries are gaining independence from their children, the presence of a child of lower developmental level whose behaviour limits the parents' activities, may lead to parents viewing the behaviour as more problematic and restrictive. This suggests that over time there may be an added risk factor for mothers as their ability to attain the type of independence from child rearing enjoyed by their contemporaries is restricted, leading to a more negative view of the child's behaviour. The sensitive provision of respite services to enable mothers to be less restricted by the child may be of benefit here.

Measures of parental appraisal of behaviour problems were not included in the earlier set of data on the cohort. However some associations within the current data and the longitudinal data do suggest that appraisal of behaviour as problematic, independently of the current level of actual problem behaviour, may be predictive of increasing behaviour problems over time. There was a very strong relationship in the current data between adaptation to the child and appraisal scores ($r = 0.46$, $p<0.001$) and, as already noted, where mothers showed low adaptation and, presumably, found the child's behaviour difficult to deal with in the past, the behaviour problems were likely to have increased over time.

The analysis of fathers' appraisal scores indicated that the child's distractability was the strongest factor in predicting fathers' appraisal of behaviour as problematic. This factor was also related to low child functioning and may reflect the difficulty fathers found in dealing with behaviour in children whose attention span was very limited and who possibly did not appear to take notice of parental attempts to influence behaviour. The fact that excitability was not related to appraisal for fathers may reflect different roles and responsibilities, where more of the caretaking tasks were undertaken by mothers, and the excitable, unpredictable, active child presented greater difficulties. The distractable child, on the other hand, may be more difficult to deal with in goal-oriented activities, where the father may play a greater role than in caretaking tasks. The additional factor related to appraisal for fathers was marital dissatisfaction. Thus, fathers' perceptions of their children's behaviour appeared to be influenced by their feelings about their relationships with their wives. This may have been through them viewing behaviours as more problematic where there was a lack of support between partners and/or disagreement about handling the child.

A number of findings from the larger study do indicate differences between fathers and mothers in their reactions to the children and in the influence of the children's behaviour and characteristics on their own adaptation. An awareness of such differences in approach and on the need to acknowledge these in interventions with families is an important factor for services.

Whilst we have concentrated here mainly on the behaviour problems of the children and the family factors which relate to these, it should be noted that, in the larger study, high levels of child behaviour problems were found to be strongly related to high levels of psychological distress for mothers (Sloper et al, 1991) and, in addition, the occurence of disturbed, socially intrusive behaviours in the children were predictive of increasing maternal distress over time in longitudinal data based on measures over two and four years. Thus, child behaviour problems can be seen as particularly salient to maternal functioning, and the necessity for services to help and support parents in dealing with such problems, even in very young children, is apparent.

IMPLICATIONS

A number of implications of these results for services to families have been suggested. The main implications concern the need for:

* Early identification of problem behaviour, particularly behaviours of the disturbed, socially intrusive variety.

* Support to parents in dealing with behaviour, in maintaining a positive parent-child relationship, and in

interpreting the reasons for such behaviours in a way that minimises harm to the parent-child relationship.

* Awareness of the effects of ill health, particularly frequent minor infections, on behaviour. Early identification and treatment of health problems and support to parents in dealing with illness-related behaviour and re-establishing positive behaviour patterns as soon as possible after the illness.

* Awareness of the influence of family factors on behaviour and the spiral effect of such influences. Thus, the need for interventions to focus on the wider family situation rather than be restricted to behavioural programmes for the child.

* The results also point to the need for the involvement of health, educational and social services in such intervention. Therefore, a coordinated multidisciplinary approach is needed which channels appropriate help to the family through a single point of contact. Organisation of services to families through a 'named' person or a 'care manager' has been recommended in a number of official reports (eg DHSS, 1976, DES, 1978, DH, 1989), yet recent research continues to find that such recommendations are not being carried out in practice (Quine and Pahl, 1989, Sloper et al, 1991, Sloper and Turner, 1992).

REFERENCES

BAYLEY N (1969). *Bayley Scales of Infant Development Manual.* New York: The Psychological Corporation.

BROOKES-GUNN J AND LEWIS M (1984). Maternal responsivity in interactions with handicapped infants. *Child Development, 55,* 782-794.

BYRNE E A, CUNNINGHAM C C AND SLOPER P (1988). *Families and Their Children with Down's Syndrome: One Feature in Common.* London: Routledge.

CRAWLEY S AND SPIKER D (1983). Mother-child interactions involving two-year olds with Down's syndrome. *Child Development, 54,* 1312-1323.

CUNNINGHAM C C, GLENN S M, WILKINSON P AND SLOPER P (1985). Relationship between measures of mental ability, symbolic play and receptive and expressive language of young children with Down's syndrome. *Journal of Child Psychology and Psychiatry, 26,* 255-265.

CUNNINGHAM C C, SLOPER P, RANGECROFT A AND KNUSSEN C (1986). The Effects of Early Intervention on the Occurrence and Nature of Behaviour Problems in Children with Down's syndrome. University of Manchester: Hester Adrian Research Centre. Final Report to the Department of Health and Social Security.

DEPARTMENT OF HEALTH AND SOCIAL SECURITY (1976). *Fit for the Future: Court Committee Report on Child Health Services.* London: HMSO.

DEPARTMENT OF EDUCATION AND SCIENCE (1978). *Special Educational Needs: Report of the Committee of Enquiry into the Education of Handicapped Children and Young People. The Warnock Report.* London: HMSO.

DEPARTMENT OF HEALTH (1989). *Caring for People.* London: HMSO

EMDE R N AND BROWN C (1978). Adaptation to the birth of a Down's syndrome infant. *Journal of the American Academy of Child Psychiatry, 17,* 299-323.

GATH A AND GUMLEY D (1984). Down's syndrome and the family: follow-up of children first seen in infancy. *Developmental Medicine and Child Neurology, 26,* 500-508.

GIBSON D (1978). *Down's Syndrome: The Psychology of Mongolism.* London: Cambridge University Press.

HART H, BAX M AND JENKINS S (1984). Health and behaviour in pre-school children. *Child: Care, Health and Development, 10,* 1-16.

JUDSON S AND BURDEN R (1980). Towards a tailored measure of parental attitudes: An approach to the evaluation of one aspect of intervention projects with parents of handicapped children. *Child: Care, Health and Development, 6,* 47-55.

McCARTHY D C (1972). *McCarthy Scales of Children's Abilities.* New York: Psychological Corporation.

MENOLASCINO F J (1967). Psychiatric findings in a sample of institutionalised mongoloids. *Journal of Mental Subnormality, 13,* 67-74.

MOORE B C, THULINE H C AND CAPES LA V (1968). Mongoloid and non-mongoloid retardates: A behavioural comparison. *American Journal of Mental Deficiency, 73,* 433-436.

QUINE L AND PAHL J (1989). Stress and Coping in Families Caring for a Child with Severe Mental Handicap: A Longitudinal Study. University of Kent: Institute of Social and Applied Psychology and Centre for Health Services Studies.

QUINTON D AND RUTTER M (1976). Early hospital admissions and later disturbance of behaviour: An attempted replication of Douglas' findings. *Developmental Medicine and Child Neurology, 18,* 447-459.

RICHMAN N, STEVENSON J AND GRAHAM P (1982). *Preschool to School - A Behavioural Study.* London: Academic Press.

SLOPER P, CUNNINGHAM C C, KNUSSEN C AND TURNER S (1988). A Study of the Process of Adaptation in a Cohort of Children with Down's syndrome and Their Families. University of Manchester: Hester Adrian Research Centre. Final Report to the Department of Health and Social Security.

SLOPER P, KNUSSEN C, TURNER S AND CUNNINGHAM C C (1991). Factors related to stress and satisfaction with life in families of children with Down's syndrome. *Journal of Child Psychology and Psychiatry, 32,* 655-676.

SLOPER P AND TURNER S (1992). Service needs of families of children with severe physical disability. *Child: Care, Health and Development, 18,* 259-282.

TURNER S, SLOPER P, KNUSSEN C AND CUNNINGHAM C C (1990). Health problems in children with Down's syndrome. *Child: Care, Health and Development, 16,* 83-97.

WING L AND GOULD J (1978). Systematic recording of behaviours and skills of retarded and psychotic children. *Journal of Autism and Childhood Schizophrenia, 8,* 79-97.

CHAPTER 5

IMPACT ON FAMILIES: YOUNG ADULTS WITH LEARNING DISABILITY WHO SHOW CHALLENGING BEHAVIOUR

Hazel Qureshi

INTRODUCTION

Young adults with learning disability who show challenging behaviour are a key group in relation to policies for Community Care. The presence of behaviour problems has been shown to be an important factor influencing levels of stress in family carers, and decisions to place people in residential care (Quine and Pahl, 1985, Wilkin, 1979). Doubts have been expressed about whether community based services are able to cope with young people in this group or to offer sufficient support to parents in circumstances where permanent admission to hospital is far less likely to be available than in the past (Audit Commission, 1989). The findings reported in this paper are derived from a study of the parents of 59 young adults who were identified by staff in services as showing challenging behaviour during the course of a large scale epidemiological study described elsewhere in this volume (Kiernan and Qureshi, Chapter 3).

Pilot work for this study had indicated that the post-school period was something of a "crunch point" in relation to family care. At this point in the life cycle of the family it seemed that a number of factors were likely to combine to increase the particular stresses upon parents giving care at home. First, there was a decline in alternative sources of informal support: the young person's siblings were likely to have become independent and left home and therefore were not really on hand to assist in case of difficulty; the young person's grandparents were likely to be becoming increasingly elderly and frail themselves, and were thus not only unable to give the kind of assistance that they might have given in the past, but were, possibly, in a situation where they would be themselves making demands for assistance upon the parents of the young person. In common with many other studies, friends and neighbours had very rarely been sources of assistance in any case and certainly there was no increase in informal support from such sources at this point in the life cycle. At the same time as informal sources of support were diminishing, parents felt that their position relative to other parents was deteriorating socially and financially. Whilst other parents might seem able to enjoy increased leisure, or opportunities to take up employment because their children had become independent, parents in the study found themselves unable to enjoy these increased freedoms. In the sense that there was an increase in the expected roles that the young person was unable to fulfil, it would be reasonable to say that their level of social handicap was increasing. Also at this time the individual's physical strength might well have increased to the point where physical control by parents was no longer possible. In addition, physical maturity might bring along with it sexual problems. Finally the parents and young people had to cope, at this point in time, with a transition to a new service situation. With the ending of compulsory schooling, some young people might not be able to find places in day centres; others might find that community based services were not able to cope effectively with the behaviour problems displayed.

Given this constellation of likely difficulties facing the parents of young adults, and concern that community care policies might impose an increased expectation of continued family care, it was decided to undertake a more intensive study of such parents. The large scale epidemiological study provided an opportunity to identify representative community-based groups of families. Of all of those young people between the ages of 18 and 26 who were identified in the epidemiological study, just under half (47 per cent) were still living in their family home; the remainder were divided equally between those who were living in long stay hospital and those who were living in community residential facilities. Among older age groups far higher proportions were living in hospital, although about the same proportion were living in community residential facilities.

Seven health districts in the North West were involved in the study and 59 parents, mostly mothers, were interviewed. This represented 70 per cent of all those parents whom we were able to approach. Since individuals were identified by staff in service facilities, we were reliant upon services to provide us with the details of the families whom we wished to approach. In a few cases (8 per cent), staff were not willing for families to be approached either because of a perception that the family was under particular stress and would not wish to be troubled by a request for an interview, or because it was felt that the family would resent the identification of their family member as being a person showing behaviour problems. Such cases were uncommon, but the reluctance of staff to allow a few parents in the latter group to be approached, does indicate some of the difficulties which may arise in trying to research a socially constructed concept such as behaviour problems, where conflict over definitions is a possibility (Qureshi, 1992). In fact, two of the parents approached did not accept that their child showed any behaviour problems and felt that this identification reflected on the incapacity of service providers to treat their child in an appropriate manner or to understand their behaviour. However, in the main, there was agreement between parents and staff that some behaviour problems were present, although the identification of the type of problem was not necessarily consistent across home and service settings. For example, 73 per cent of the young people were identified as making physical attacks upon staff, whilst only 49 per cent were identified as attacking family members.

The aims of the study of parents were: to describe the reality of caring at home for a young person with learning disability and behaviour problems; to investigate the costs to parents of providing such care; to discover these informal carers' evaluations of services; and to consider the factors influencing an expressed preference for alternatives to family care. The data were collected through one tape-recorded interview with the main carer within each family; one single parent father was interviewed, six married couples were interviewed jointly and in two of these cases the father was the main carer; in the remainder of cases the mother alone was interviewed. All the mothers and fathers were aged 40 years or more, with the median age for both being 52 years. The median age of the young adults was 21 years and three fifths of the young people were male. The majority (64 per cent) were fully mobile with one in five experiencing some difficulty walking and only one in six suffering severe restrictions in mobility. Half suffered from fits, with one third having one or more major seizures per month. The young people tended to be rated by staff as 'severely mentally handicapped', two thirds of those in services were rated severe and half of those not rated severe were categorised by staff as 'not assessed/cannot say'. Only one third were said by parents to be able to understand information about things outside their own experience and under half were able to regularly communicate using varied phrases or sentences. Unwillingness to co-operate with self care tasks in just over half the cases makes the comparative assessment of self care skills difficult. Only one in five of those in services were rated as fully competent in feeding, washing and dressing, although there were some differences between staff and parents in these ratings, with parents likely to rate their children as more dependent. This last may indicate a difference in ratings made by staff, which reflect the perceived or measured capacity to undertake a task, as opposed to ratings made by parents on the basis of whether or not the person actually does undertake such a task in the course of their normal life. However, we did not pursue these particular differences in depth. Staff ratings suggested that young people whose parents were included did not differ significantly from those whose parents did not take part. No staff ratings were available for six people excluded from services.

PLAN OF THE CHAPTER

There are two main parts to this chapter. The first part will consider parents' attitudes towards alternatives to family care, and will investigate the factors associated with an expressed preference for such alternative care. An integral part of this discussion will be consideration of the role of psychological distress in mothers, which was measured in this study using the Malaise Inventory (Rutter et al, 1970), a checklist of psychosomatic symptoms. Initially, it had been expected that the level of symptoms of distress would be related to the expressed desire for alternatives to family care but this did not prove to be the case. Indeed, it seemed that these two factors were related to quite different features of the caring situation. A number of potentially influential features of the caring situation were investigated, including the characteristics and behaviour of the young adult, the costs borne by parents and the level of services received. Levels of distress and the expressed desire for alternatives to family care were seen as possible outcomes of these factors. Costs to parents are interpreted much more widely than merely as financial costs; there are opportunity costs in terms of lost employment or lost social activities, as well as negative effects of care such as sleep deprivation or the need to undertake additional domestic work. Previous research had indicated that these were important areas (Carr, 1985, 1990, Quine and Pahl, 1985), and structured questions designed to investigate them were included in the research interview. As will be discussed, the relationship between these features of the caring situation and our two possible outcomes of care was not as had been initially expected, and the findings give rise to a number of recommendations about the kinds of services which might reduce stress in carers and those which might help to maintain or preserve care in the community by parents.

The second part of the paper will discuss parents' evaluations of the advice that they have received from professionals on handling behaviour problems at home, and will outline the characteristics and activities of professionals who were considered by parents to have been helpful. First it is necessary to discuss in some detail the question of parents' attitudes towards the future care of their son or daughter. As might be expected this was not necessarily an easy area for parents to discuss and a small number of parents were unwilling to approach the subject at all. Within the research interview, discussion of this issue was open-ended, as it was felt that a structured approach might seem to be insensitive in approaching a subject likely to give rise to some distress. The categorisation of parents' attitudes towards future care was constructed from transcriptions of these open-ended discussions. The next section will try to give some indication of the richness and diversity of parents' views, and of the context within which they were making their choices about the future, before we go on to consider the division of parents into two groups representing those who wished to carry on giving care at the time they were interviewed, as opposed to those who wished to find alternatives forms of care immediately or soon.

PARENTS' ATTITUDES TOWARDS FUTURE CARE

Previous research undertaken with parents of adults with learning disability (Richardson and Ritchie, 1986, Grant, 1986) suggested that it would be possible to divide parents into a number of groups according to the degree to which they wished to consider alternatives to family care for their son or daughter. Richardson and Ritchie suggested three categories of response reflecting the feelings of parents. Effectively these were: those who were currently trying to find a place for their son or daughter outside the home; those who were not currently looking for alternative provision; and finally, those who were highly ambivalent about the question. Later work by Grant (1988), suggested that parents could be broadly divided into those whom he described as 'family reliant' in terms of their attitudes towards future care, and those who were 'agency reliant'. The latter being those who looked to health or social services to assume responsibility in the future. Within the family reliant group Grant distinguished three sub groups: those for whom dependence on the family was a positive wish; those who hoped the person might become independent; and those whose main orientation seemed to be not so much a preference for family care as a rejection of services for ideological or historical reasons leading to a belief that there was no real alternative to carrying on the family care. With slight variations according to age, the family reliant group comprised almost half of the families surveyed by Grant, although it is of interest from the point of view of the current study to note that there were higher rates of challenging behaviour in the agency reliant group. Certainly, in the current study, a much larger proportion (73 per cent) anticipated agency responsibility in the future and even those few families who expressed an orientation towards family care seemed to feel some ambivalence. For example, one mother who had initially said that she was just hoping to live long enough for her younger daughter to be 18 and take over, subsequently said:

> "The ideal situation would be that he died the day before me to
> be honest ... I don't really want (his sister) to ruin her life with
> him"   (Interview 860)

Other parents who were not expecting family care to continue after the point at which they would have to give up, explicitly stated that they did not wish their other children to have the burden of care whichhad affected their own lives. The full categorisation of responses is given in Table 1.

Although the majority of parents were agency reliant in terms of their orientation towards the future, there were clear differences between those

Table 1 Parents attitudes towards future care.

	Response	No.	%
1.	Does not want to think about it	3	5
2.	Hopes for independent living	4	7
3.	Hopes for continuing family care	8	14
4.	Non-family alternative needed eventually	23	39
5.	Non-family alternative needed soon	14	24
6.	Non-family alternative wanted now	6	10
7.	Other	1	2

who wished to carry on the caring for the time being and merely anticipated that services would have to take over when they became too old, or otherwise unable to cope, and those who were already seeking some kind of residential services or who were feeling that they could not cope for much longer at home. Some of the people in this latter group simply felt that care was getting beyond their resources:

"I have realised in the past 12 months that I too, am getting older and it is getting harder. He is getting awkwarder and harder to handle because of his weight and because of his tempers you know. And you think Oh God! how am I going to keep on doing this you know."   (Interview 220)

"We're both finding it difficult to handle him now, it takes two of us sometimes, doesn't it? Well it takes three of us to get him on the bus".   (Interview 794)

It seemed possible that in some instances an improvement in service provision might enable these parents to cope for longer. Certainly, some of them suggested that this might be the case:

"I would like the help to keep him at home ... you see, we've always looked after Ewan, we've done the best we can for Ewan and I think because of that we've been penalised ... if we had neglected him I think we'd have got all the help we wanted." (Interview 144)

A single parent mother argued:

> "Really what it is, it's me now that needs some help to cope with him or to be able to pay somebody to look after him."
> (Interview 250)

Other parents, however, were clearly coming to feel that they had done their bit and that their health and increasing age meant that it was right for them to be thinking of giving up. These were mostly parents who were at or past retirement age:

> "I've always said that by the time I'm 60 I'd not carry on, I always thought about 60 I'd have done my service."
> (Interview 794)

A number of themes cut across discussion of the future for all groups. First, there was a perception that there was a shortage of suitable residential care for young people with challenging behaviour in the community. Some parents made it clear that even if they did wish to give up there were no services available, as far as they were concerned, that would be suitable as an alternative to their own care. Those who did not wish to give up caring immediately or soon were able to live in hope that a suitable service would come about by the time they did wish to do so. For those who did wish to give up the problems posed were clearly more immediate. However, parents across all groups pointed to the difficulty of achieving any kind of arrangements which would ensure the gentle phasing in of alternative care so that their son or daughter would not be too disturbed at the final break with the family. Very few parents were able to achieve any such gentle transitional arrangements. It was ironic that in some districts there were imaginative schemes for supporting people with learning disability who had been discharged from hospital and these schemes were located in ordinary housing with staff support. However, parents who had seen these schemes and felt that they would provide a suitable service for their own child found that, because their children had never been permanently admitted to hospital, they were not able to obtain access to such services. Hardy, Wistow and Rhodes (1990) have commented on the fact there may seem to be a two-tier service in the community, with those people who have never been admitted to hospital being relatively disadvantaged, and certainly this was how some parents in the study perceived their current situation.

One mother had finally succeeded in achieving the admission of her daughter to a local hostel for people with learning disabilities but this was only after great persistence in the face of initial discouragement:

"It was getting a bit of a struggle and I said this to the social worker and she said "well would you like us to find long term residential accommodation?" and I said yes, she said "Oh! good lets get things moving" then she came back a few weeks later and said "there isn't anywhere so forget it."   (Interview 723)

Another mother, who had been less successful in finding alternative care, had already felt, at one point, driven to refusing to have her son back home from short stay residential care:

"I think he were in a fortnight or something like that. In fact in the first week I said I weren't having him back. And after that there was case conferences, and you name it I have to go through it. Because I put him in they wanted to know why and all the rest of it you know. And I said "I just can't cope ..." He doesn't go enough to stop the frustration in us you know. If ... he went every weekend that would suit me fine. We'd have a break every weekend. But no, he is not in again until next September. I mean, I know September is not long, but it is in weeks and days you know ... but you think Oh June to September it's only three months. But it's three months. It's twelve weeks. But it's all them days, you know." (Interview 220)

This parent felt compelled to continue caring because of the lack of alternatives. The degree to which parents may be thought to be making choices about continuing care in highly stressful circumstances has to be understood in the light of such experiences.

In summary a majority of parents felt that the care of their children would eventually be the responsibility of statutory services. Supportive services were often felt to be inadequate, but parents made their decisions about carrying on caring in a context where there were perceived to be few suitable alternative residential services in the community and a lack of willingness on the part of statutory services to provide for gentle transition into alternative forms of care. The next section goes on to consider those factors which were associated with the expressed desire for alternatives to family care to be found immediately or soon.

The desire for alternative care and psychological distress

As already mentioned, quantitative analysis showed that the desire for alternative care and the level of symptoms of psychological distress were not associated. That is to say, some parents suffering high levels of distress wished to carry on caring and some parents whose distress levels were not high were among those who wished to find alternatives. This was not as initially expected. However the investigation of the features of the caring situation which were associated with each of these possible outcomes of care cast some light on the question of why they were not related. Table 2 indicates the factors which were most strongly and significantly associated with these two outcomes.

The table suggests that the kind of factors which are associated with high distress scores are those which are related to the "daily (and nightly) grind" of caring: the ever present and continuous nature of the caring task. Sleep deprivation has often been found to be related to distress in carers (Pahl and Quine, 1985, Levin, Sinclair and Gorbach 1989), and the relationship to the health of the carer has also been previously reported (Gilleard et al, 1984, Quine and Pahl, 1989, Sloper et al, 1991). The level of extra domestic work generated and the total number of behaviour problems to be dealt with all seem to have a longer term effect in undermining mental health. Similar results have been reported in the other studies cited. It makes sense, therefore, that the quantity of day care shows an inverse relationship to the level of distress. The more day care one receives presumably the greater the relief from the "daily grind".

Table 2 Factors associated with malaise (distress) and the wish for alternative care.

Malaise (distress)	Wish for Alternative Care
Sleep Disturbance	Mother would otherwise be in employment
Additional Domestic Work	Loss of social activities
Number of Behaviour Problems	Self-injury as a severe problem
Health of Carer	Perceived lack of cooperation in care
Amount of Day Care	Amount of short-term care
(The more day care the less distress)	(The more care the more likely to wish to give up)

In contrast, the expressed desire to give up care is related to quite a different set of factors. First, to the opportunity costs of caring, reflected both in the perception that the mother would otherwise be in work if it were not for the responsibilities of caring, and also in the degree to which social activities such as visiting, outings and holidays were perceived to have been sacrificed for the demands of caring. In addition, in common with other research, the degree of co-operation shown by the young adult in the process of care was related to the expressed desire to give up (Lewis and Meredith, 1988). Finally, if the main behaviour problem shown by the young person was identified as self injury both at home and in the service facility, then this was related to the expressed desire to give up. This too, is consistent with other research that suggests that self injury is a particularly difficult problem to cope with in a domestic situation and is more likely to lead to a person being placed in institutional care (Emerson, 1992, Murphy and Wilson, 1985).

Quantity of day care is not related to the expressed desire to give up but, interestingly, the higher the number of nights of short term care received in the past year, the more likely it was that the mother would express a desire to give up. At first sight this might seem to be a rather disturbing result if we assume that the purpose of short term care is preventative. Of course it may well be that those factors which lead to a desire for short term care are also those which in the end lead to the wish for long term care. However, it also seems possible that short term care could have a **precipitative effect,** particularly if it is in short supply and only given when the situation becomes intolerable. Certainly one mother in pilot interviews had argued that short term care had enabled her and her family to rediscover normal life and made them feel that they no longer wished to have their son living permanently at home.

The situation among parents in the study was that very few received quantities of short term care which they considered to be adequate. Seventy per cent of those interviewed said that they would have liked more short term care although half of these did not feel that any of the forms of short term care which are actually available to them were satisfactory. Several had been asked to take their children home from short term care in the middle of planned stays because staff could not cope with their behaviour. Some had been asked to be on the other end of a phone throughout the stay, and in one case the mother had been asked to remove her son from respite care during each day of his stay because the local day centre could not provide day care for him. Only around half of the parents who used short term care felt that their children enjoyed their stays.

What then are the service implications which may be drawn from these results? First, we may identify a number of services which might reduce levels of distress in mothers. These would be domiciliary assistance, or someone to mind the young person while the mother performed domestic tasks unhindered. Second, carers at night or overnight care so that the parents who are missing out on sleep could catch up on this. Quine and Wade (1991), and Quine, (Chapter 12), have indicated that it is possible to teach parents behavioural methods which are demonstrably successful in reducing sleep problems in young children who show behavioural difficulties. It would be of interest to discover whether or not these techniques could be used in relation to adults with sleep disturbance, although equally it would probably be beneficial to ensure that these techniques were used on a wider scale with children, as this might prevent such problems from persisting into adulthood. Direct attention to the mother's physical and mental health might also reduce distress. Of course, levels of distress as reflected in the Malaise Inventory may not be a consequence of caring at all but could be related to other life circumstances such as poor housing, financial problems or marital problems. Thus assistance given in other areas of life might also be instrumental in reducing distress levels (Sloper and Turner, Chapter 4). Finally, it seems that additional hours of day care might be a way of reducing distress.

However, as we have seen, it might be possible to provide such services and reduce levels of distress without necessarily reducing any expressed wish for alternatives to family care. It has often been assumed that reducing levels of distress is the same as, or is a way of, preserving or maintaining family care and preventing admission to institutions. However, it is clear that something more is required of services which are designed to prevent caring breakdown. Such services it seems would have to take into account the carer's own needs and opportunity costs and, therefore, services would have to be provided which would supply care at unsocial hours, weekends and holidays, thus enabling mothers to take employment if they so wished and to undertake social activities and holidays. To deal with problems in the relationship it might be helpful to have help and counselling in dealing with unco-operative behaviour and in handling behaviour problems, particularly self injury. A focus on situations where long term care is likely to be sought would suggest that services should target help on people who are making high use of short term care as this seems to be associated with an eventual permanent admission. Of course, it may be argued that it is perfectly proper for increasing periods of short term care to be used as a bridge to long term care, but this sits uncomfortably with the current expressed aim of government policy which is to preserve and maintain informal care. It has been stated that a key objective of government policy is to foster independence (DHSS, 1989) and for these young people it may be that their independence is best fostered by the ending of family care. However, without providing the right packages of services and seeing whether or not this does enable some parents to carry on caring for longer and enable others who choose to do so to give up, it is not possible to reliably say which parents could have been helped by additional services, and for which parents a phased transition to a residential service needed to be planned as soon as possible.

There are ways of providing the kind of flexible and intensive services which would seem to be necessary for parents in these kinds of situation, but they do require some initial investment of resources which certainly did not seem to be forthcoming at the time of the study. Parents had, of course, had quite substantial dealings with large numbers of professionals and their general evaluations of services are dealt with in another paper (Qureshi, 1991-2). Given the focus on challenging behaviour, the final section of this paper will concentrate on parents' evaluations of the advice that they have received from professionals on how to handle behaviour problems at home.

ADVICE FROM PROFESSIONALS

Parents were asked a number of open ended questions designed to discover whether they had ever had any advice from professionals about how to handle behaviour problems at home. If they had received advice, they were asked how useful this had been. Browne (1982) argued that advice and support in dealing with behaviour problems may well require specialised help because the techniques of verbal admonition or praise, or physical control or punishment, which parents find effective with their other children, may not seem to work with the child with learning disability. Browne indicated that many social workers and other staff working with children with learning disability believed that parents 'spoiled' the disabled person by overprotection and over-indulgence. However, parents in her study experienced considerable uncertainty as to the best or most appropriate approach in the light of their child's learning disability.

For the past three decades behavioural theory has been the common underpinning of the analysis by many professionals of problem behaviour in the field of learning disability (Kiernan, 1989). It is recognised that such methods may be less useful when there is a known organic factor underlining the behaviour, for example, in certain particular syndromes such as Lesch-Nyhan (Nyhan, 1985), or some forms of epilepsy (Gedye, 1989). However, in general, adherents of a behavioural approach argue that making abstract causal inferences about problem behaviour is less important than a careful analysis of the circumstances in which the behaviour occurs, and the consequences which result for the individual by performing the behaviour (Zarkowska and Clements, 1988). The behavioural tradition is a dynamic, developing field in which, and about which, major debates are still taking place. However, it has been argued that advances in the development of theory have not necessarily been reflected in changes in practice, and that attempts to implement behavioural techniques have been prone to over simplification and misunderstanding of the basic ideas (Kiernan, 1985, Remington, Chapter 6).

The strategies which behaviour analysis may suggest can seem counter-intuitive or, at least, contrary to a care providers normal impulses to intervene, may also worsen the behaviour in the short term. There has been some interest in the literature, and in practice, in the possibility that parents could be trained as behaviour therapists in relation to their own children (Forehand and MacMahon, 1981, Moreland et al, 1982).

There is some evidence that behavioural methods can succeed in modifying unacceptable behaviour in young children, irrespective of their intellectual level (Callias & Carr, 1975), and there are other accounts of evaluated attempts to teach numbers of parents behavioural methods specifically directed towards changing unacceptable behaviour (Firth, 1983, Scott and Stradling, 1987). However, such methods are not successful in every case; for example, approximately 40 per cent success in reaching set targets was achieved in Firth's study and only 50 per cent of those who were aggressive were rated as improved in Callias and Carr. All these studies related to children under 15. There are, of course, examples in the literature of the successful use of behavioural techniques to modify the behaviour of adults with learning disabilities, but these are largely individual case studies and therefore do not cast light on the likely levels of success that would be achieved across all cases.

The purpose of this brief section is not to explain the basics of behavioural theory but to introduce the parents' descriptions of the kind of advice they received about controlling their son or daughter's problem behaviour. It will become clear that only a very few appeared to have received advice which was based on a thorough-going behavioural approach, and that rather more appeared to have received some distorted and filtered half truths which bore only a vague and tenuous relationship to the ideas of the discipline. Most commonly parents had been advised to ignore the behaviour (even in cases where the function of the behaviour was clearly demand avoidance rather than attention seeking), or to take a firm line (even in relation to children who were considerably larger and stronger than they were). Of course, this study has collected only the parents' views of the advice received and it may well be in some cases that the parents simply did not understand or take in the principles underlying the actions they were asked to undertake. Even if this is so, there are still lessons here for professionals who wish to undertake work with parents in attempting to modify behaviour at home.

Responses to the question on advice from professionals could be broadly categorised into three groups:

> None at all (26%)
> None helpful (61%)
> Yes useful (13%)

Some parents had received some advice which had been useful and some which had not; if any advice was useful the response has been classified as "yes useful". In general, there was a strong wish for help and understanding in coping with behaviour problems and people who could offer insight were valued:

> "Even the mental handicap team came in, I mean, we had the clinical psychologist in. Nobody seemed to be able to get to the bottom of it. I think the first time we've had anything sensible about her has been Dr K (psychiatrist). Time and time again, we'd be crying out, will somebody tell us why she is doing this". (Interview 723).

As indicated, the majority of parents (61 per cent) made responses categorised as having received advice but not having found it useful in their current situation. Although as many as one in four simply said they had received no advice at all. One mother commented:

> "I can't say there was any advice as to what to do ... there's no real advice as to how to cope with it, I wish there were." (Interview 239)

What were the characteristics of advice that was not useful?

A few parents had received advice which did not go beyond platitudes "The doctor just said "A firm hand at all times". (Interview 871). But the most common reasons advanced by parents for lack of usefulness of advice were that it was not possible for them to implement the advice in a day to day domestic context, or that parents disagreed with the professional's assessment of the causes of the behaviour. In the accounts of those who felt that the advice was impossible to implement, a prominent theme was that professionals failed to understand the reality of the situation which faced parents on a day to day basis:

> "Actually they want to live with it. I mean doctors have said don't feed him, don't have food in your cupboards because he used to smash our cupboards up for food ... and I said it's easy to say don't feed him you want to live with it you know".
> (Interview 220)

> "Yes, I think Dr D (psychiatrist) thinks I'm too easy going. She did say to me once that Brenda rules ... our lives ... well it was true, I mean we ... couldn't sort of like come home and relax with dinner when someone was throwing a tin of soup at you really. And bottles of milk ... I mean you sort of can't say right we're having our tea at 6 o'clock and what have you ... we used to have it when we could".   (Interview 785)

The mother quoted above graphically described her attempts to follow the advice that she was given which was to ignore the behaviour:

> "Most of the advice we have had from the Unit has been to ignore what she does, even the throwing and the tantrums, they even did a video at the Unit and asked me to watch it when she was having all the behaviours - screaming, throwing things - how they coped with it and they wouldn't even look her in the eye. She got no eye contact, which we can't do at home. They never even uttered a word. (Did you find that advice useful for your situation here?) No I didn't. No. You couldn't really because there was nothing there (at the Unit) that she could get hold of she was doing it in her room. And there was hardly anything in the room. Where as here I mean she was throwing tins of soup and jars of pickle or something; milk bottles - I mean I could get rid of the milk bottles, I had plastic bottles in the end ... when she's thrown eggs on the floor and somebody came to the door or whatever I could walk over them and not comment on it I could leave it there for three hours ... that I could do. And even the milk - running down the walls - I wasn't

you know that bothered. But I couldn't, not with the violence and the you know the chairs - the dining chairs. You'd have to duck or you'd have to - if it hit you or whatever - you'd have to react."
(Interview 785)

When she received short term residential care in a local hospital the person above was sedated to control her behaviour. Her mother described the feelings she had, which were never expressed to the psychiatrist involved with her daughter's case:

> "I think she felt as though I had coped very well in the fact that I had not gone to pieces, but I had let her (daughter) get away with too much. Then again, when she was faced with it she gave her an injection".

Some of the difficulties involved in implementing full scale behavioural programmes in the domestic context are well illustrated by two parents who were both Registered Nurses in Mental Handicap and who therefore used such techniques in their everyday professional work, but who frankly and honestly described some of the difficulties in translating these particular techniques into methods which could be used in family life. As the father commented:

> "Structured programmes like that are so difficult to implement especially with somebody so close to you ... that sometimes you must question it. And as I say many a time she would be acting the goat at table with us and she was having a paddy of some sort sat at the table and you'd say to her "Look if you don't behave I'll take it away from you and I'll scrape it in the bin, if you can't behave we will take it away" Now you knew what was going to happen the minute you removed that food ... you could forget your meal then ... because you weren't just destroying her food you were destroying your own because there'd be no way you'd be able to eat then ... and there's many a time you've thought to yourself is it really worth it?"
> (Interview 580)

In contrast to parents who were told to ignore behaviour were those who were advised that they should take a firm line or that they should chastise their son or daughter. One father commented:

> "This man (from Social Services) said, he said "Oh you don't

mess about like that - you just chastise him" now you can't just start chastising a lad like Eric you've got to use your brain a bit ... of course he's a bigger lad now so he wants a lot more handling ... if he has a tantrum. When he's little you can handle him."   (Interview 974)

In this case the son far outweighed the father in size and strength and the father had been attempting, successfully in the short term, to control his son's behaviour by sending him fake 'official' letters threatening him with admission to 'mental handicap hospital' if his behaviour did not improve. Chastisement was the alternative strategy suggested by the social worker.

The other main area of disagreement centred around the perceived cause of the behaviour problems. Difficulties arose when parents felt that professionals gave the impression that the young person should be able to control their behaviour when parents had come to the conclusion that there were times when this was not possible. For example, one mother argued:

"My husband and I are still somehow convinced that it's still something to do with hormones, chemicals, call it what you will. Something inside of him that he has no more control over than I would say PMT or something like that and that's how we think of it that's how my husband and I think it is ... nobody's been able to talk us out of it. The doctor does not always agree with us but that's how we feel, I instinctively feel that and that's not a cover up, I really do, that's really how we see it."
(Interview 788)

Orford (1987), in a review of studies of families coping with disordered behaviour, identified four factors which had been shown to be associated with less successful family coping: 1. Attributing the person's behaviour to personality constructs such as laziness. 2. Assuming the behaviour to be fully under the deliberate control of the person. 3. Thinking the behaviour to be intentionally provocative. 4. Blaming one's self by attributing problems to one's own past treatment of the person. If it is the case that beliefs that the behaviour is not fully under the deliberate control of the person, and that it is not intentionally provocative, are the kind of beliefs which are associated with successful coping, then it seems likely that parents who have managed to survive as carers into their child's adulthood will be likely to hold such beliefs and to resist contrary explanations or attributions if they believe that statutory workers are trying to impose them. If accepted, such attributions could undermine the caring relationship. The perception that difficult behaviour, especially at its worst, was not a deliberate act on the part of the young person was very widespread amongst parents, although not universal, and advice from professionals was sometimes rejected because it seemed to contradict this belief.

Useful advice

Despite these difficulties, there were, as we have seen, 13 per cent of parents who had received advice which they considered had been useful. Sometimes advice had focussed on techniques for parents to use at home. In these instances professionals had come to the home, demonstrated the techniques to parents, and showed that they could be successful. In other instances, there was clear evidence of consistent work across all settings and this seemed to increase parents confidence and help them to cope:

> "We were all doing the same thing and that's helped a lot I'm sure".   (Interview 784)

> "Whatever they do at the centre we carry on here and if I start something here then they carry on at the centre". (Interview 560).

Once convinced that a technique might work, parents would go to considerable lengths and show perseverance in implementing it, although they were correspondingly disappointed if professionals did not then match their persistence:

> "We were doing it at home with filling in graphs and everything but they never kept in touch with us they just left us doing it all the time and nothing. They don't finish it they never do, they do nothing for you".   (Interview 853)

However some attempts to observe and record behaviour by parents had resulted in the identification of possible solutions:

> "We started charting it that it is showing a peak not pre-menstrually but mid-cycle and so he's done some progesterone levels on her and she's definitely low mid-cycle so at the moment he's just put her on vitamin B6, he's got this theory, it's another factor but it seems to be working."   (Interview 723)

In short, useful advice was advice which worked in controlling the behaviour or in achieving some lesser goal; it also involved professionals demonstrating or showing a willingness to try using the techniques which they suggested themselves, and networking across different carers to make sure that responses were consistent in different settings. Finally, there was continuing contact and assessment during the implementation of particular programmes.

Aside from behaviour modification, the other common method of intervention is the use of drugs, and in the 46 cases where information was available, 11 people were taking antipsychotic drugs and a further seven were taking minor tranquillisers only. There was no doubt that in some cases, drug treatment had brought about a dramatic improvement in the person's behaviour. But in others, parents had found the side effects of drugs to be quite undesirable and indeed had decided that they would rather put up with behaviour problems than have their child reduced to what several described as a zombie state:

> "I said I want him off and I don't want a cabbage in a wheelchair, I said that's not Howard anymore ... I said I would keep them for when he had these mad outbursts you know to calm him".   (Interview 220)

Professionals judged to be helpful by parents

The interview included open ended discussion about professionals whom parents identified as having been helpful. From this discussion a number of dimensions were identified which parents used in making judgments about helpfulness. The most frequently identified dimension centred around the provision of practical or instrumental help. Twenty one parents mentioned a worker who had helped in this way; the assistance might be material or financial or it might have involved arranging access to services or ensuring people received their full benefit entitlement. This provision of practical or instrumental help linked into a highly valued characteristic of showing competence in handling the service system and doing so vigorously on behalf of parents. Such a successful **advocacy role** was clearly valued by parents and was contrasted by them with workers who came and went and made promises which were never followed up. Workers who took on this role came from a variety of professions:

> "This was a relief GP and he was fantastic it was just unbelievable how much he did in such in a short time you know not just saying it actually doing it."   (Interview 220)

"She would do what she said she was going to do, if she said I
will try she followed it through and made the arrangements she
did what she said. She was good the social worker."
(Interview 785)

The feeling that a professional was on the side of parents was something
recalled by those who felt that they no longer had anyone acting in this
capacity for them:

"It would be great if we could have someone like him carrying
on, he tried to do his best for you, you felt as if somebody was
helping you out. You wasn't alone, you wasn't fighting anything
alone at least he was helping you."   (Interview 209)

Professionals perceived as helpful kept to agreed arrangements, were
accessible when parents tried to contact them and kept parents informed of
progress when they had promised to try and ensure that things happened.
They also showed respect for parents and their knowledge of their child
though without using this as an excuse for not offering any help. Another
highly valued quality was showing respect for and a willingness to get to
know the young adult with challenging behaviour:

"He's a person that is concerned you know and he's the only
one that has shown me how concerned he is about Kate. He
goes to the centre and has a look at her."   (Interview 245)

"Mr N (community nurse) was very very good of course. He
spent a lot of time with Brian, he used to go up and see him
and he took him out."   (Interview 585)

Professional knowledge and skills were valued especially if they had proved
able to achieve results which parents were not able to achieve. Or perhaps
professionals might have a particular status or resource which enabled them
to have more influence over the person with disability than parents had:

"The community policeman would have a talk with him and say
'Now look Eric I think you've been a bit of a naughty lad
haven't you?' and you'd be amazed, we could get four good
weeks out of the lad."   (Interview 974)

In accepting advice from professionals it was noted that parents often
perceived that statutory workers have no real conception of the day to day

reality that they face. In a study linked to the All Wales strategy, (McGrath, 1989), parents gave this as one of the important reasons as to why consumers should be involved in planning services. Among parents in the current study, professionals who did seem to appreciate the difficulties were much valued as were those who recognised and tried to meet parents' own needs. This recognition of parents' own needs included an acceptance of shared responsibility for the care of the young person. Some parents felt that there were staff who could not wait to give them a litany of their child's bad behaviour in services:

> "One of the things parents like us suffer from are people who tell you what your son's been up to ... Over the years you can meet two types of people ... those who help you and wouldn't tell you if he did anything wrong, come what may, because they know that puts pressure on you, and those who just can't wait to tell you what's gone wrong."   (Interview 487)

To some parents professionals seemed to be preoccupied with their own needs and the needs of the service system, in a way which was both bewildering and irrelevant:

> "I just couldn't understand the way they were all going on, it was like they were in their own little world. And yet their job was to do with me and my daughter and that's what their job is all about, their service is about and yet I felt alien to what they were all talking about. It was as though it was nothing at all to do with me all that" (So they were talking about the service and the systems and these sorts of things) "That's right and I didn't want to know about that, I just wanted to know about a night's sleep and a break you know and things like that."
> (Interview 975)

CONCLUSIONS AND IMPLICATIONS

This study raises issues of considerable relevance to policy and practice. Sooner or later, the care of the majority of these young adults with learning disability and challenging behaviour will become the responsibility of the State, whether as purchaser or provider of residential services. The questions which therefore arise concern the determination of when and how this should happen, and what kinds of support are best provided for parents in the intervening period. With few exceptions, the overall picture of services received and costs borne by parents is not encouraging, and can only serve to illuminate in depth the comments of the Audit Commission (1989) about the relative neglect of people remaining in the community compared with those who are being relocated from hospital. The Government's avowed aims to give more choice to consumers and to foster independence seem to sit uneasily with their accompanying view that services should aim to maintain the contribution of informal carers and thereby reduce demands for expensive residential care. For people in this age group after all, independence frequently means moving away from the parental home, and for most, if not all, of the young people in the study this could not be accomplished without sustained assistance from formal services. Few parents felt that a realistic choice about continuing care was available to them. The one in three parents who wanted alternative care in the near future were rarely being assisted to find this, and the larger number who felt that residential care would be needed eventually, often commented on the difficulty of achieving any sensible planning with services towards a phased transition in later life.

There is no escaping questions about the relative priority of different possible service objectives. Is the aim to preserve family based care for as long as possible by enhancing willingness to care, or to reduce the psychological distress suffered by carers irrespective of whether they wish to give up, or to assist the young adult to achieve a managed transition to independence from their family? As we have seen, these aims carry quite different service implications. A desire for alternatives to family care was associated with the level of opportunity costs to the main carer, the difficulties of dealing with un-cooperative or self-injurious behaviour, and the amount of short term care received. This last association brings the question of objectives into sharp focus. What is the role and purpose of short-term residential care for adults? What quality and frequency of service achieves a preventative as against a precipitative outcome, and when should a decision to be made to use the service positively as a bridge towards a permanent alternative to family care, rather than as a way of maintaining such care?

The kind of services which may effectively reduce distress by tackling the "daily and nightly grind" of caring may not enhance willingness to continue caring if carers' opportunity costs are not addressed. This does not mean that carers will be arguing that their needs should be the focus of intervention. Few explicitly made a connection between failure to meet their own needs for employment, or for a social life, and their wish for alternative care. Nevertheless, such an association did exist.

The quality of advice on handling behaviour at home must be improved. Workers should be trained to understand and appreciate the difficulties for parents operating in a domestic context, and should refrain from giving advice "in passing" without careful consideration of the realities of the situation, and a willingness and committment to devote the necessary resources to implementing and following up the advice given. When working with parents, care should be taken around the attributions made, or implied, about the causes of the behaviour, or the degree to which it is seen as deliberate, so that existing beliefs which facilitate coping are not threatened or undermined. Early intervention would seem to have considerable potential, for example in dealing with difficulties such as night disturbance in children, before patterns of behaviour become too well established and while physical control is still possible.

Health and Social Service workers were involved with many of these families. Potentially, new Community Care arrangements could be of great assistance to them, although parents are likely, quite rightly, to be rather more interested in the outcomes for themselves and their children, rather than the minutiae of organisational arrangements or the difficulties of inter-agency cooperation. Given the difficulties involved in the care of this group of disabled people, and the stresses upon their family carers, a neglect of their needs can only be a short term solution, leading to later crises.

REFERENCES

AUDIT COMMISSION (1989). *Developing community care for adults with a mental handicap.* London: HMSO.

BROWNE E (1982). *Mental Handicap: the Role for Social Workers.* Social Services Monographs, JUSSR, University of Sheffield.

CALLIAS M AND CARR J (1975). Behaviour modification programmes in a community setting. IN C Kiernan and F Woodford (Eds) *Behaviour Modification with the Severely Retarded.* Amsterdam: Associated Scientific Publishers.

CARR J (1985). The effect on the family of a severely mentally handicapped child. IN A M Clarke , A D B Clarke and J Berg (Eds) *Mental Deficiency: the Changing Outlook.* London: Methuen.

CARR J (1990). Supporting the families of people with behavioural/psychiatric difficulties. *International Review of Psychiatry, 2*, 33-42.

DEPARTMENT OF HEALTH/DSS (1989). *Caring for people: Community care in the next decade and beyond.* London: HMSO.

EMERSON E (1992). Self-injurious behaviour: an overview of recent trends in epidemiological and behavioural research. *Mental Handicap Research, 5*, 49-81.

FIRTH H (1983). Difficult behaviour at home: a domiciliary service for handicapped children. *Mental Handicap, 11*, 61-64.

FOREHAND R AND McMAHON R (1981). *Helping the Non-compliant Child: a Clinicians' Guide to Parent Training.* New York: Guilford.

GEDYE A (1989). Extreme self-Injury attributed to Frontal Lobe Seizures. *American Journal on Mental Retardation, 94*, 20-26

GILLEARD C, BELFORD H, GILLEARD J, WHITTICK J AND GLEDHILL K (1984). Emotional distress amongst the supporters of the elderly mentally infirm. *British Journal of Psychiatry, 145*, 172-177.

GRANT G (1986). Older carers, interdependence and the care of mentally handicapped adults. *Ageing and Society, 6*, 333-351.

GRANT G (1988). Letting Go: Tracing reasons for the different attitudes of informal carers towards the future care of people with mental handicap. Paper presented at the 8th International Congress of IASSMD, Dublin, 1988.

HARDY B, WISTOW G AND RHODES R (1990). Policy networks and the implementation of community care policy for people with mental handicaps. *Journal of Social Policy, 19*, 141-168.

KIERNAN C (1985). Behaviour Modification. In A M Clarke, A D B Clarke and J Berg (Eds) *Mental Deficiency: the Changing Outlook*. London: Methuen.

KIERNAN C (1989). The Analysis and Management of Problem Behaviour. Paper presented to the Seventh International Congress of the National Association for Special Education, Bergamo, Italy.

LEVIN E, SINCLAIR I AND GORBACH P (1989). *Families, Services and Confusion in Old Age*. Aldershot: Gower.

LEWIS J AND MEREDITH B (1988). *Daughters who Care*. London: Routledge.

McGRATH M (1989). Consumer participation in service planning - the AWS experience. *Journal of Social Policy, 18,* 67-89

MORELAND S, SCHWEBEL A, BECK S AND WELLS K (1982). Parents as therapists: a review of the behaviour therapy parent training literature 1975 to 1981. *Behaviour Modification, 6,* 250-276

MURPHY G AND WILSON B (Eds) (1985). *Self-Injurious Behaviour*. Kidderminster: BIMH.

NYHAN W (1985). Behaviour in the Lesch-Nyhan syndrome. In G Murphy and BWilson (Eds). *Self-Injurious Behaviour*. Kidderminster: BIMH.

PAHL J AND QUINE L (1985). Families with Mentally Handicapped Children: a study of Stress and Service Response. Health Services Research Unit, University of Kent, Canterbury.

ORFORD J (Ed) (1987). *Coping with Disorder in the Family*. Beckenham: Croom Helm.

QUINE L AND PAHL J (1985). Examining the causes of stress in families with severely mentally handicapped children. *British Journal of Social Work, 51,* 510-517.

QUINE L AND PAHL J (1989). Stress and Coping in Families Caring for a Child with Severe Mental Handicap: a Longitudinal Study. Institute of Social and Applied Psychology/Centre for Health Service Studies, University of Kent, Canterbury.

QUINE L AND WADE K (1991). Helping parents of children with severe disabilities manage sleep disturbance. *Social Care Research Findings No. 16.* York: Joseph Rowntree Foundation.

QURESHI H (1992). Integrating methods in applied policy research: a case study of carers. IN J Brannen (Ed) *Mixing Methods: Qualitative and Quantitative Research.* Aldershot: Avebury.

QURESHI H (1991-2). Young adults with learning difficulties and behaviour problems: parents' views of services in the community. *Social Work and Social Sciences Review. 3,* 104-123.

RUTTER M, TIZARD J AND WHITMORE K (1970). *Education, Health and Behaviour.* London: Longman.

RICHARDSON A AND RITCHIE J (1986). *Making the Break: Parents Views about Adults with a Mental Handicap Leaving the Parental Home.* London: King's Fund.

SCOTT M AND STRADLING S (1987). Evaluation of a group programme for parents of problem children. *Behavioural Psychotherapy, 15,* 224-239.

SLOPER P, KNUSSEN C, TURNER S and CUNNINGHAM C (1991). Factors related to stress and satisfaction with life in families of children with Down's Syndrome. *Journal of Child Psychology and Psychiatry, 32,* 655-676.

WILKIN D (1979). *Caring for the mentally handicapped child.* Beckenham: Croom Helm.

ZARKOWSKA B AND CLEMENTS J (1988). *Problem Behaviour in People with Severe Learning Disabilities: a Practical Guide to a Constructional Approach.* Beckenham: Croom Helm.

PART 3

ANALYSIS AND MANAGEMENT

CHAPTER 6

CHALLENGING BEHAVIOUR IN PEOPLE WITH SEVERE LEARNING DISABILITIES: BEHAVIOUR MODIFICATION OR BEHAVIOUR ANALYSIS?

Bob Remington

INTRODUCTION

The way that services for people with challenging behaviour develop is, without doubt, multiply determined. Social and cultural values, ethical beliefs, and financial considerations necessarily play their part in shaping the methods of care and management that are deployed. Such a statement would of course be equally true in any clinical field, but it would be necessary to add that a scientific understanding of the problem should play a major role in determining the nature of the intervention. In the case of challenging behaviour, the relevant science in which to look for understanding is psychology, conceptualised as the scientific study of behavioural processes. Certainly psychologists have been involved in work with people with learning disabilities for many years, but their contributions have sometimes been controversial. My aim in this paper is to provide a rationale for an approach to intervention based on behavioural psychology, and then to touch on some of its implications for practice, the funding of future research, policy and management. The account will not be unduly technical; it is not written for the specialised audience of psychological researchers and practitioners, but more generally for those involved at all levels of service development.

The need for effective services for the management of people with severely challenging behaviour was recently highlighted by a report that appeared in the Hampshire local press (Davies, 1992). Under the headline **'Abandoned by the NHS'**, the report referred to a 20 year old man, resident with his parents, who had a lifelong history of challenging behaviour that had never been successfully managed. Problems arose because local services simply did not have the resources - in terms of either cash or trained staff - to provide the kind of support required. Parents thus faced the impossible dilemma of choosing between full residential accommodation in the local hospital or no service at all. Moreover, the nature of the challenging behaviour was such that recent attempts at management had been through the use of psychoactive drugs, the effects of which had deeply upset his parents. Drug-based intervention is sometimes an unavoidable crisis management technique, but it can reduce clients' capabilities and undermine their dignity. Hubert (1992) has interviewed parents whose children have challenging behaviour. Comments such as those cited below indicate the personal distress that drug-based intervention can cause:

> "They said, "... she's a bit under the weather, not quite herself, we had to give her some sedative because she was quite high".

> She was absolutely like a zombie ... she stared straight ahead, she could hardly walk " (p 33)

> "It was a terrible time then - they'd increased her Tegretol and the Melleril and she just went all floppy ... the doctor kept saying "This Melleril, it's one of the finest ones on the market" " (p 28)

Apart from the consumers' negative rating, research suggests that drugs have many unwanted side effects (Hubert, 1992) and that up to 55 per cent of prescriptions may be inappropriate (Bates, Smeltzer and Anoczky, 1986). Under these circumstances it is appropriate for service providers to consider other techniques of management for the most serious cases of challenging behaviour.

BEHAVIOURAL APPROACHES

Behaviour modification, which provides a psychological approach to behavioural management, has a long and sometimes troubled history in the treatment of challenging behaviour. For something like 30 years, the principles of operant conditioning have been applied in attempts to produce constructive changes in the behaviour of people with severe learning disabilities. This approach to intervention has proved immensely influential in the USA but, for a number of complex reasons, it has never achieved the same degree of acceptance in the UK. Rather than review the vast literature that has been generated, my aim here is to focus attention on the sea-change in emphasis that has transformed this area over the last decade, and to discuss its implications for clinical work with challenging behaviour. This critical change can be characterised as the decline in behaviour modification as technique per se, and the ascendance of behaviour analysis. Despite the fact that such a change has occurred, and has been widely documented in the technical literature (eg Remington, 1991, Repp and Singh, 1990), its significance may have escaped many service providers because the fundamental principles which underlie old and new approaches, and much of the technical vocabulary, has not changed. The next sections of this chapter therefore contrast behaviour modification, with its emphasis on change techniques, and behaviour analysis with its emphasis on interpreting the functions of challenging behaviour prior to intervention.

Behaviour modification as a technique

From its beginnings, behaviour modification offered fast solutions to previously intransigent problems. The rallying cry was "bring us your worst cases and let us work with them". Many successes were achieved. The style of intervention was based on a good theoretical grasp of the principles of learning, reliable behavioural measurement, rigorously applied intervention techniques, and a searching evaluation of outcome. In working with people with learning disabilities, the aim was - and remains - to develop new and socially valued forms of behaviour, such as self-care skills. The methods used are familiar to most people who work in the field: positive reinforcement is used to shape new ways of acting (operant behaviours), together with supplementary principles such as chaining or stimulus shaping to develop more complex repertoires. A very successful example of this approach in the UK has been the EDY staff training project (McBrien and Foxen, 1981).

The use of positive reinforcement principles to develop new behaviour has been widely accepted, but the use of behavioural methods to reduce existing forms of challenging behaviour has been much more controversial. Two kinds of solutions have been proposed: punishment and differential reinforcement.

Punishment: By the late 'sixties, basic research had isolated how, by varying the conditions under which punishment was delivered - schedule, delay, amount, and so on - it could function as a very effective method of suppressing behaviour (Azrin and Holz, 1966). Inevitably, some clinicians were tempted to use punishment techniques with challenging behaviour. For example, Lovaas and Simmons (1969), working with 'retarded' children, showed how very brief electric shocks, delivered immediately following self-injurious behaviour (SIB), could effectively suppress it over long periods of time. Lovaas justified what seemed to most a harsh approach in utilitarian terms; the SIB itself was horrendous, and only very few shocks were needed to suppress it. At that point, he argued, the real task of teaching new behaviour via positive reinforcement could begin.

Although punishment has been widely proscribed in recent years, research has continued. The kinds of stimuli used as punishers have increased, and now includes such techniques as timeout, water sprays in the face, bad odours, and so on. Moreover, the technology of punishment administration using shock has been considerably refined. For example, Linscheid, Iwata et al (1990) have recently evaluated a high-tech device that both detects self-injurious blows to the head and punishes them automatically, using a 0.08

sec mild shock to a limb (the intensity resembles a rubber band 'twanged' against the wrist).

Many studies of punishment have shown it can be enormously effective - at least in the short term. But the approach has attracted severe criticism, largely because of the 'aversive' nature of the stimuli employed. In fact, as we will see later, aversiveness is in the eye of the beholder, and the concept cannot be easily detached from its scientific origins in behaviour analysis. For the moment, however, consider alternatives to punishment for reducing challenging behaviour.

Differential reinforcement: A second class of response-reductive techniques, typically described as non-aversive (see, eg, LaVigna and Donnellan, 1986), is also based on operant principles. These attempt to reduce challenging behaviour by using positive reinforcement to increase the frequency of some other forms of acceptable behaviour, with the hope that by so doing the problem behaviours will be 'crowded out'. For example, differential reinforcement of other behaviour (DRO) might involve delivering a reinforcer every minute provided that no challenging behaviour had occurred during that minute, with the clock resetting to zero on each occurrence of the target behaviour (Repp and Dietz, 1974). Jones (1991) has recently reviewed a variety of these methods, and there is substantial research evidence to support claims of their effectiveness.

Punishment or differential reinforcement?: With a burgeoning research literature indicating that both punishment and differential reinforcement methods can successfully reduce challenging behaviour, it seems reasonable to ask whether there are ways in which we can choose between aversive or non-aversive techniques. If we ignore ethical issues for a moment (for as we will see later, reinforcement may be no less constraining than punishment), the decision about which technique is better seems on the surface to be a clear example of a difference in opinion about the effectiveness of different forms of behavioural intervention. Certainly, comparative experiments have been conducted (eg Corte, Wolfe and Locke, 1971) and reviews written (eg Lancioni and Hoogeveen, 1990) in an attempt to establish which approach is the more effective.

There is, however, a major problem with the very process of attempting to make comparisons of this kind. Although comparative evaluations have a superficially behavioural orientation, the philosophy that underlies them is not rigorously behavioural. In one sense, the logic of comparing punishment and reinforcement owes more to a medical than a behavioural model, at least in the sense that operant contingencies are seen as different treatments that might be applied to existing behaviour to produce a cure. Such a comparison is not dissimilar from comparing Melleril with Tegretol in a clinical trial. In both cases, the hope is that by adding an effective ingredient - a particular drug in one case and a particular operant contingency in the other - behaviour will be successfully modified. In this sense, behaviour modification is nothing more than the use of a 'bolt-on extra' operant contingency. Despite any technical sophistication, at bottom the question with this approach is always: Do we use the carrot or do we use the stick? And this is the wrong question. We should be asking: Do we merely try to modify behaviour, or do we try to understand the purpose of the behaviour first? Understanding of this kind involves behaviour analysis.

Behaviour analytic principles

Behaviour analysis begins with the idea that before we can permanently reduce the likelihood of challenging behaviour, we have to know about its causes. There are two senses in which we can provide useful and satisfying explanations: the first is historical; and the second functional.

Historical explanations: Challenging behaviour is often the product of a long history of person-environment interactions. Skinner (eg 1981) has frequently described an operant selection process in which reinforcing consequences of a behaviour at time t1 affect the likelihood of that behaviour recurring at time t2. Just as with Darwinian natural selection, a simple process of behavioural selection by consequences operating over a period of time can plausibly account for the emergence of quite remarkable new forms. Oliver (Chapter 7), has provided a speculative account of the selection of challenging behaviours in exactly these terms.

There are, however, notorious difficulties in trying to establish a behavioural history retrospectively. The failure of psychoanalysis stemmed more from the unreliability of retrospective data than from the fact that the past was unimportant in understanding the present (there were some other problems as well!). In this context, the key point is that although an understanding of the origins of behaviour is theoretically important, the here-and-now approach of bolt-on behaviour modification excludes this issue from consideration.

Functional analytic explanations: While there are practical reasons for avoiding a retrospective analytic approach, there are no such problems with a dynamic approach to current behaviour. Understanding the dynamics of behaviour - for example as in transactional analysis or family therapy - is all about discovering the functions of the behaviours that can be currently observed. If we adopt a behaviour analytic approach to challenging behaviour, the aim is always to understand what purpose it serves for the person we are considering. This way of working is thus intrinsically individualistic, because the same pattern of challenging behaviour, say SIB, may serve completely different functions for different people, or indeed for the same person at different times.

The aims and methods of behaviour analysis

The behaviour analyst's task is to detect the relations between challenging behaviour and its environmental antecedents and consequences, and to describe these relationships in terms of behavioural theory. The point of this exercise is to generate testable hypotheses concerning factors that maintain challenging behaviour. For example, such behaviour may function to produce positively reinforcing consequences (eg gaining tangibles or attention) or negatively reinforcing consequences (eg reducing boredom, or escaping from pressure to perform). These consequences may only occur in certain contexts, for example in particular physical locations or with particular people. Cues of this kind act as potential 'triggers' (discriminative stimuli) which control behaviour by virtue of their relationship with the availability of reinforcement. Moreover, some consequences will only be effective only under certain conditions. For example the reinforcement effectiveness of a drink of iced water will vary with the ambient temperature. These setting, or establishing, conditions also need to be taken into account in a functional analysis. Such a formulation is critically important because its results are used to inform any subsequent behaviour change attempt. Thus, intervention is based on manipulation of the existing environmental contingencies hypothesised to be responsible for the occurrence of the behaviour in question (eg Repp, Felce and Barton, 1988).

As the foregoing makes clear, behaviour analysis is a form of ecological research. Trained staff observe a client, sometimes over extended periods and in different settings. The most successful techniques for doing this are direct observation and analogue assessment. In the former, a client's behaviour-environment interactions in everyday settings are logged (often using a microcomputer), then analysed to identify any conditional relationships between them (eg the probability that SIB will be followed by staff attention). In analogue assessment, similar recording and analytic techniques are used, but the client is observed for short periods in environments that are specially created by the interventionist to model situations where challenging behaviour is likely to occur.

Given the published success of straightforward behaviour modification, the more elaborate behaviour analytic approach may seem unnecessarily time-consuming and complex. Why then has it become so important?

BEHAVIOUR MODIFICATION VERSUS BEHAVIOUR ANALYSIS

A simple example illustrates the differences between the two approaches described above. Imagine a client who engages in severe SIB but, as an observational assessment has shown, this is frequent only in teaching situations involving high task demand. The hypothesis would be that SIB was maintained by negative reinforcement - its function was to produce escape from demanding situations. Would we expect intervention based on either bolt-on reinforcement or punishment contingencies to be effective in this case? The punishment technique selected could involve using an aversive stimulus such as water spray delivered contingent on SIB. If so, the need to escape from the situation would become greater, and the probability of self-injury increase - punishment would be ineffective even in the short term. On the other hand, if timeout punishment was used it would be rapidly effective because the function of the behaviour itself is to produce seclusion. The problem is that when demand recurred, so would SIB. Thus timeout punishment would be effective only in the short term. Taking a wider perspective it would strengthen the challenging behaviour.

Suppose now that a differential reinforcement procedure was used. As noted previously, there are several techniques based on this idea. If differential reinforcement of **incompatible** behaviour was used, toy-play may be encouraged because it is incompatible with SIB. But this would once again increase social demand and make escape more necessary, so the approach would fail. However, if differential reinforcement of **other** behaviour was used, the client would be left to his own devices and reinforced perhaps with a favourite food when a minute passed without self-injury. Again, this approach would incidentally produce the seclusion that a behavioural analysis shows is maintaining the SIB, and would work very effectively, again in the short term.

We can see that bolt-on behaviour modification techniques may make matters better, but they may equally well make them worse. Unfortunately, it is difficult to predict what the effect will be without the understanding of behavioural function that comes from behaviour analysis. Intervention based on such an analysis adopts a completely different tack. If the client's behaviour is escape motivated, the aim must be to reduce the need to escape, and - should that need arise - to provide some other more efficient method of achieving it. Intervention would involve restructuring the task to reduce its aversiveness or, as in many recent studies, teaching a functionally equivalent response to the challenging behaviour (Durrand and Crimmins, 1991). Where functional analysis suggests challenging behaviour may function as a means of social control, intervention often involves teaching some way of communicating that requests either help, or that the demanding situation be terminated. Because the effort involved in such verbal communication is so much less than that involved in SIB, and the cost in pain is removed, functionally equivalent behaviour can often be quickly established and easily maintained (eg Durrand and Carr, 1991).

AREAS FOR FUTURE BEHAVIOUR ANALYTIC RESEARCH

The functional approach draws heavily on a research base. Both laboratory-based work and applied studies are pushing back the frontiers of our understanding of the nature of challenging behaviour. For the most part, however, these ideas have not yet fully been taken on board by clinical practitioners. The paragraphs that follow describe two interrelated behavioural phenomena that have implications for clinical practice.

The systemic nature of the behavioural repertoire

Recent research has told us much more about the complexity of relations between behavioural and environment events. The key change is from a focus on individual responses to a systemic approach. A person's behavioural repertoire should not be thought of as a collection of unrelated behaviours but as a complex interacting system (Scotti, et al, 1991). When this system is disturbed by particular environmental constraints, it adapts in subtle and sometimes unexpected ways. Some forms of challenging behaviour may be seen as adjustments to simple constraints. For example, very many laboratory studies have shown that when important events such as reinforcers occur regularly in time, but intermittently, an individual's behavioural system in some sense 'resonates' to this temporal constraint (Falk, 1986). Just before the reinforcer is due, anticipatory behaviours occur, but when reinforcement is unlikely, ritualistic patterns of behaviour often emerge. These behaviours, which are described as adjunctive (or schedule-induced), include aggression, pica, and other forms of stereotyped activity that are not maintained by the eventual recurrence of the reinforcer, but reflect other sources of motivation. It is not difficult to see how many forms of challenging behaviour might be adjunctive. For example, consider the temporal constraints imposed by room management. Here, one carer attends to each of several individuals in turn, providing precisely the temporally-spaced pattern of social reinforcement that could give rise to adjunctive behaviour. Functional analysis can reveal whether challenging behaviour occurring in these circumstances is adjunctive. If so, it makes more sense to change the room management procedure than impose an additional contingency to try to reduce its effects.

The nature of 'aversiveness' The idea of a behaviour system also raises some fundamental questions about reinforcement and aversion. Recent theoretical interpretations see operant contingencies as constraints on action or choice. This way of thinking about reinforcement dramatically undermines the distinction between aversive and non-aversive procedures (eg Remington, 1991). This is important given the current debate about the defensibility of aversive methods. Consider the following simplified example. Imagine two people in a small group home: by preference person A spends 70 per cent of her day watching TV and 10 per cent on occupational therapy (OT); person B spends her time the opposite way around. According to the well-known Premack principle (Premack, 1959), TV watching should reinforce OT for person A (who prefers TV watching), but the reverse would be the case for the person B (OT should reinforce TV). Thus, there are no events that can be absolutely specified as reinforcers because reinforcement is based on relative preference for activities. And, just as the higher probability behaviour is relatively reinforcing, so the lower probability behaviour is relatively aversive. Thus there are no absolute aversive stimuli for different individuals. TV is relatively aversive for B; OT is relatively aversive for A.

Thinking in these terms rapidly leads to questioning the distinction between reinforcement and punishment as normally conceived. For example, in the case of person A, a reinforcement contingency for OT might involve allowing TV when she has done more OT than usual. But a punishment contingency to reduce time watching TV would involve insisting that she does more OT than usual following a bout of TV watching. More generally, it is possible to show (Rachlin, et al, 1981) that both reinforcement and punishment can involve exactly the same constraints on free choice between two activities, except that the order in which the preferred and non-preferred activities occur is reversed (reinforcement involves non-preferred followed by preferred activity; punishment, preferred followed by non-preferred activity).

In sum, because there are no absolute aversive events, there are logical difficulties with proscribing aversive procedures per se. The constraint on free choice involved in a positive reinforcement procedure may be as great as the constraint involved in a punishment procedure. We can take this a step further. The two different free choice baselines might have been obtained from the same person at different times, for example depending on whether or not she had just been on a trip out to the shops. Thus specific setting conditions determine whether or not an event or activity will be relatively reinforcing or aversive - even for a particular person.

As far as challenging behaviour is concerned, the point is that - rather than imposing additional constraints in the name of behaviour modification using either differential reinforcement or punishment - we should be analysing the constraints that exist in the person's 'natural environment', then teaching the most effective ways of overcoming them.

IMPLICATIONS OF A BEHAVIOUR ANALYTIC APPROACH

Implications for practice

Unlike the bolt-on approach of behaviour modification, behaviour analysis is decisively not a crisis management technique. In fact, such an analysis identifies the behavioural skills that are ways of avoiding crisis situations as targets for teaching. Thus, intervention involves **teaching** effective behaviour at times when a crisis is not occurring rather than **treating** the challenging behaviour during a crisis. As Carr, Robinson and Palumbo (1990) have pointed out, this means that the aims of functionally-based intervention are education and empowerment. Clients are taught skills that will lead to desirable consequences in a wide range of situations, and will thus be generalised and maintained. The time spent in functional analysis and intervention is well spent if it produces permanent long-term change. Note also that the functional approach is about permanently eradicating the antecedent conditions that give rise to challenging behaviour on a long-term basis - unacceptable conditions of living. Here, the behaviour analytic approach makes strong contact with normalization principles (Emerson and McGill, 1989).

Finally, once we get away from the bolt-on characterization of behavioural psychology, we can begin to look differently at other approaches to working with people with challenging behaviour. For example, as Jones and McCaughey (1992) have shown, it is possible to analyse and understand aspects of Gentle Teaching procedures (McGee et al, 1987) in terms of behavioural principles - despite the fact that the approach is apparently hostile to that of behavioural psychology. Thus, establishing a bonded relationship between a carer and a client may equate with an informal version of functional analysis. Alternatively, the social pressure of interactions in Gentle Teaching may amount to nothing more than an effective negative reinforcement contingency for compliant behaviour.

Research funding implications

While the theoretical and applied developments discussed above have begun to alter the way in which we understand challenging behaviour, they raise many more questions to which answers are needed. In most cases, we must look to the USA for research that will develop the science of behaviour analysis; the research base in the UK is particularly weak in terms of the funding of basic science in this area. In the field of challenging behaviour, British research funding has been directed primarily at service evaluation oriented projects. While there is no doubt that the information gleaned from work of this kind is important in monitoring the effects of policy and management decisions, it can do little to develop new ways of thinking or acting that will have profound benefits for people with challenging behaviour. It will tell us much about whether people have or have not been 'abandoned by the NHS', but little that is new about the nature of their disabilities or how to ameliorate them

Policy and management implications

The discussion of behavioural systems and of aversiveness reflects a far richer and more complex understanding of behaviour than underlies the past simplicities of the kind of carrot-and-stick behaviourism recklessly 'given away' to care staff in the immediate past (see Kiernan, 1991, for discussion). We have seen that the value of drug-based treatment for challenging behaviour can be questioned in terms of both research findings and consumer satisfaction. Equally, little is to be gained from the insensitive application of simplistic behaviour modification techniques. Both of these solutions are relatively straightforward, they are relatively inexpensive in terms of trained staff resources - but they don't work. To manage challenging behaviour, we first have to understand it. This is not easy. The behaviour we see in a mature person today has a long developmental history, and it occurs in a complex social environment where a multiplicity of potential causes occur in an apparently chaotic fashion. Fortunately, there are some tools available. Although a great deal more research needs to be done, the beginnings of a sound methodology for observing and analysing behaviour-environment interactions is now emerging (eg Iwata, et al, 1982, Oliver, 1991, Repp, Felce and Karsh, 1991). The approach is not simple, and it does require trained professionals with the time to do it - but it does work.

Thus, the key issue in improving the care and management of people with challenging behaviour must be staff training. At present, it remains the case that most routine behavioural 'programmes' make little use of the more sophisticated behavioural theory and methodology outlined above. Fortunately, at least two centres in the UK (the Hester Adrian Research Centre and the University of Kent) have now begun to meet these needs by offering courses designed to develop the behavioural skills of nurses, social workers, and other professions allied to medicine (McGill and Bliss, Chapter 13). Ensuring the continuation and expansion of this kind of training, while maintaining an adequate supply of clinical psychologists with high-level research skills in addition to a professional interest in learning disabilities, is essential for the future development of effective services for people with challenging behaviour.

REFERENCES

AZRIN N H AND HOLZ W C (1966). Punishment in W K Honig (Ed) *Operant Behavior: Areas of research and application*. New York: Appleton-Century-Crofts.

BATES W J, SMELTZER D J AND ANOCZKY S M (1986). Appropriate and inappropriate use of psychotherapeutic medication for institutionalised mentally retarded persons. *American Journal on Mental Deficiency, 90,* 362-370.

CARR E G, ROBINSON S AND PALUMBO L W (1990). The wrong issue: Aversive versus nonaversive treatment. The right issue: Functional versus nonfunctional treatment. IN A C Repp and N Singh (Eds). *Nonaversive and Aversive Interventions for Persons with Severe Developmental Disabilities*. De Kalb, Illinois: Sycamore Press.

CORTE H E, WOLFE M M AND LOCKE B J (1971). A comparison of procedures for eliminating self-injurious behaviour of retarded adolescents. *Journal of Applied Behavior Analysis, 4,* 201-213.

DAVIES S (1992). Abandoned by the *NHS. Southampton Advertiser,* 6 March.

DURAND V M AND CARR E G (1991). Functional communication training to reduce challenging behavior: Maintenance and application in new settings. *Journal of Applied Behavior Analysis, 24,* 251-264.

DURAND V M AND CRIMMINS D (1991). Teaching functionally equivalent responses as an intervention for challenging behaviour. IN B Remington (Ed), *The Challenge of Severe Mental Handicap: A behaviour analytic approach.* Chichester: J Wiley and Sons.

EMERSON E and McGILL P (1989). Normalization and applied behaviour analysis: Values and technology in services for people with learning difficulties. *Behavioural Psychotherapy, 17,* 101-117.

FALK J L (1986). The formation and function of ritual behavior. IN T Thompson and M D Zeiler (Eds) *Analysis and Integration of Behavioural Units.* Hillsdale, N J: Erlbaum.

HUBERT J (1992). *Too Many Drugs, Too Little Care.* London: Values in Action.

IWATA B A, DORSEY M F, SLIFER K J, BAUMAN K E AND RICHMAN G S (1982). Towards a functional analysis of self-injury. *Analysis and Intervention in Developmental Disabilities, 2,* 3-20.

JONES R S P (1991). Reducing inappropriate behaviour using non-aversive procedures: Evaluating differential reinforcement schedules. IN B Remington (Ed) *The Challenge of Severe Mental Handicap: A behaviour analytic approach.* Chichester: J Wiley and Sons.

JONES R S P AND McCAUGHEY R E (1992). Gentle Teaching and Applied Behavior Analysis: A critical review. *Journal of Applied Behavior Analysis, 25,* 853-867.

KIERNAN C (1991). Professional ethics: Behaviour analysis and normalization. IN B Remington (Ed) *The Challenge of Severe Mental Handicap: A behaviour analytic approach.* Chichester: J Wiley and Sons.

LANCIONI G E AND HOOGEVEEN F R (1990). Non-aversive and mildly aversive procedures for reducing problem behaviours in people with developmental disorders: A review. *Mental Handicap Research, 3,* 137-160.

LaVIGNA G AND DONNELLAN A M (1986). *Alternatives to Punishment: Solving behavior problems with non-aversive strategies.* New York: Irvington

LINSCHEID T R, IWATA B A, RICKETTS R W, WILLIAMS D E AND GRIFFIN J C (1990). Clinical evaluation of the self-injurious behavior inhibiting system (SIBIS). *Journal of Applied Behavior Analysis, 23,* 53-78.

LOVAAS I O AND SIMMONS J Q (1969). Manipulation of self-destruction in three retarded children. *Journal of Applied Behavior Analysis, 2,* 143-157.

McBRIEN J A and FOXEN T H (1981). A pyramid model of staff training in behavioural methods: The EDY project. IN J Hogg and P Mittler (Eds) *Staff Training in Mental Handicap.* London: Croom Helm.

McGEE J J, MENOLASCINO F J, HOBBS D C, MENOUSEK P E (1987). *Gentle Teaching: a non-aversive approach to helping persons with mental retardation.* New York: Human Sciences Press.

OLIVER C (1991). The application of analogue methodology to the functional analysis of challenging behaviour. IN B Remington (Ed) *The Challenge of Severe Mental Handicap: A behaviour analytic approach.* Chichester: J Wiley and Sons.

PREMACK D (1959). Towards empirical behavior laws: Positive reinforcement. *Science, 136,* 255-257.

RACHLIN H, BATTALIO R, KAGEL J and GREEN L (1981). Maximization theory in behavioral psychology. *Behavioral and Brain Sciences, 4,* 371-417.

REMINGTON B (1991). Behaviour analysis and severe learning difficulty: The dialogue between research and application. IN B Remington (Ed) *The Challenge of Severe Mental Handicap: A behaviour analytic approach.* Chichester: J Wiley and Sons.

REPP A C and DIETZ S M (1974). Reducing aggressive and self-injurious behavior of institutionalized retarded children through reinforcement of other behaviors. *Journal of Applied Behavior Analysis, 7,* 313-325.

REPP A C, FELCE D and BARTON L E (1988). Basing the treatment of stereotypic and self-injurious behavior on hypotheses of their causes. *Journal of Applied Behavior Analysis, 21,* 281-289.

REPP A C, FELCE D AND KARSH K G (1991). The use of a portable microcomputer in the functional analysis of maladaptive behaviour. IN B Remington (Ed) *The Challenge of Severe Mental Handicap: A behaviour analytic approach.* Chichester: J Wiley and Sons.

REPP A C AND SINGH N (1990) (Eds). *Nonaversive and Aversive Interventions for Persons with Severe Developmental Disabilities.* DeKalb, Il: Sycamore Press.

SCOTTI J, EVANS I M, MEYER L H AND DI BENEDETTO A (1991). Individual repertoires as behavioural systems: Implications for program design and evaluation. IN B Remington (Ed) *The Challenge of Severe Mental Handicap: A behaviour analytic approach.* Chichester: J Wiley and Sons.

SKINNER B F (1981). Selection by consequences. *Science, 213,* 501-504.

CHAPTER 7

SELF-INJURIOUS BEHAVIOUR: FROM RESPONSE TO STRATEGY

Chris Oliver

INTRODUCTION

> "Think not that everything is pleasant that men for madness
> laugh at. For thou shalt in Bedleem see one laugh at the
> knocking of his own head against a post, and yet there is little
> pleasure therein."

>   Sir Thomas More,
>   (Visitor to Bedlum)
>   De Quator Novissmus

A shared and perhaps definitive feature of challenging behaviours is the immediate and evocative effect they have on the behaviour of others. This can be observed at the individual level of social interactions, perhaps in the form of immediate prevention of further occurrences, and at a broader level, for example the channelling of resources and energy into containment services or intervention delivery. Both of these responses are understandable. Their short term goals are to stop the behaviour occurring again and reduce its apparent prevalence. Although these responses may frequently be effective in the short term, whether these responses comprise an effective long term strategy, particularly when pursued in isolation, is debatable.

The most common response to challenging behaviour in the past 30 years has been the use of psychoactive medication (eg Oliver, Murphy and Corbett, 1987). Empirical research however, has demonstrated the most effective response to be interventions based on the psychological theory of operant conditioning. Initially this approach was derived directly from fundamental psychological research and then translated into techniques which could be applied by practitioners. In the USA the early development of behaviour modification, as it became known, took place in an academic culture which derived the technology from the experimental analysis of behaviour. However as the techniques became widely disseminated and practised so the link with theory and fundamental research weakened (Michael, 1985, Remington, 1991 and Chapter 6). Ultimately, isolated practitioners had little to guide them except their own experience and a battery of methods.

In the UK the dissemination of behaviour modification lagged behind that in the USA but was similarly rapid. A critical difference however, was the absence of a pervasive academic culture in the UK sympathetic to behavioural theory. Consequently the behavioural approach was rapidly disseminated and applied predominantly in the form of techniques only. When this dissemination occurred there was a period of optimism, followed by disillusionment and, more recently, occasional, but increasing outright, rejection of any behaviour modification procedures. The factors which influenced this course were diverse and a few were critical. These were:

* the demand for rapid results for limited input (similar to the sedative effects of psychoactive medication).

* the dissemination of techniques alone.

* the lack of available theoretical knowledge that practitioners could readily access.

Immediate success with little labour is one feature of what are commonly deemed to be successful treatments. The demand or expectation for this to be delivered may have contributed to the increasing use of aversive methods and the general absence of the application of functional analysis prior to interventions being implemented. When this demand is combined with the available product, techniques alone, when interventions do not give early success the tendency is to add a technique or move to another. There is little evidence that, in practice, a failed technique leads to a re-evaluation of functionally related determinants of challenging behaviour. Finally this tendency is exacerbated when practitioners cannot easily access the products of either fundamental or applied research which may better inform decisions on intervention strategies.

The dissatisfaction with behaviour modification has spread to behavioural psychology itself and led many to reject the whole approach. The vacuum left behind has been quickly filled by other approaches, many of which lack a basis in empirical or theoretical mainstream psychology, have superficial and seductive appeal and are evangelically disseminated. This development will further isolate people with learning difficulties from others by cultivating the notion of a distinct psychology (Clements, 1992). The uncritical acceptance of these approaches is an indictment of the failure of dissemination of mainstream psychology.

This trend is particularly lamentable when the psychological approach to challenging behaviour is undergoing a renaissance. The dissatisfaction with technique dominated behaviour modification has been expressed within behavioural psychology as well as by opponents (eg Carr, Robinson and Palumbo, 1990). The last decade has seen a significant shift toward evaluation of the determinants of challenging behaviour and the application of this understanding, for example via functional analysis, to intervention design (Durand and Crimmins, 1991, Oliver, 1991a). As the understanding of the determinants of challenging behaviour expands so does the potential for more effective interventions.

This aspect of research in challenging behaviour will grow rapidly in the nineties and needs to be capitalised on. More critically this must happen in conjunction with a return to an empirical approach.

Whilst this body of knowledge expands, the approach of made-to-measure interventions will not be adopted by practitioners unless there is active dissemination of contemporary applied behaviour analysis. There are lessons of history which should guide this process. Given the above analysis of the demise of technique based behaviour modification there are two obvious guidelines:

* greater emphasis placed on the theoretical basis to methods of analysis and intervention.

* continuing easy access for practitioners to recent basic research, available technology and information.

A more obvious condition is that there is better understanding of the determinants of challenging behaviours. Without this there will only be a stagnant stockpile of assessment and intervention techniques. Whilst there has recently been some limited growth in this area, constant proactive support is required to expand the knowledge base.

The empirical study of self-injurious behaviour is an illustrative example of the introduction to this chapter. The earliest empirical literature demonstrated the role of operant conditioning in maintaining SIB (Lovaas et al, 1965, Lovaas and Simmons, 1969). There was then a major shift toward the study of interventions which primarily manipulated contingencies without prior functional analysis (see Singh, 1981). The bulk of the ensuing empirical literature about SIB then consisted of demonstrations of the impact that implementing new contingencies can have (Footnote 1, page 177). Throughout this period applied behaviour analysis commanded little attention, as increasing types of reinforcers and punishing stimuli were demonstrated in increasingly elaborate single-case designs and then applied by practitioners. There is little doubt that this period of development substantially contributed to the well-being of many people for whom there was no alternative help. The demonstration of operant conditioning also firmly located the study of challenging behaviour within the discipline of psychology.

This resume of the history of the application of behavioural psychology helps focus attention on its current position. The major problem would appear to be the technological drift away from applied behaviour analysis. This has led to two problems:

* When established techniques fail, practitioners are unable to call upon 'first principles' to examine failures and develop further interventions.

* The technological approach, by its very nature, is unable to substantially contribute to a basic understanding of challenging behaviour.

This current state is unlikely to change without a deliberate move toward applied behaviour analysis and active dissemination of this approach. This chapter is intended to be help stimulate this process.

There are a number of specific aims for this chapter. The main one is to expand the operant model within the sphere of applied behaviour analysis. The reason for this is that there is little explanation in the operant literature which sufficiently explains:

* Why SIB only occurs in some people with learning disabilities, particularly those with severe learning disabilities. Currently, explanations would seem to rely predominantly on chance.

* Why there is an association between some individual characteristics and SIB.

* What determines some of the parameters of self-injurious responding at a given point in time such as rate, intensity and topography.

* Why individuals should have a given function to their SIB and not others.

A second aim is to integrate empirical evidence that comes from different approaches, more specifically, the operant and biological approaches. Finally, the concluding sections will examine the implications of the determinants of SIB for practice.

THE APPLICATION OF OPERANT THEORY

Social conditioning

There is a wealth of literature that provides evidence that SIB is an operant maintained by reinforcing consequences (Lovaas et al, 1965, Carr, 1977, Durand and Crimmins, 1988). This literature will not be extensively reviewed or discussed here except in passing. Instead it will be interpreted to present a model of the development and maintenance of SIB over time. This model has been presented before in different forms (Oliver, 1986, Oliver and Head, 1990) and the version here is a revision of previous descriptions.

It is clear that SIB may be maintained by the presentation of social reinforcement, either positive (usually described under the rubric of attention) or negative (most commonly demonstrated by escape from demands),(see Carr and McDowell, 1980; Gaylord-Ross, 1982; Iwata et al, 1982, Carr and Durand, 1985a). A critical aspect of understanding this maintenance by social reinforcement is the effect that SIB has on others and how the responses to SIB are themselves reinforced by the person showing SIB (Ferster, 1961, and see Patterson, 1982, Emery et al, 1983). This may best be achieved by considering the general case for socially determined SIB in a stepwise fashion.

This is done below and the description should be read in conjunction with the flow diagram in Figure 1. (In this stepwise description, normal text indicates the behaviour of, or effect on, the person showing SIB, bold text indicates the behaviour of, or effect on, another person).

* Self-injurious behaviour occurs

* **An aversive stimulus (the SIB) is presented to others (see Carr, Taylor, Robinson, 1991, Hall and Oliver, 1992).**

* **The aversive stimulus acts as an establishing operation (Footnote 2) which evokes escape behaviour from others, for example social intervention. That is, the SIB establishes the significance of escape from SIB as a reinforcing consequence of a social intervention.**

* The social intervention acts as positive or negative reinforcement for the SIB. (Why the intervention should be a reinforcing one, ie the right one, given the circumstances that exist at the time of the SIB, is an interesting question addressed later).

* As a reinforcing stimulus has been presented the SIB ceases, as an abolishing operation of either reinforcer satiation, in the case of

positive reinforcement, or the removal of the aversive stimulus, in the case of negative reinforcement, has occurred.

* As a result of reinforcement the probability that SIB will occur in the future when the same discriminative stimuli and/or establishing operations occur, is raised.

* **When the SIB ceases there is the removal of the presentation of an aversive stimuli to others, consequently the social intervention that was presented by another person is negatively reinforced.**

* **As a result of the negative reinforcement for the social intervention the probability that the same intervention will be presented in the future is raised.**

By considering the effect that SIB has on the behaviour of others, as well as the effect that others have on SIB, a more complete explanation of SIB is possible. The aversive property of SIB is critical, as it establishes escape from SIB as potential reinforcement and thus determines its power to evoke responses from others and raise the probability that it will be selectively reinforced over other behaviours which are not aversive to others. This may explain why SIB becomes dominant in the behavioural repertoire of individuals. There is a useful analogy here in evolutionary theory, particularly as expressed by Dawkins (1988) in "The Blind Watchmaker" (Footnote 3).

Dawkins lucidly presents the thesis that during evolution organisms survive because of their adaptive properties in the prevailing environment. Those that survive breed, and consequently pass on similar properties to their offspring via genetic code. Those that do not have adaptive properties, do not survive and consequently the genetic code for their properties and the properties themselves become extinct. There is therefore a constant selection for given features. Dawkins illustrates the gradual nature of extensive change by computer simulations of the cumulative effect which can result from numerous small changes which occur between generations (see Dawkins, 1988, p58). Thus in each new generation there will be a variety of potential forms each differing slightly from the previous generation by virtue of a small difference in the genetic code for given features. Gradually over a long period of time complex organisms can evolve with the cumulative effect of successive changes, each selected for in single generations. Dawkins also makes the point that when a complex form is viewed at a single point in time, in isolation from previous forms, then it may appear that a creationist force (a "watchmaker") has been at work.

Figure 1 Flow diagram illustrating social conditioning of SIB and the conditioning of the other person in the interaction. (Normal text indicates the effect on, or behaviour of, the person showing SIB, italicised text indicates the effect on, or behaviour of, the other person).

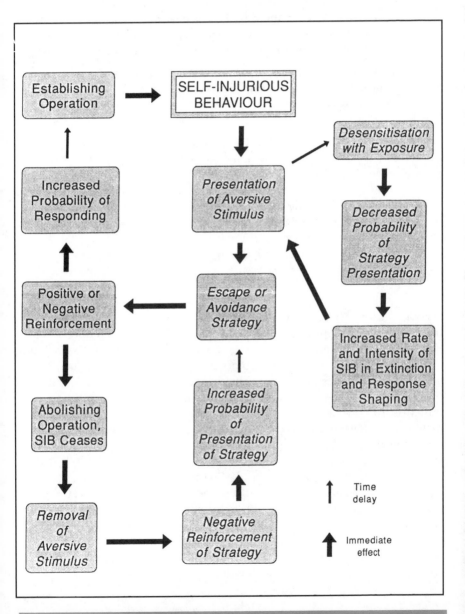

In evolutionary theory selection of, for example physical features, is by environmental factors. SIB maintained by social reinforcement is also selected for from the behavioural repertoire of an individual by environmental factors, in this case the process of reinforcement by others. It is here that the aversive property of SIB is critical to its survival. SIB is more likely to be reinforced precisely because it is aversive to others. As SIB is aversive to others, it acts as an aversive establishing operation thus providing negative reinforcement for others if the SIB is itself temporarily terminated by being reinforced. Other behaviours (in fact probably all those not labelled challenging) tend not to have this property. Thus, when they occur, they do not comprise an aversive stimulus and consequently do not evoke behaviour from others. SIB is therefore more likely to be reinforced than other behaviours which are not challenging. For this reason SIB may rise to a dominant position in the repertoire.

This selection of a behaviour in the repertoire of the person showing SIB is not the only potential application of the analogy to the model. A second is in the explanation of why the other person in the interaction necessarily presents a reinforcer contingent on the SIB. In this case the reinforcer for the other person's behaviour is escape from or avoidance of SIB. The most likely explanation is that any interventions which the other person presents which do not terminate the SIB will not be negatively reinforced (ie selected for in their repertoire), in fact they are punished. Those that do terminate the SIB will be negatively reinforced and consequently selected for. As the SIB ceases only when a reinforcer is presented (via the abolishing operation of reinforcer satiation or the removal of an aversive stimulus) there are punitive consequences for presenting unreinforcing interventions and reinforcing consequences for presenting reinforcing interventions. For this reason the presentation of reinforcing interventions is selected for and comes to be dominant in the repertoire of others when SIB occurs. Here the evolutionary analogy requires expansion as the form of the blind watchmaker is itself subject to evolutionary selection.

This description of the interaction between someone showing SIB and others is open to empirical evaluation and was examined in an observational study of the effects of head and body hitting and banging on the behaviour of others (Hall and Oliver, 1992). The analysis in this study comprised deriving the mean trend in social contact prior to, during and following a burst of SIB. The results of these observations are presented in a revised format in Figure 2, together with an interpretation of the flow of events.

From the data presented in Figure 2 it appears that the effect of the SIB on the behaviour of others is consistent with the model proposed in Figure 1 when self-injury is maintained by positive reinforcement of social contact. There are other points of interest which arise from this analysis:

* An establishing operation of reinforcer deprivation appears to be the influential antecedent that evokes SIB. Whilst this finding requires replication and further examination, there are two major implications. Firstly, functional analysis employing A-B-C recordings should specifically seek to describe the absence of events which may be influential antecedents as well as their presence(cf Maurice and Trudel, 1982). Secondly, the potential role played by discriminative stimuli in evoking SIB may be minimal (this is discussed in more detail later).

* Not only does SIB evoke social contact from others, it also appears to be almost the only antecedent to social contact. Once SIB has ceased the probability of social contact declines, presumably as there is no other establishing operation for social contact. Consequently an establishing operation of reinforcer deprivation occurs again. When SIB occurs, the social contact is negatively reinforced by the termination of SIB.

* Reinforcement for SIB is presented at the point of reinforcer deprivation (thus enhancing its potency) (see Vollmer and Iwata, 1991) and on a variable, intermittent schedule. The probability of reinforcement rises throughout the burst of SIB and peaks immediately after SIB. It is difficult to construct a situation more conducive to both learning and long term maintenance.

The detailed analysis in Figure 2 appears to provide support for the theoretical model in Figure 1 and also demonstrates a method of functional analysis (see Hall and Oliver, 1992 for details). From the model in Figure 1 it is also possible to generate a testable hypothesis about the form of the plot if the function of SIB was escape from aversive stimuli (eg demands, social interactions) as opposed to maintenance by social interactions. (If the y axis represented the probability of the presentation of the aversive stimulus then the plot should be a mirror image of the curve in Figure 2).

In this section the reinforcement of SIB and the reinforcement for the social interaction which maintains SIB have been considered at one point in time. The development of SIB and the parameters of the severity of SIB requires this analysis to be considered over time.

Figure 2 Plot of the mean probability of social contact prior to, during and following a long burst of SIB, for SIB maintained by positive reinforcement from social contact (see Hall and Oliver 1992). The flow diagram below is an interpretation of the sequence of events based on the social conditioning model described in Figure 1.

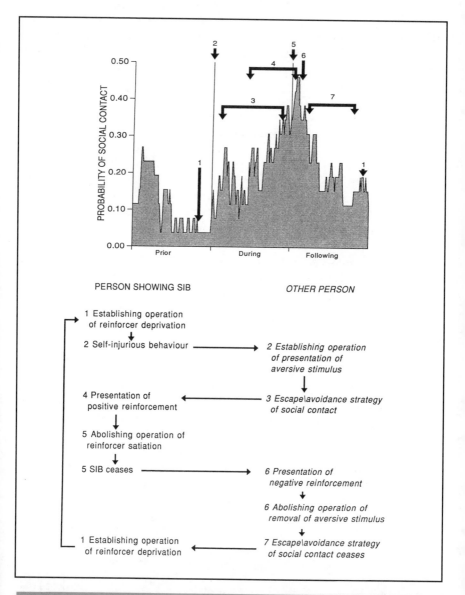

Establishing more severe SIB by social conditioning

Very severe SIB, in terms of rate, intensity and topography, requires further explanation. It is useful here to again apply the analogy of evolution because when very severe SIB occurs, then creationism (Viennese or otherwise) often comes to the fore. It was argued above that the critical feature of SIB that governs its selection over other behaviours is its aversive property. Similarly it may be argued that more aversive SIB may be selected over less aversive SIB. Clearly how aversive self-injury is to others is variable. The variability may be determined by parameters of self-injurious responding (rate, intensity and topography), context or a host of other variables (Footnote 4). There are predictions that may be made about some of the parameters of SIB. These basically rest on the premise that more damaging SIB is likely to be more aversive, and thus more likely to be reinforced (ie selected for), than less damaging SIB. This assumption may be examined empirically.

One aspect of the relative aversive property of SIB, that of burst duration, was examined in the study by Hall and Oliver (1992). In this study the probability of social contact following long bursts of SIB was compared to the probability of social contact following short bursts of SIB (Footnote 5). Revised results of this comparison are shown in Figure 3.

Clearly longer bursts were more likely than short bursts to evoke social contact from others. Additional analysis also showed burst length to be significantly correlated with the probability of contingent social contact. Consequently longer bursts of SIB were systematically differentially reinforced and thus selected for.

A second aspect of the aversive property of SIB, that of intensity, is illustrated in a case study of a young girl with Rett syndrome (Oliver, Murphy et al, 1993). Informal observations revealed two types of mouth hitting which differed primarily in intensity. (Inter-observer reliability indices showed that the two could be satisfactorily differentiated.) Analogue methodology revealed that the harder mouth hits were reinforced by the termination of social interactions, whilst softer hits were reinforced by the resultant sensory stimulation. Figure 4 shows the mean frequency per minute of both types of hitting throughout analogue conditions in which others were present or the girl was alone.

The high intensity SIB is clearly most influenced by the conditions in which others were present whilst low intensity SIB is unaffected. Additionally the data reveal a pattern which is suggestive of fixed interval escape responding

Figure 3 Plot of the mean probability of social contact following long and short bursts of SIB for SIB maintained by positive reinforcement from social contact (see Hall and Oliver, 1992).

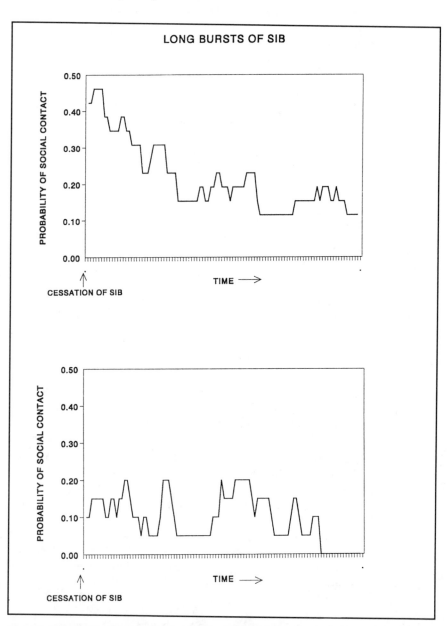

(see Carr, Newsom and Binkoff, 1976, Carr and Durand, 1985a). These results demonstrate that the socially reinforced SIB (ie reinforced by escape from social interactions) is that which is harder and it seems reasonable to assume that this is because it was more aversive to others and thus more likely to evoke in others the escape behaviour of terminating social contact. Historically, harder SIB was therefore systematically differentially reinforced and thus selected for.

Other parameters of the aversive property of SIB such as topography and potential for damage may also be selectively reinforced. This may explain why head to object banging sometimes occurs on the corners of tables as opposed to the flat surface, and a behaviour such as head slapping is more common than hand to hand slapping (both are easy). It may also help to explain why head to window banging often occurs (high danger with low pain), banging on cupboard doors often occurs (sounds worse than it is) and hard surfaces may be selected (more damaging).

There is therefore some evidence which suggests that more severe SIB is selected for at a given point in time. This does not however, explain the initial occurrence of more severe SIB. When high rate or high intensity SIB is considered in isolation in this way there is a tendency toward rejecting an operant interpretation. The evolutionary analogy employed above is helpful here as it encourages consideration of the evolutionary history of the more severe behaviour in order to explain its current form and thus lay to rest any creeping creationism.

The development of more severe SIB

More severe SIB is differentially reinforced, and therefore selected for, by virtue of its greater aversive property, which acts as an establishing operation evoking reinforcing responses from others. SIB of greater severity may occur initially, and so come to be selectively reinforced, for a number of reasons. These essentially rest on the premise that repeated exposure to aversive stimuli results in desensitisation to those stimuli (Footnote 6). Consequently if others are repeatedly exposed to SIB, stable in terms of parameters such as rate, intensity, dangerousness, etc, they are likely to find the SIB decreasingly aversive with repeated exposure. As the aversive property decreases, so the SIB (at that level) loses its property as an establishing operation and consequently may not evoke reinforcing responses from others. This process of desensitisation may drive the development of more severe SIB in three ways.

Figure 4 Overall mean frequency per minute of high and low
intensity SIB over time, within combined analogue
conditions expressed as a three point moving mean
(see Oliver, Murphy et al, 1993).

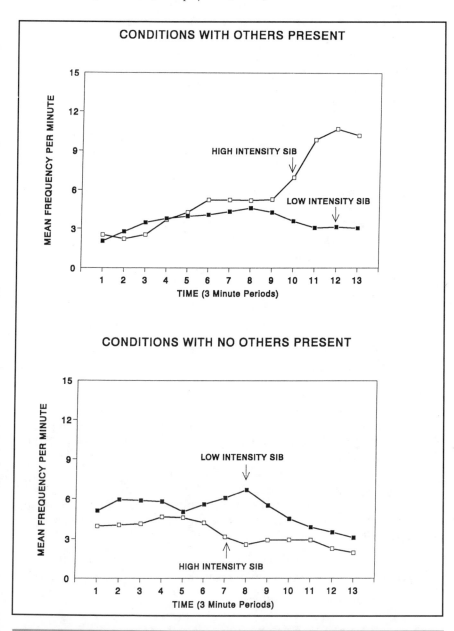

1. Desensitisation contributes to the formation of intermittent schedules of reinforcement

Initially single self-injurious responses may be sufficiently aversive to evoke reinforcing responses from others. With repeated exposure to single responses, the aversive property of a single response decreases, an establishing operation is therefore not in effect and consequently a reinforcing response from others does not occur. If however, a number of responses occur together the aversive stimuli may again be presented, by a cumulative effect, and the establishing operation becomes operative. A reinforcing response is then evoked and higher numbers of responses are differentially reinforced over single responses. For this reason responding comes to be maintained on an intermittent schedule of reinforcement which is almost certainly variable. This schedule is critical to the further development of more severe SIB for two reasons:

* The behaviour becomes resistant to extinction and occurs at a higher frequency (the partial reinforcement effect or "Humphreys' paradox"; see Rachlin,1991). This ensures that the behaviour will remain to the fore in a behavioural repertoire by surviving episodes of the nonpresentation of reinforcement.

* The behaviour has opportunities to generalise to more environments (people and places), condition others and become subject to further conditioning.

2. Desensitisation promotes the probability of episodes of the non-presentation of reinforcement

Further development of more severe SIB occurs during periods in which reinforcement for SIB does not accrue (the importance of these periods is discussed below). Given the evocative property of SIB, in terms of the behaviour of others, it is necessary to explain why these periods should occur at all. There are two possible reasons:

* With repeated exposure to frequent SIB desensitisation will occur. Others may then not respond immediately, as an establishing operation is not in effect. When the response is withheld, albeit 'passively', the early stage of extinction is operative.

* Once others have become desensitised to the frequent SIB they may then decide to actively attempt extinction.

The desensitisation process therefore cultivates high rate responding and an increased probability that periods of non-reinforcement (ie extinction) will occur.

Periods of non-reinforcement are, ironically, influential in contributing to more severe SIB. There are three main ways in which this occurs:

* In the early stages of extinction, behaviour increases in both frequency and intensity. Under these circumstances SIB will comprise a more aversive stimulus than pre-extinction SIB, an establishing operation will become operative and the higher rate, higher intensity SIB will be differentially reinforced and thus selected for. This single process may be repeated many times and each time the starting point (in terms of frequency and intensity) is different (the behaviour is more severe). Figure 1 should then be viewed as a repeating cycle moving through time. The analogy with evolutionary theory is self-evident. Each small (unsuccessful) trial of extinction gives rise to a generation differing only slightly from that which preceded it but viewed over many generations the cumulative change is substantial.

* When responding is not reliably reinforced there is a general rule that may come into operation. This is the win stay/lose shift rule. This means that when reinforcement is not presented for a given behaviour, different behaviours will occur. Given the propensity for others to reinforce behaviours that are aversive to them, it is likely that more challenging behaviours, possibly a new form of SIB, will be selected for under these conditions. The addition of more forms of SIB is an increase in the severity of SIB.

* Schedules of reinforcement will become increasingly lean as the number of responses which comprise an aversive stimulus of sufficient strength to be an establishing operation increases. This will generally, and gradually, raise the frequency of SIB

3. Desensitisation systematically determines selection when behavioural variability is evident

No two self-injurious responses are exactly the same. In fact, they will vary on a number of dimensions of severity (exact site, intensity, responses per burst, etc) in a way best described by a normal distribution curve around a hypothetical mean of severity. The hypothetical mean will be determined by the reinforcement history for a given response. Obviously some responses will be of lesser severity (ie below the mean) whilst others will be of greater severity. In general, by the process of desensitisation, others are less likely to find responses below the mean as aversive as responses above the mean. Consequently responses below the mean will not be as reliably reinforced as those above the mean. There is therefore a constant and steady selection pressure for an increase in the severity of responding. A second implication of variability in severity is that self-injurious responses which differ greatly from those already in the repertoire are unlikely but nevertheless possible. Those that are much more severe are much more unlikely (a property of the normal distribution) but if they occur they will present a relatively extreme aversive stimulus and thus they have a high probability of being reinforced.

An example of this may be seen in the development of severe head to object banging. Banging on the flat surface of a table may yield a given aversive level. However a low probability (but possible) bang on a sharp corner of a table is likely to be extremely aversive to others and thus evoke a reinforcing response. Consequently such banging may enter a behavioural repertoire.

These explanations of the increase in frequency and severity are best considered by applying the evolutionary analogy. The change to very severe SIB is very unlikely to be sudden and more commonly occurs over many trials of learning (generations). Each generation may vary only a little from the previous generation but it is the cumulative effect from the overall number of generations which determines the extent of change. Large jumps in severity may occur but are of low probability (Footnote 7). (An analogy from evolution for these jumps may be discontinuities in fossil records). Self-injury can and does occur at extremely high rates (anything up to hundreds of responses a day) consequently there are numerous opportunities for selection to occur. Given these circumstances SIB of immense severity can and does develop just as an immensely complex product of evolution such as the eye has developed (Footnote 8).

When severe SIB is dominant in the behavioural repertoire of an individual there are numerous ways in which it may attain further 'functions' for an individual. High frequency SIB for example, may become subject to 'superstitious' conditioning and subsequently functional for a given reinforcer. Changes or additions of function therefore, are possible over time. (The evolutionary analogy here is 'functional change in structure continuity'; see Gould's, (1992), chapter 'Not Necessarily a Wing'; pp 139-151). Once SIB attains more than one function, functional analysis becomes problematic and the behaviour modification rule of consistent response to behaviours may be of dubious value.

This section has examined how applied behaviour analysis can contribute to an understanding of severe SIB. The analogy of evolutionary theory has been employed to illustrate the importance of considering the derivation of apparently bizarre and severe behaviour. There is a point however at which the evolutionary analogy becomes inappropriate. Evolutionary theory considers the arbitrary development of organisms as a product of the impact of environmental features. The direction of the development of SIB does not appear to be arbitrary and nor is there just a one-way effect. Instead, because SIB interacts with its environment in particular ways, the direction is most likely to be one of increasing severity. This gives the behaviour immense 'survival value' because of its perfect adaptive properties.

Conditioning by sensory reinforcement

SIB maintained by social reinforcement (either positive or negative) represents one aspect of the application of operant theory. The maintenance of SIB by unmediated reinforcing sensory consequences has also been demonstrated via a number of paradigms (see Meyerson et al, 1967, Rincover and Devany, 1982). These studies show that a self-injurious response, such as eye poking or pressing, may occur because it yields rewarding stimulation, in this case the impression of bright 'patterns' of apparent lights (see Thurrell and Rice, 1970 Jan et al, 1983). This form of maintenance is commonly distinguished from socially mediated forms of reward because of the nature of the reinforcement (intrinsic versus extrinsic) but it should be noted that there are probably more similarities between the types of maintenance than differences.

BIOLOGICAL THEORIES

In terms of robust evidence the operant theory as an explanation of the general case is currently dominant. There is however an expanding body of literature which documents the potential role of neurotransmitters and neuromodulators as determinants of SIB. The contention that there is a biological basis to SIB is resolutely separated from the operant theory in the literature. Consequently these two positions are viewed as incompatible. This need not necessarily be the case and it may be unproductive to accept this position.

Currently the study of biological determinants of SIB is fragmented both in terms of paradigms and the operative neurochemical systems studied. Interest is predominantly focused on the endorphins (naturally occurring endogenous opiates with analgesic and euphorogenic properties) and the dopaminergic system. Evidence for the involvement of the endorphins comes from a number of sources:

* The reduction of SIB in some subjects following the administration of the opiate blockers Naloxone and Naltrexone (Richardson and Zaleski 1983, Sandman et al 1983, Davidson et al 1983, Sandyk 1985; Leboyer et al 1988, Barrett et al 1989).

* The observation that metenkephalins are raised in people who show "delicate cutting" (Coid et al, 1983).

* the observation that autistic children who show SIB show raised plasma levels of endorphins (a statistically non-significant result, but nevertheless suggestive), (Gillberg, 1988).

On the basis of this evidence a number of roles for the endorphin system in the cause of SIB have been generated. These are:

* that SIB is reinforced in an operant fashion by the contingent euphorogenic effect of the release of endorphins.

* that endorphins induce analgesia to self-injurious acts.

* that the chronic release of endorphins raises the sensitivity of dopaminergic receptors thus increasing the likelihood of dopaminergic involvement (see below), (Smee and Overstreet, 1976, Gillman and Sandyk 1985).

Evidence for the involvement of the dopaminergic system in the cause of SIB is equally fragmented and is based on the findings that:

* Self-biting may be induced in animals by the administration of pemoline, clonidine, caffeine, amphetamines and other dopaminergic agents. (Peters, 1967, Genovese et al 1969, Mueller and Hsiao 1980, Mueller and Nyhan 1983).

* The dopaminergic system is disturbed in Lesch-Nyhan syndrome in which SIB is always observed. (Christie et al 1982, Baumeister et al 1985, Harris 1992).

* Some trials of dopamine blockers have yielded reductions in SIB. (Gualtieri et al, 1986).

* Stereotyped behaviour in animals may be induced by dopaminergic agents.

The nature of the association between dopaminergic disturbance and SIB is unclear. Why SIB should result from a disturbance of dopamine has not really been adequately discussed, nor has the associated question of why SIB does not always arise from dopaminergic disturbance. The only clear statement that can currently be made is that under some circumstances SIB is correlated with dopaminergic disturbance.

INTERACTIONS BETWEEN OPERANT AND BIOLOGICAL THEORIES

The preceding account is necessarily an oversimplification of the current biological theories of SIB. However when considered in conjunction with the evidence for operant conditioning of self-injurious responding a number of useful questions are generated.

* If SIB is only ever influenced by environmental contingencies:
    * why is its occurrence ever influenced by opiatergic and dopaminergic agents?
    * why is it associated with syndromes in which the opiatergic and dopaminergic systems are disturbed?

* If SIB is only ever influenced by the euphoric effects of the release of endorphins:
    * how can it ever be reduced or increased by the manipulation of environmental contingencies?
    * how did the SIB become severe enough for endorphins to be released?
    * why are Naloxone and Naltrexone not always successful?

* If SIB is only ever influenced by the analgesia to responding resulting from the release of endorphins:
    * how can it ever be reduced or increased by the manipulation of environmental contingencies?
    * what precipitates its occurrence? (Footnote 9).

* If SIB is only ever influenced by a disturbance of the dopaminergic system:
    * how can it ever be reduced or increased by the manipulation of environmental contingencies?

* why are dopamine blockers not always successful and when they are successful why do they not completely eradicate the SIB?

Putting to one side the fairly critical issue of strength of evidence, a reasonable resolution to these discrepancies would seem to be that for a given individual any of these influences may be operative to some degree at any one time. Which determinant is most influential may vary over time and may also be determined by some individual characteristics (this is discussed in more detail in the next section). This interpretation suggests that biological and operant determinants are not incompatible, rather they exert a joint influence on the probability that SIB may occur.

The interaction between endorphins and operant conditioning in determining the probability of SIB occurring and its severity is interesting because of the variety of ways the interaction may operate. There are two main possibilities:

* Operant conditioning shapes SIB by the processes of differential reinforcement and intermittent schedules to a level of severity sufficient for endorphins to be contingently released and consequently positively reinforce SIB. The operant 'function' may then become comparatively less influential, although still operative. The introduction of an opiate blocker may therefore only eliminate one function (by extinction) and thus only some of the SIB.

* The analgesic effect of endorphins reduces the response cost inherent in SIB thus there is an absence of a naturally occurring punitive contingency. SIB maintained by social reinforcement may then occur with greater severity than would otherwise be the case (Footnote 10). The SIB of greater severity may then be subject to differential reinforcement by social contingencies. The introduction of an opiate blocker may therefore reintroduce the naturally occurring punitive contingency of pain. (It is a testament to the operant/biological split that this intervention is not considered relevant to the "aversive/nonaversive" debate). Under these conditions SIB may reduce, but may also still be evoked by previously significant environmental antecedents.

In both cases it is clear that a complete long term reduction of SIB resulting from the administration of opiate blockers is unlikely and that their efficacy is directly related to the role played by endorphins (for example, low intensity SIB which may not yield a painful contingency may be unaffected).

If this rationale is ignored and opiate blockers are employed as the treatment for SIB, then the mistakes made in the implementation of technological behaviour modification will be repeated. A second implication arising from this interpretation is for the use of combined interventions employing both operant procedures and opiate blockers.

The role of dopamine receptor supersensitivity as a determinant of SIB is less clear. The evidence is predominantly tangential and dopamine blockers have not yielded consistent effects, even in Lesch-Nyhan syndrome for which there is some direct evidence of dopaminergic disturbance. Further critical findings are that SIB in Lesch-Nyhan syndrome may be influenced by environmental contingencies and may also be reduced by behavioural interventions (Anderson et el 1978, Buzas et al, 1981, Duker, 1975). At present it seems safe to only conclude that dopamine receptor supersensitivity raises the probability of SIB occurring and the mechanism is unclear. If this is the case then there are some interesting possibilities:

* In Lesch-Nyhan syndrome the initial primary determinant of SIB may be dopamine receptor supersensitivity. Responding may then become subject to operant conditioning with a decreasing role played by dopamine. Under these circumstances dopamine blockers may have only a limited effect, as may behavioural interventions.

* More generally dopamine receptor supersensitivity may occur in people showing SIB as the result of a sequence of related events. It is argued above that SIB of sufficient severity for endorphin involvement is likely to have been cultivated by operant conditioning. The chronic release of endorphins may in turn raise dopamine receptor sensitivity and thus increase the probability of SIB occurring. This combined with a heightened analgesia to self-injurious responding. There is therefore the interesting possibility of a "disordered" behaviour ultimately causing neurotransmitter disturbance which then contributes to the occurrence of the behaviour.

Both of these interpretations of the available evidence again point to the need for interventions which acknowledge the probable involvement of both the environment and neurotransmitters as determinants of SIB. This may indeed be why some of the successful interventions described by Gualtieri et al (1986) employed both dopamine blockers and differential reinforcement procedures.

Figure 5   Flow diagram illustrating the interactions between social conditioning, stimulatory conditioning and biological factors.

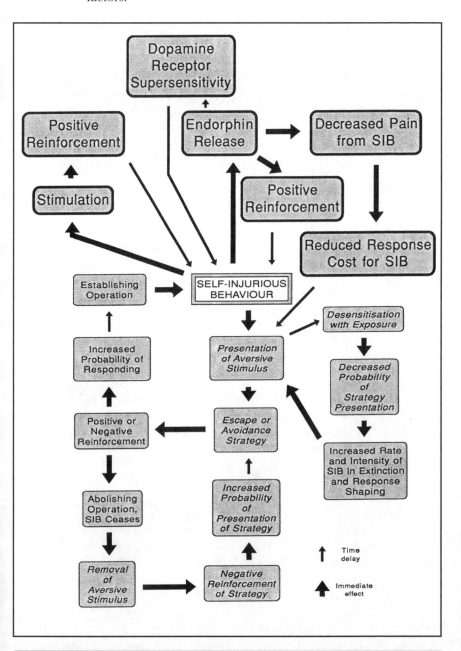

It is clear from the preceding discussion that it is more productive to consider operant and biological determinants of SIB as compatible. The model of the operant conditioning process described in Figure 1 may therefore be expanded. The result is shown in Figure 5.

The model outlined in Figure 5 represents the active processes which govern the probability of SIB occurring in the immediacy. Whilst these processes indicate how SIB develops and persists, they do not explain why people with a learning disability should be more likely to show SIB than those who do not have a learning disability. The processes themselves are applicable to both people with a learning disability and others. They are therefore insufficient as a complete account of the determinants of SIB in people with a learning disability. These processes need to be related to other findings, particularly those arising from prevalence and cohort studies, in order to expand the account.

THE PREDISPOSITION TO DEVELOP SIB AND THE MEDIATION OF ACTIVE PROCESSES

Predisposing factors

From examining the findings of prevalence and descriptive cohort studies there are clearly individual characteristics which are correlates of SIB. The three main characteristics are:

* Sensory and physical disabilities (Schroeder et al, 1978, Kiernan and Kiernan, 1987, Oliver 1991b).

* Particular syndromes (eg *Lesch-Nyhan; Smith-Magenis.* Colley et al, 1990: *autism.* Schroeder et al, 1978, Bartak and Rutter, 1976:*Gilles de la Tourette.* Robertson et al, 1989).

* An increased degree of learning disability. Data supportive of this conclusion are given in Tables 1 and 2. Additional evidence comes from the studies of Bartak and Rutter (1976) and Ando and Yoshimura (1978).

Table 1 Data reanalysed from prevalence studies showing a breakdown of the percentage of people who show SIB by degree of learning disability.

AUTHOR(S)	PROFOUND OR SEVERE LEARNING DISABILITY	MODERATE OR MILD LEARNING DISABILITY
Singh (1977)	56%	44%
Maisto et al (1978)	95.6%	4.4%
Kebbon and Windahl (1986)	87.2%	12.8%
Griffin et al (1986)	89.9%	10.1%
Rojahn (1986)	59%	41%
Oliver et al (1987)	88%	12%

Table 2 Data reanalysed from prevalence studies showing the percentage of people with given degrees of learning disability who show SIB.

AUTHOR(S)	DEGREE OF LEARNING DISABILITY			
	PROFOUND	SEVERE	MODERATE	MILD
Ballinger (1971)	29.4%	17.8%	10.4%	5.6%
Ross (1972)	26%	25%	18%	13%
Eyman and Call (1977)	35%	20%	8%	
Maisto et al (1978)	20.7%		3.4%	0%
Schroeder et al (1978)	14%		9%	2%
Jacobson (1982)	16.9%	7.2%	3.4%	2.6%
Kebbon and Windahl (1986)	12.7%	7.1%	1.4%	0.2%

None of these characteristics can be said to directly "cause" SIB as it is evident that not all people with these characteristics, or any combination of them, show SIB. They are then perhaps better construed as predisposing factors which increase the probability that SIB may become prominent in an individual's repertoire. As the evidence for the active processes described above is substantial, it is apparent that the correlational link between these characteristics and SIB rests on the characteristics directly or indirectly stimulating the active processes. An understanding of how this occurs is important as potential interventions of a more general nature may become clear.

Mediating conditions

The three characteristics above give rise to mediating conditions which may affect the processes maintaining SIB. These mediating conditions are:

* A handicap in expressive communication. This term is perhaps too specific but still usefully descriptive. It refers not only to formal or informal communication systems but to the extent of the behavioural repertoire of an individual that can reliably affect the behaviour of others.

* Operant vulnerability and susceptibility. This is a clumsy term to encapsulate in operant terms the notion of "motivation". It refers to the enhanced probability of being subjected to establishing operations of reinforcer deprivation and aversive stimuli and the frequently concomitant susceptibility to particular reinforcers.

* Pre-existing neurotransmitter disturbance.

Each mediating condition is discussed below in terms of its relationship to predisposing factors and the processes which maintain responding. The complete model is shown in Figure 6.

A handicap in expressive communication

One of the more obvious disabilities associated with a greater degree of learning disability is a handicap of expressive communication and this type of disability appears to be related to the presence of SIB (Shodell and Reiter, 1968, Ando and Yoshimura, 1979a, b, Carr and Durand 1985a and see Murphy et al, Chapter 1). Perhaps the major impact of this handicap on an individual's life is that they are unable to affect the behaviour of others in a reliable way. This is not critical when people are independent, but its

Figure 6 Diagram to illustrate the association between operant and biological processes which maintain SIB, the factors which mediate these processes and the conditions which give rise to mediating factors.

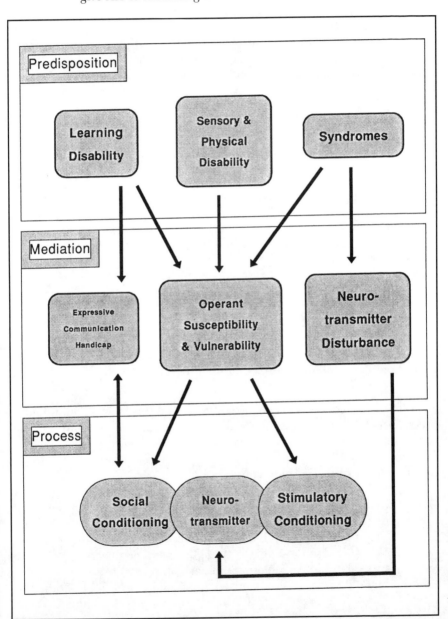

impact increases as a function of dependence. A handicap in expressive communication may be related to a general learning disability for a number of reasons:

* Because of developmental delay language simply fails to develop normally.

* Because of a limited behavioural repertoire alternative communicative responses may not be present.

* More general "social skills" related to communication may not develop (see Murphy et al, Chapter 1).

* Physical, auditory and visual impairments may further hamper the development of a communicative behavioural repertoire.

A greater degree of learning disability and physical or sensory disabilities therefore predisposes a condition of expressive communicative handicap. This handicap may be further compounded by environmental conditions. An authoritarian service culture, for example, has as one defining characteristic limited choice for individuals and a negative response to expressions of choice. Similarly many residential environments are characterised by low support worker to service user ratios, relative to individuals' levels of dependence. Under either of these conditions even normally robust communication may fail to affect the behaviour of others.

The relationship between this handicap and SIB is fairly clear. If an individual is unable to communicate to others, ie reliably affect the behaviour of others, by exhibiting communicative behaviours which are responded to, it is made more likely that a behaviour which has this effect, in this case SIB, may function in this way (Footnote 11). It is important to note that this may not be just a one-way effect, because if SIB functions in the way that another form of communication may, and is reliably reinforced, it is unlikely that the individual will develop other forms of expressive communication. The finding that individuals who show SIB have poorer expressive than receptive communicative skills may therefore be caused by SIB attaining communicative properties and be an effect on the probability of showing SIB (see Murphy et al, Chapter 1).

It is also important to note that a disability in expressive communication is not a necessary condition for the development of SIB (for an excellent illustration see, Foxx and Dufrense, 1984). A more critical condition may be that the behaviour of others is unaffected by potentially communicative behaviours in a repertoire. An example of this was reported in a Sunday newspaper article describing a young offenders' institution:

> On one occasion he was slashed with a razorblade across the face to a depth of nearly half an inch. He said: "There was no way I could go to the screws: if I'd grassed, I would have been battered much worse, probably by several people. One lad in our unit was beaten up on the stairs, where there are no screws, and was so frightened he cut himself all the way up his arms to try to get moved, rather than grass...".

> Observer 31 May, 1992

In this example a simple request to be moved without good reason (the reason was good enough but could not be imparted) would fail to be effective. The SIB presumably would result in a move for medical attention.

Operant vulnerability and susceptibility

A second link between the individual characteristics described above and the operant process which maintain SIB can be broadly subsumed under the rubric of operant vulnerability and susceptibility. In terms of vulnerability a greater degree of learning disability, physical and sensory impairments, and some syndromes, may raise the probability that commonly occurring situations are aversive.

Examples of this may be:

* being required to participate in an activity which:

    * Is commonly reinforced by contingencies which are either remote or not operative for that individual in the prevailing environment, eg others' critical remarks about hygiene in the case of self-care skills, the avoidance of future discomfort in the case of subjecting one's self to a medical examination (see Iwata et al 1990).

    * Whilst yielding reinforcement is too difficult to complete given the individual's level of learning disability and/or sensory impairments (see Gaylord-Ross, 1982).

    * Is paired with aversive stimuli (eg a high demand rate).

* Social interactions void of any demands in the case of a developmental phase in Rett's syndrome (Coleman et al, 1988).

* In the case of autism:

  * The interruption of rituals.

  * Changes in routines.

* Being in physical discomfort, for example, poorly supported in a wheelchair.

These kind of situations may arise frequently during a day and are not easily managed by people with severe physical, sensory or learning disabilities who, for example, are unable to vote with their feet or draw from an extensive repertoire of alternative behaviours. They are, therefore, additional aversive uncontrollable situations (and thus establishing operations) experienced by people with characteristics which are associated with SIB.

Operant susceptibilities refers to the enhanced potency of some reinforcers precisely because people have a learning disability, physical or sensory impairments or syndromes. Examples of this are:

* Social interactions by virtue of their conditioned reinforcement property. As the degree of learning disability, physical and sensory impairments increases so does the individual's dependence on others. Consequently access to most (if not all) reinforcers is mediated via social interactions. There is therefore an increased susceptibility to finding such interactions reinforcing.

* States of deprivation of reinforcers, such as social interactions or sensory stimulation. More specifically:

  * In environments which aggregate people with multiple and severe disabilities and or challenging behaviours, social interactions may be limited in quantity. When such interactions are positively reinforcing (see above) a prevailing state of reinforcer deprivation (an establishing operation) exists.

  * People with sensory impairments are (by definition) deprived of a source of stimulatory reinforcement. Perhaps the clearest example of this is damage to the eye

rendering it completely ineffective when the occipital cortex is intact. This combination is commonly correlated with the presence of eye pressing or poking (Jan et al, 1983).

* An inherent susceptibility to a particular reinforcer as a feature of a syndrome. This is perhaps a contentious statement but it may help to explain why some behaviours reliably occur in some syndromes. An example relevant to SIB is the rapid hand to mouth movements commonly seen in Rett's syndrome (see Oliver et al, 1993). These potentially injurious movements may be reduced by sensory extinction procedures (Swahn, 1988). This suggests that the movements are not a movement disorder as such (the procedure does not interfere with the motion) but rather that the movements were maintained by the resultant stimulation most economically attained by the rapid hand mouth movement (Footnote 12).

The characteristics that are associated with SIB therefore give rise to an increased range and potency of potential establishing operations and an enhanced susceptibility to some forms of reinforcement.

When these are combined with the handicap in expressive communication the probability of challenging behaviour featuring in an individual's repertoire is raised. For most of the vulnerabilities and susceptibilities described above, if the individual was able to affect the behaviour of others in a reliable way and thus control the presentation of aversive or reinforcing stimuli, then challenging behaviours would be unlikely to occur. Similarly, as has been noted above, if individuals could easily escape from aversive situations in other ways, or easily access reinforcers, then the establishing operations are simply removed.

Pre-existing neurotransmitter disturbance

It is evident that endorphins may be a contributory determinant to SIB as an active process. Similarly there has been some speculation about the role of dopamine receptor sensitivity as a determinant of SIB and the way it may be affected by chronic endorphin release as well as being potentially associated with some syndromes. Consequently the possibility arises that a fundamental pre-existing disturbance of either endorphins or dopamine receptor sensitivity can detrimentally mediate the neurotransmitter process. There is evidence that endorphin levels are raised in people with autism (Gillberg, 1988). This may then increase the possibility that, when SIB occurs in people with autism, the influence of endorphins is greater than would otherwise be the case. This can occur by social or stimulatory operant conditioning giving rise to SIB and interacting with neurotransmitter processes as indicated above to yield more severe SIB. An initially raised endorphin level, combined with further endorphin release would lead to raised dopamine receptor sensitivity, thus increasing the potential for SIB. Similarly for syndromes in which dopamine disturbance is hypothesized (Lesch-Nyhan and Gilles de la Tourette syndromes) and SIB is common, the initial disturbance increases the potential for SIB which may then be maintained operantly. Syndromes therefore may come to predispose the development of SIB by a pre-existing neurotransmitter disturbance mediating the neurotransmitter process.

THE IMPLICATIONS OF RESEARCH INTO THE DETERMINANTS OF SIB FOR PRACTICE

A stated aim of this chapter was to integrate and interpret empirical evidence which provided insight into the determinants of SIB within the framework of mainstream psychological theory. The model which has been developed represents the general case, a concept not readily adopted by applied behaviour analysis (see Sidman, 1988), but nevertheless helpful. It was also argued in the early part of the chapter that understanding determinants contributes to the efficacy of interventions. This concluding section will address this issue.

There are three main levels of intervention for challenging behaviour. There is a level of immediate response by others in the regular contact with the individual, guided by those from whom intervention advice is sought. The nature of this response will depend on a second level of service content and operation. This in turn depends on a broader strategic response to the needs of services such as training, access to technology and knowledge, and the knowledge base itself.

From the operant model developed in earlier sections a number of points relevant to interventions have been made. The most important of these are:

* The natural course of SIB (and probably most challenging behaviours) is toward greater severity because of its evocative power over the behaviour of others.

* There are mediating factors which drive the development of SIB.

* For most people, for most of the time, SIB is functional.

* The determinants of SIB may vary between individuals, topographies and over time.

These critical points should determine aspects of all three levels of intervention.

IMMEDIATE RESPONSES

Prevention

Clearly as SIB develops and more learning and generalisation takes place, so the behaviour becomes more established in a behavioural repertoire. It would be better therefore, if it did not come into the repertoire in the first place. Preventative strategies at this level may include:

* Ensuring that minor illnesses (middle ear infections, dermatitis), which may evoke a potentially self-injurious response initially, are immediately and effectively treated.

* Ensuring that those in regular contact with children who have predisposing characteristics are aware of how self-injurious responding may be reinforced.

* Ensuring that early self-injurious responding is not reinforced.

* Minimising the conditions that mediate operant conditioning by ensuring individuals can reliably affect the behaviour of others, that appropriate responses occur when operant vulnerabilities are likely to be operative and reducing states of reinforcer deprivation.

Obviously many of these pre-emptive strategies are 'easier said than done'. It is at the level of service delivery that this problem needs to be addressed (see below).

Early intervention

If prevention is not possible then early intervention is crucial, even though the self-injury may be mild and not yet 'challenging' services. The reasons for this are similar to those given for prevention. Additionally it may be possible to attempt some strategies when SIB is not yet dangerous (eg extinction as part of a broader intervention).

Responsive interventions

This section on interventions for established SIB requires a chapter on its own. It is only possible therefore to allude to some general implications for interventions which arise from the proposed model:

* There is a growing body of evidence which demonstrates the value of assessment to intervention design. All determinants of SIB should be evaluated and those which are influential, no matter how indirectly, should be favourably manipulated. In terms of operant determinants this means:

    * functional analysis comprised of all of its defining properties (see, Kiernan, 1973, Blackman, 1985, Oliver and Head, 1993).

    * acknowledging the conditioning of others by the person showing SIB.

    * repeating functional analyses when interventions are in place and on behaviours which have replaced SIB.

    In more broad terms this means addressing both operant and biological determinants in assessment and intervention.

* It is essential that a constructional approach (Goldiamond, 1974) is adopted alongside any direct intervention. This is not just a statement arising from dogma. If SIB has a function in the life of an individual and the SIB is removed from a repertoire, then it will naturally come to be replaced by another behaviour with the same function, in just the same way that SIB became established. For this reason the behaviour is likely to be challenging because it can affect the behaviour of others. Equally SIB is likely to rise in the hierarchy again if no replacement behaviour is present. This is because SIB is never removed from a repertoire, it just attains a lower position in the hierarchy.

    The evidence for the contention that a constructional approach is more effective in the long term is beginning to appear (Durand and Carr, 1992) and now requires translation into practice. The critical issue is how a replacement behaviour can be established to reliably affect the behaviour of others in the way that SIB does, without having the same property of being aversive (and therefore challenging) to others. This is a problem that needs to be addressed at a service level.

This all too brief section can only touch on some of the broad implications for direct responsive interventions for SIB. How these interventions are put into effect is dependent on the available services and their operation.

SERVICE RESPONSES

There are two major implications from the model for service responses. One is that, at an early stage, services are proactive and the second is that they recognise the potency and tenacity of SIB.

Proactive prevention and early intervention

In the opening paragraph of this chapter it was suggested that a defining feature of challenging behaviour is that it evokes responses from others. This creates a problem for preventative and early intervention strategies precisely because when SIB is not present or is mild, it will not evoke a response, social or strategic. For this reason services have to be proactive. Specifically they have to:

* Actively identify children with predisposing characteristics which are associated with the development of SIB.

* Actively identify children who show behaviours which may become self-injurious (mild body contact 'stereotypies', rubbing etc).

* Actively screen for mild illnesses, such as middle ear infection, in children who are unable to communicate.

* Actively support service users in attempts to mitigate the conditions which mediate the operant conditioning process (eg easy access to communication therapists, advice from agencies with knowledge about ameliorating the effects of sensory impairments, etc).

* Be responsive to challenging behaviour when it is not yet severe or fulfilling the broadly accepted definition of challenging behaviour (Emerson et al, 1987)

The common theme to these points is obviously the **proactive nature of services.** While there is a paucity of informative data on the chronicity of

SIB, common experience suggests it is indeed a chronic problem (see, Murphy et al, Chapter 1). An investment in services which operate in a proactive fashion may prove to be economically prudent as well as humane (Footnote 13).

Interventions within services

More general residential and 'day' services for people who show SIB should recognise the natural development of SIB toward greater severity when no intervention is in place and the influence SIB has on others. The combination of these two factors will allow SIB to develop in any environment in which those in contact with the person showing SIB are not able to:

* constantly monitor their own responses to SIB or potential SIB in the face of its evocative power.

* constantly reinforce behaviours which are appropriate functional replacements for SIB even though they have less evocative power than SIB.

From the operant model described in Figure 1, and supported by data in Figure 2, it is clear that the exact opposite of these two conditions will naturally occur. It is necessary therefore to create environments which are in one sense unusual, as they contradict a natural course. To put such environments into effect there are a number of conditions which should be met:

* The behaviour of all people in the environment requires active management in the broadest sense of the term. This means interactions require constant monitoring by others or by those involved in the interactions.

* Antecedent and contingency management of this kind is effective when it is constantly sustained. Interventions for those who are vulnerable to showing SIB (either by virtue of reinforcement history or predisposing factors) should therefore also be constantly sustained. Hit and run interventions will be fragile and prone to attrition because of the natural propensity of SIB to rise in a behavioural hierarchy.

* Both of these implications for services, require service providers to recognise that the amelioration of SIB involves skills in people which have to be cultivated by training and management (from trained

managers). The services that are offered should have more in common with intensive care units than faith healing.

These points relate directly to residential and day services where it is possible to exert control over the potential reinforcement of SIB by others via a management system. Clearly a different situation arises when the person with SIB is living at home with parents. Under these circumstances a great deal of external support is needed, particularly as the model may predict that SIB has a more powerful evocative effect with parents than others. Again intervention will need to be sustained and skilled practitioners will need to spend lengthy periods helping parents to understand SIB, and thus their role in the behaviour, and manage antecedents and contingencies in the home environment.

STRATEGIC RESPONSES

Although the efficacy of the two types of response to SIB described above, immediate and service, critically depends on resources, there are two other determinants which are less well recognised: basic research; and dissemination.

Basic research

In this chapter findings from basic research have been integrated to examine implications for decreasing SIB, both in individuals and in terms of prevalence. This is clearly one productive role for basic research into the determinants of SIB and other challenging behaviours. There is however a need for more powerful explanatory models of the determinants of SIB which draw on the available evidence. SIB should be fully understood simply because it is not. If this argument is insufficient, then there are others:

* Psychological interventions which require people to interact with others in prescribed ways, require thorough justification to those involved. Simple explanations may not convince and this may detrimentally effect interventions.

* Advances in intervention efficacy and sophistication do not appear to simply arise via systematic improvements in intervention techniques. Rather they appear to be fostered intermittently by reviews and critical studies of determinants. (Note the impact of Lovaas et al, 1965, Carr, 1977, Iwata et al, 1982 and Carr and Durand, 1985a,

1985b). The former have stimulated both conceptual shifts (eg the advent of the 'communication' hypothesis) and changes in emphasis (eg the resurrection of functional analysis and the 'nonaversive' approach) which are gradually modifying practice.

* It is incorrect to speak of **'the cause'** of self-injurious behaviour. At any given point in time for any individual there are a number of factors which determine the probability of SIB occurring. It is then more accurate to refer to the determinants of SIB. By acknowledging this possibility and then attempting to document the relative influence of determinants which may operate simultaneously it is then possible to implement multimodal interventions to increase efficacy.

* By examining the determinants of SIB from the onset and having a good understanding of factors that affect its probability of occurring at all in an individual, and those that affect its development, it should be possible to generate broad and effective strategies for prevention and early intervention.

* A full understanding of all potential determinants of SIB has clear implications for assessment. If a determinant can be discovered for the general case its influence can be assessed for individuals. Recently there has been an increase in the number of studies which report the results of a functional analysis and use the data to determine the intervention (see Durand and Crimmins 1991, Mace et al, 1992 and Pyles and Bailey 1992). This is an indication that applied behaviour analysis is beginning to replace behaviour modification. These studies are establishing the value of assessing the determinants of SIB for intervention efficacy and this body of literature will thrive. Its impact and vigour however will not just depend on outcome but more decisively on the knowledge base which feeds it.

* A comprehensive and clear statement of the determinants of SIB would allow the profile of inconsistent evidence to be raised. This would require revision of some stated assumptions.

Currently, research into the determinants of SIB is quite simply limited, both in scope and quantity. There appears to be a straightforward behavioural/organic split in the literature and in research strategies. Evidence for this can easily be gleaned from a swift scan down the reference list of nearly all published papers. Organic papers almost exclusively cite organic papers and behavioural papers almost exclusively cite behavioural papers. There is a need to meaningfully integrate these bodies of literature. Both have an empirical basis and consequently neither should be ignored.

Basic research is not a common feature of services or the job descriptions of those involved in services. Service evaluation is a more common topic of research for many practitioners who have some research skills (Footnote 14). This situation is unlikely to change with the greater emphasis placed on service delivery in a market culture. There is a need therefore for basic research to be strategically and actively cultivated in the long term. There are two reasons for this proposal:

* Long-term research is incompatible with short term funding. Follow-ups of cohorts are problematic mainly because of the need to keep contact with a cohort and prevent attrition of numbers. This is relevant to:

    * Developing preventative strategies by studying early development of SIB over a sustained period.

    * Examining chronicity and the determinants of chronicity.

    * Long term follow up of intervention studies to examine efficacy and the determinants of efficacy.

    * Easy access to subjects with known characteristics and histories.

* Access to research findings derived from a project and known to a project is limited by the temporary nature of projects. When project staff move or change, resources, both tangible and intangible, move or more commonly are simply lost. This situation is compounded by the delay in dissemination of research findings from completion of a project to the most common means of dissemination, publication.

The product of these limitations is that there is no sustained and accessible resource of research findings which can beneficially influence immediate responses and service responses. This limitation is also linked to dissemination.

Dissemination

The contrast between the optimism evident in research and the pessimism often pervading services is a testament to the failure of dissemination. The process of dissemination needs to be guided by the question: who will disseminate what, to whom, and how?

Currently dissemination is most commonly undertaken by academics and researchers who are active in the field (less than 10 in the UK at any one time) and those with a training role in services. The latter are more likely to be recipients of information as well as sources and thus rely on the former as well as the available literature. There is therefore quite simply limited access to up to date research, information and technology because of a lack of people whose role it is to collate and generate it. Moreover, active and wide dissemination is not necessarily a dominant part of any individual job description.

Exactly what is disseminated is partly determined by what is available for dissemination and what is requested. Active dissemination of the following should beneficially guide immediate and service responses:

* Mainstream psychological theory as applied to challenging behaviour. This should:

    * Locate practice and philosophy within the boundaries of an approach dedicated to understanding disordered human behaviour via an understanding of all human behaviour (Clements, 1992).

    * Enable those involved in service delivery to effectively use techniques which have their basis in theory.

* Interpretations of and the results of research into the determinants of challenging behaviour. This would enable:

    * The development and modification of strategies to prevent challenging behaviour.

    * Assessment of determinants to be more complete.

    * Interventions to be derived from theoretical, not just technological, perspectives.

    * Predictions to be made about the likely level of service delivery.

* Interpretations of, and the results of, intervention studies to guide and inform decision making.

Who this information is disseminated to is perhaps easily decided. It should be disseminated to anybody who can make use of it to decrease challenging behaviour either in one individual or in terms of prevalence. The form of the information, its content and complexity, can be varied to suit the recipient.

How dissemination takes place is a critical question. The most common forms appear to be academic conferences and hit and run training. Consequently the majority of people who deal with challenging behaviour for the majority of time are simply not exposed to the available information.

There are two general guidelines which should determine how dissemination of information about challenging behaviour takes place:

* It should be active. Recipients of information about challenging behaviour cannot be expected to know when information has become available or where it is located, given its general inaccessible nature.

* It should be in an accessible format. Research papers are written primarily for the consumption of other researchers. They require transforming into materials which are appropriately designed.

At present there is no strategy for dissemination of information about challenging behaviour in general or SIB in particular. This situation will not change without active intervention. A valuable resource exists but is not readily available to those who would use it.

CONCLUSION

In this chapter it has been argued that the most critical feature of SIB (and challenging behaviour in general) is its power to evoke responses from others. Commonly these responses have the effect of removing SIB in the short term (in interactions) or from the view of society (via the use of isolated containment services). Neither response can be part of an effective long term strategy for an individual or society respectively. They do however remove an aversive stimulus and thus make those who effect the removal feel better in the short term. There should be no confusion about what comprises a response and what comprises a strategy.

At an individual level, an examination of the determinants of SIB allows productive and constructive long term strategies to become apparent. The same is true of the development of a broader model of the determinants of SIB in people who have learning disabilities and some of these strategies for reducing prevalence have been proposed above. Whether these strategies are adopted depends on the willingness of service providers to put resources into prevention and early intervention, and the availability of those resources. The likelihood is that scarce resources will continue to be used to respond to problems rather than to develop strategies to pre-empt them.

FOOTNOTES

1. This type of research has led Bob Remington to remark that the law of effect has yet to be repealed!

2. An establishing operation momentarily alters the reinforcing effectiveness of other events, and momentarily alters the frequency of the kind of responses that have been reinforced by those events (see Michael, 1982).

3. This analogy has been examined and employed in behavioural literature elsewhere. See for example, the opening of Rachlin's (1991) chapter on 'Patterns of Behaviour' and Catania's (1992) chapter of 'Evolution and Behaviour'. For a more broad ranging discussion see Catania and Harnad (1988).

4. One subject described by Oliver (1991b) punched the site of a Spitz-Holt shunt. There was therefore an additional aversive component to this person's SIB, ie concern for the effective operation of the shunt.

5. Long bursts were approximately 17.4 times the length of short bursts (see Hall and Oliver, 1992).

6. This is a well documented phenomenon therapeutically employed in interventions for phobias.

7. Chris Cullen has suggested that these jumps may also be a product of rule governed behaviour.

8. See Dawkins, 1988, pp 77-86, for a full description of this example.

9. The fact that no pain is experienced after a behaviour has occurred is insufficient as an explanation of why a behaviour should occur at all.

10. This may explain why SIB is reported to occur in people with syndromes in which insensitivity to pain is one feature (Altman et al, 1983, Roach et al, 1985).

11. A complete account of the 'communication theory' is to be found in the excellent chapter by Carr and Durand (1985a).

12. A related example of this is seen in Prader-Willi syndrome. Here the disorder is essentially one of appetite. Consequently the individual is in a constant state of deprivation of reinforcement from food. An establishing operation for food acquiring behaviours (including challenging ones) is therefore constantly operative.

13. Schroeder, Bickel and Richmond (1984) estimated that there were 34,100 "SIB clients" in the USA, whose SIB cost USA society one billion dollars (ie USA billion) a year, over and above the cost of offering a general service because of their learning disability.

14. Service evaluation research is more correctly described by another term: service evaluation.

REFERENCES

ALTMAN K, HAAVIK S AND HIGGINS S T (1983). Modifying the self-injurious behavior of an infant with spina bifida and diminished pain sensitivity. *Journal of Behavior Therapy and Experimental Psychiatry, 14,* 165-168.

ANDERSON L T, DANCIS J, ALPERT M AND HERRMAN L (1977). Punishment learning and self-mutilation in Lesch-Nyhan Disease: a negative report. *Neuropadiatrie, 7,* 439-442.

ANDO H AND YOSHIMURA I (1978). Prevalence of maladaptive behaviors in retarded children as a function of IQ and age. *Journal of Abnormal Child Psychology, 6,* 345-349.

ANDO H AND YOSHIMURA I (1979a). Comprehension skill levels and prevalence of maladaptive behaviors in autistic and mentally retarded children: a statistical study. *Child Psychiatry and Human Development, 9,* 131-136.

ANDO H AND YOSHIMURA I (1979b). Speech skill levels and prevalence of maladaptive behaviors in autistic and mentally retarded children: a statistical study. *Child Psychiatry and Human Development, 10,* 85-90.

BALLINGER B R (1971). Minor self-injury. *British Journal of Psychiatry, 118,* 535-538.

BARRETT R P, FEINSTEIN C AND HOLE W T (1989). Effects of naloxone and naltrexone on self-injury: a double-blind, placebo-controlled analysis. *American Journal on Mental Retardation. 93,* 644-651.

BARTAK L AND RUTTER M (1976). Differences between mentally retarded and normally intelligent autistic children. *Journal of Autism and Childhood Schizophrenia, 6,* 109-120.

BAUMEISTER A A, FRYE G AND SCHROEDER S R (1985). Neurochemical correlates of self-injurious behavior. IN J A Mulick and B L Mallory (Eds). *Transitions in Mental Retardation: Advocacy, Technology and Science.* Norwood, NJ: Ablex Publishing Corporation.

BLACKMAN D E (1985). Contemporary behaviourism: a brief overview. IN C F Lowe, M Richelle, D E Blackman and C M Bradshaw (Eds). *Behaviour Analysis and Contemporary Psychology.* London: Lawrence Erlbaum Associates Ltd.

BUZAS H P, AYLLON T AND COLLINS R (1981). A behavioral approach to eliminate self-mutilative behavior in a Lesch-Nyhan patient. *The Journal of Mind and Behavior, 2,* 47-56.

CARR E G (1977). The motivation of self-injurious behavior: A Review of some hypotheses. *Psychological Bulletin, 84,* 800-816.

CARR E G AND DURAND V M (1985a). The social-communicative basis of severe behavior problems in children. IN S Reiss and R Bootzin (Eds) *Theoretical Issues in Behavior Therapy*. New York: Academic Press.

CARR E G AND DURAND V M (1985b). Reducing behavior problems through functional communication training. *Journal of Applied Behavior Analysis, 18,* 111-126.

CARR E G AND McDOWELL J J (1980). Social control of self-injurious behavior of organic etiology. *Behavior Therapy, 11,* 402-409.

CARR E G, NEWSOM C D AND BINKOFF J A (1976). Stimulus control of self-destructive behavior in a psychotic child. *Journal of Abnormal Child Psychology, 4,* 139-153.

CARR E G, ROBINSON S AND PALUMBO L W (1990). The wrong issue: Aversive versus non-aversive treatment. The right issue: Functional versus non-functional treatment. IN A Repp and N Singh (Eds) *Perspectives on the Use of Non-aversive and Aversive Interventions for Persons with Developmental Disabilities*. Sycamore, IL: Sycamore Press.

CARR E G, TAYLOR J C AND ROBINSON S (1991). The effects of severe behavior problems in children on the teaching behavior of adults. *Journal of Applied Behavior Analysis, 24,* 523-535.

CATANIA A C (1992). *Learning*. New Jersey: Prentice-Hall.

CATANIA A C AND HARNAD S (1988). *The Selection of Behavior: The operant behaviorism of B F Skinner: Comments and consequences*. New York: Cambridge University Press.

CHRISTIE R, BAY C, KAUFMAN I A, BAKAY B, BORDEN M AND NYHAN W L (1982). Lesch-Nyhan disease: clinical experience with nineteen patients. *Developmental Medicine and Child Neurology, 24,* 293-306.

CLEMENTS J (1992). I can't explain... "Challenging Behaviour": towards a shared conceptual framework. *Clinical Psychology Forum, 39,* 29-37.

COID J, ALLOLIO B AND REES L H (1983). Raised plasma metenkephalin in patients who habitually mutilate themselves. *The Lancet, 2,* 545-546.

COLEMAN M, BRUBAKER J, HUNTER K AND SMITH G (1988). Rett syndrome: A survey of North American patients. *Journal of Mental Deficiency Research, 32,* 117-124.

COLLEY A, LEVERSHA M, VOULLAIRE L AND ROGERS J (1990). Five cases demonstrating the distinctive behavioural features of chromosomal deletion 17(p11.2p11.2) (Smith-Magenis syndrome). *Journal of Paediatrics and Child Health, 26,* 17-21.

DAVIDSON P W, KLEENE B M, CARROLL M AND ROCKOWITZ R J (1983). Effects of naloxone on self-injurious behavior: a case study. *Applied Research in Mental Retardation, 4,* 1-4.

DAWKINS R (1988). *The Blind Watchmaker.* London: Penguin.

DUKER P C (1975). Intra-subject controlled time-out (social isolation) in the modification of self-injurious behaviour. *Journal of Mental Deficiency Research, 19,* 107-112.

DURAND V M AND CARR E G (1992). An analysis of maintenance following functional communication training. *Journal of Applied Behavior Analysis, 25,* 777-794.

DURAND V M AND CRIMMINS D B (1988). Identifying the variables maintaining self-injurious behavior. *Journal of Autism and Developmental Disorders, 18,* 99-117.

DURAND V M AND CRIMMINS D (1991). Teaching functionally equivalent responses as an intervention for challenging behaviour. IN: B Remington (Ed) *The Challenge of Severe Mental Handicap: A behaviour analytic approach.* Chichester: Wiley and Sons.

EMERY R E, BINKOFF J A, HOUTS A C AND CARR E G (1983). Children as independent variables: some clinical implications of child-effects. *Behavior Therapy, 14,* 398-412.

EMERSON E, BARRETT S, BELL C, CUMMINGS R, TOOGOOD S AND MANSELL J (1987). *Developing Services for People with Severe Learning Difficulties and Challenging Behaviour.* Canterbury: University of Kent.

EYMAN R K AND CALL T (1977). Maladaptive behavior and community placement of mentally retarded persons. *American Journal on Mental Deficiency, 82,* 137-144.

FERSTER C B (1961). Positive reinforcement and behavioral deficits of autistic children. *Child Development, 32,* 437-456.

FOXX R M AND DUFRENSE D (1984). "Harry": the use of physical restraint as a reinforcer, timeout from restraint and giving restraint in treating a self-injurious man. *Analysis and Intervention in Developmental Disabilities, 4,* 1-13.

GAYLORD-ROSS R J (1982). Curricular considerations in treating behavior problems of severely handicapped students. IN K D Gadow, and I Bialer (Eds) *Advances in Learning and Behavioral Disabilities, 1.* Greenwich, CT: JAI Press.

GENOVESE E, NAPOLI P A and BOLEGO-ZONTA N (1969). Self-aggressiveness: A new type of behavioral change induced by pemoline. *Life Sciences, 8,* 513-515.

GILLBERG C (1988). The role of endogenous opioids in autism and possible relationships to clinical features. IN L Wing (Ed) *Aspects of Autism:biological research.* Oxford: Gaskell.

GILLMAN M A AND SANDYK R (1985). Opiatergic and dopaminergic function and Lesch-Nyhan syndrome. *American Journal of Psychiatry, 142,* 1226.

GOLDIAMOND I (1974). 'Toward a constructional approach to social problems: Ethical and constitutional issues raised by behavior analysis'. *Behaviorism, 2,* 1-84.

GOULD S J (1992). *Bully for Brontosaurus:* London: Penguin.

GRIFFIN J C, WILLIAMS D E, STARK M T, ALTMEYER B K AND MASON M (1986). Self-injurious behavior: a state-wide prevalence survey of the extent and circumstances. *Applied Research in Mental Retardation, 1,* 105-116.

GUALTIERI C T, SCHROEDER S R, KEPPEL J M AND BREESE G R (1986). Rational pharmacotherapy for self-injurious behavior: testing the D1 model. Paper presented at the 19th Gatlinburg conference on research and theory in mental retardation and developmental disabilities.

HALL S AND OLIVER C (1992). Differential effects of severe self-injurious behaviour on the behaviour of others. *Behavioural Psychotherapy, 20,* 355-365.

HARRIS J (1992). Biological Factors in Self-injury in Mental Retardation. IN J K Luiselli, J L Watson, N N Singh (Eds) *Assessment, Analysis and Treatment of Self-injury.* New York: Springer-Verlag

IWATA B A, DORSEY M F, SLIFER K J, BAUMAN K E AND RICHMAN G S (1982). Toward a functional analysis of self-injury. *Analysis and Intervention in Developmental Disabilities, 2,* 3-20.

IWATA B A, PACE G M, KALSHER M J, COWDERY G E AND CATALDO M F (1990). Experimental analysis and extinction of self-injurious escape behavior. *Journal of Applied Behavior Analysis, 23,* 11-27.

JACOBSON J W (1982). Problem behavior and psychiatric impairment within a developmentally disabled population. 1: behavior frequency. *Applied Research in Mental Retardation, 3,* 121-139.

JAN J E, FREEMAN R D, McCORMICK A O, SCOTT E P, ROBERTSON W D AND NEWMAN D E (1983). Eye-pressing by visually impaired children. *Developmental Medicine and Child Neurology, 25,* 755-762.

KEBBON L AND WINDAHL S I (1986). Self-injurious behaviour: results of a nationwide survey among mentally retarded persons in Sweden. IN J M Berg and J M Dejong (Eds) *Science and Service in Mental Retardation.* London: Methuen.

KIERNAN C (1973). Functional analysis. IN P Mittler (Ed) *Assessment for Learning in the Mentally Handicapped.* London: Churchill Livingstone.

KIERNAN C AND KIERNAN D (1987). Challenging behaviour in schools for students with severe learning difficulties. Paper presented at the TASH conference. Chicago, 1987.

LEBOYER M, BOUVARD M P and DOUGAS M (1988). Effects of naltrexone on infantile autism. *The Lancet, 26,* 715.

LOVASS O I, FREITAG G, GOLD V J AND KASSORLA I C (1965). Experimental studies in childhood schizophrenia: Analysis of self-destructive behavior. *Journal of Experimental Child Psychology, 2,* 67-84.

LOVAAS I AND SIMMONS J Q (1969). Manipulation of self-destructive behavior in three retarded children. *Journal of Applied Behavior Analysis, 2,* 143-157.

MACE F C, LALLI J S AND SHEA M C (1992). Functional analysis and treatment of self-injury. IN J K Luiselli, J L Matson and N N Singh (Eds) *Self-injurious behavior: Analysis, assessment, and treatment.* New York: Springer-Verlag.

MAISTO C R, BAUMEISTER A A AND MAISTO A A (1978). An analysis of variables related to self-injurious behaviour among institutionalised retarded persons. *Journal of Mental Deficiency Research, 22,* 27-36.

MAURICE P AND TRUDEL G (1982). Self-injurious behavior: Prevalence and relationship to environmental events. IN J Hollis and C E Meyers (Eds) *Life Threatening Behavior: Analysis and Intervention.* Washington DC: American Association of Mental Deficiency.

MEYERSON L, KERR N AND MICHAEL J L (1967). Behavior modification in rehabilitation. IN S Bijou and D Baer (Eds) *Child Development: reading in experimental analysis.* New York: Appleton-Century-Crofts.

MICHAEL J (1982). Distinguishing between discriminative and motivational functions of stimuli. *Journal of the Experimental Analysis of Behavior, 37,* 149-155.

MICHAEL J (1985). Fundamental research and behaviour modification, IN C F Lowe, M Richelle, D E Blackman and C M Bradshaw (Eds) *Behaviour Analysis and Contemporary Psychology.* New York: Erlbaum.

MUELLER K AND HSIAO S (1980). Pemoline-induced self-biting in rats and self-mutilation in the de Lange syndrome. *Pharmacology, Biochemistry and Behaviour, 13,* 627-631.

MUELLER K AND NYHAN W L (1983). Clonidine potentiates drug induced self-injurious behaviour in rats. *Pharmacology, Biochemistry and Behaviour, 18,* 891-894.

OLIVER C (1986). Self-injurious behaviour. *Talking Sense, 33,* 23-24.

OLIVER C (1991a). The application of analogue methodology to the functional analysis of challenging behaviour. IN B Remington (Ed) *The Challenge of Severe Mental Handicap: A behaviour analytic approach.* Chichester: Wiley and Sons

OLIVER C (1991b). Self-injurious behaviour in people with mental handicap: prevalence, individual characteristics and functional analysis. Unpublished PhD thesis, University of London.

OLIVER C AND HEAD D (1990). Self-injurious behaviour in people with learning disabilities: Determinants and interventions. *International Review of Psychiatry, 2,* 99-114.

OLIVER C AND HEAD D (1993). Self-injurious behaviour: functional analysis and interventions. IN R S P Jones and C B Eayrs (Eds) *Challenging Behaviour and Intellectual Disability: A psychological perspective.* Clevedon, Bristol: BILD Publications.

OLIVER C, MURPHY G H AND CORBETT J A (1987). Self-injurious behaviour in people with mental handicap: a total population study. *Journal of Mental Deficiency Research, 31,* 147-162.

OLIVER C, MURPHY G, CRAYTON L AND CORBETT J A (1993). Self-injurious behavior in Rett Syndrome: Interactions between features of Rett syndrome and operant conditioning. *Journal of Autism and Developmental Disorders, 23,* 91-109.

PATTERSON G R (1982). *Coercive Family Process.* Eugene OR: Castalia.

PETERS J M (1967). Caffeine-induced haemorrhagic automutilation. *Archives Internationales de Pharmacodynamic et al Therapie, 169,* 139-146.

PYLES D A M AND BAILEY J S (1992). Behavioral Diagnostic Interventions. IN J K Luiselli, J L Matson and N N Singh (Eds) *Self-injurious Behavior.* New York: Springer-Verlag.

RACHLIN H (1991). *Introduction to Modern Behaviorism.* New York: W H Freeman and Company.

REMINGTON B (1991). *The Challenge of Severe Mental Handicap: A behaviour analytic approach.* Chichester: Wiley and Sons

RICHARDSON J S AND ZALESKI W A (1983). Endogenous opiates and self-mutilation. *American Journal of Psychiatry, 143,* 938-939.

RINCOVER A AND DEVANY J (1982). The application of sensory extinction procedures to self-injury. *Analysis and Intervention in Developmental Disabilities, 2,* 67-81.

ROACH E S, ABRAMSON J S AND LAWLESS M R (1985). Self-injurious behaviour in acquired sensory neuropathy. *Neuropediatrics, 16,* 159-161.

ROBERTSON M M, TRIMBLE M R AND LEES A J (1989). Self-injurious behaviour and the Gilles de la Tourette syndrome: a clinical study and a review of the literature. *Psychological Medicine, 19,* 611-625.

ROJAHN J (1986). Self-injurious and stereotypic behavior of non-institutionalised mentally retarded people: prevalence and classification. *American Journal of Mental Deficiency, 91,* 268-276.

ROSS R T (1972). Behavioral correlates of level of intelligence. *American Journal of Mental Deficiency, 76,* 545-549.

SANDYK R (1985). Naloxone abolishes self-injuring in a mentally retarded child. *Annals of Neurology, 17,* 520.

SANDMAN C A, DATTA P C, BARRON J, HOCHLER F K, WILLIAMS C AND SWANSON J M (1983). Naloxone attenuates self-abusive behavior in developmentally disabled clients. *Applied Research in Mental Retardation, 4,* pp. 5-11.

SCHROEDER S R, BICKEL W K AND RICHMOND G (1984). Primary and secondary prevention of self-injurious behaviors: a lifelong problem. IN K D Gadow (Ed) *Advances in Learning and Behavioral Disabilities, 5.* Greenwich, CT: JAI Press.

SCHROEDER S R, SCHROEDER C S, SMITH B AND DALLDORF J (1978). Prevalence of self-injurious behavior in a large state facility for the retarded: a three year follow-up study. *Journal of Autism and Childhood Schizophrenia, 8,* 261-269.

SHODELL M J AND REITER H H (1968). Self-mutilative behavior in verbal and nonverbal schizophrenic children. *Archives of General Psychiatry, 19*, 453-455.

SIDMAN N (1988). *Tactics of Scientific Research: Evaluating Experimental Data in Psychology*. Boston: Authors Cooperative Inc.

SINGH N N (1977). Prevalence of self-injury in institutionalised retarded children. *New Zealand Medical Journal, 86*, 325-327.

SINGH N N (1981). Current trends in the treatment of self-injurious behavior. *Advances in Paediatrics, 28*, 377-440.

SMEE M L AND OVERSTREET D H (1976). Alterations in the effects of dopamine agonists and antagonists on general activity in rats following chronic morphine treatment. *Psychopharmacology, 49*, 125-130.

SWAHN O (1988). Some parameters of self-injurious behaviour. Paper presented at the Behaviour Therapy World Congress, Edinburgh.

THURRELL R J AND RICE D G (1970). Eye rubbing in blind children: application of a sensory deprivation model. *Exceptional Children, 10*, 325-330.

VOLLMER T R AND IWATA B A (1991). Establishing operations and reinforcement effects. *Journal of Applied Behavior Analysis, 24*, 279-291.

PART 4

SERVICE ORGANISATION

CHAPTER 8

SUPPORTING PEOPLE WITH SEVERE LEARNING DISABILITIES AND CHALLENGING BEHAVIOURS IN ORDINARY HOUSING

David Felce and Kathy Lowe

INTRODUCTION

Traditionally people with learning disabilities and challenging behaviours have a high probability of spending most of their lives in large, poor quality institutions, which have been subject to an ever increasing catalogue of criticism over the last three decades. The presence of challenging behaviours is commonly cited among the reasons for admission or readmission to such settings (Campbell et al, 1982, Hemming, 1982, Pagel and Whitling, 1978, Sherman, 1988, Sutter et al, 1980). As a consequence, the prevalence of severe challenging behaviour is higher in institutional than community populations (DHSS, 1971 and 1972, Russell and Harris, 1989, Chapter 2, Kiernan and Qureshi, Chapter 3, Kushlick and Cox, 1973, Oliver et al, 1987). Such a situation is still current today. The fact that challenging behaviour occurs in community settings and is a primary cause of community placement breakdown does contribute to the view that there is a continuing need for specialist services. Differences between and within professional, campaign, parent,and academic groups on the correct design brief to provide such specialism seem to have generated inaction. People with challenging behaviour have typically not been included in the moves to community services to date as the rundown of traditional hospitals has progressed (DH, 1989). Experience of providing support such people in ordinary housing services is still, therefore, relatively thin on the ground.

The need for the development of expertise concerning people with challenging behaviour in mainstream ordinary housing is now becoming urgent. As reduction in institutional size proceeds to eventual closure, we are reaching the point when the future options need to be determined and developed successfully. Sufficient is known about the disadvantageous characteristics of institutional services - their excessive size, isolation and segregation from the outside world, the separation of residents from their family and friends and from the general life of the community, the poverty of the material and social environment, and absence of stimulation and of meaningful pursuits - for these to be rejected as the basis of creating a progressive service for this client group capable of achieving the goals and quality of life articulated in contemporary policies (eg, DHSS, 1971, O'Brien 1987, Welsh Office, 1983). Recent research of new 'housing-style' specialist provision on an institutional campus serves only to emphasise such a conclusion (Emerson et al, 1992). Moreover, the prevalence of challenging behaviours among people with severe or profound learning disabilities is sufficiently high (Footnote 1, page 202) that, even if some form of specialist back-up facility to the mainstream ordinary housing provision were to be countenanced, competence within mainstream services would still be essential for such specialist units to avoid either silting up or becoming so large that they come to possess all of the deficiencies which characterised institutional provision.

Nor does the advent of specialist support teams (Emerson et al, Chapter 10) change this perspective. Such teams may be an important source of professional advice and practical help. However, they typically work with individuals considered to have the most severely challenging behaviour over protracted periods of time and, therefore, carry small case loads (Emerson et al, Chapter 10, Lowe et al, in press). Competence in relation to challenging behaviour is required in mainstream services as they will serve a wider spectrum of people with challenging behaviour than specialist teams can possibly support. Moreover, specialist teams are likely to be overwhelmed by demand and to be relatively ineffective if the system they work within is devoid of the basic building blocks for successful response to challenging behaviour (see Durand and Kishi, 1987, Lowe et al, in press for extensions of this line of reasoning).

Given the debate about whether ordinary housing services can provide for people with severe learning disabilities and challenging behaviours, two types of question have been raised. The first concern is whether it is feasible to provide residential services to this group using ordinary community housing; can such behaviour be contained in such settings, can staff cope, will the community be sufficiently receptive? The second concern is whether individuals benefit from such a service; do they experience an enhanced quality of life, do they gain skills, does their challenging behaviour decrease? This chapter reflects on both of these questions by reviewing the lessons from the Andover (Felce, 1989) and NIMROD (Lowe and de Paiva, 1991a) ordinary housing developments, which have tested the water in this area.

THE FEASIBILITY QUESTION: CAN PEOPLE WITH CHALLENGING BEHAVIOUR BE SERVED IN MAINSTREAM HOUSING ALONGSIDE OTHER PEOPLE WITH SEVERE OR PROFOUND LEARNING DISABILITIES?

The NIMROD and Andover developments

The NIMROD and Andover schemes, both first operational in 1981, are important and relevant to the current purpose because they set out to provide comprehensively for adults with severe or profound learning disabilities who required a residential service, whether or not they had challenging behaviours. People with challenging behaviours were not the exclusive focus of concern but were not to be excluded. Demographically defined catchment areas were followed rigorously to determine service availability in both cases, a fact which provides a sampling basis to the accompanying research which helps overcome some of the problems of generalising experience from one area to another.

The NIMROD service was designed to serve all people with a learning disability living in or, for those in residential care, originating from an area of Cardiff which had a total population of approximately 60,000. Extensive cross checking of service and research records was undertaken (Footnote 2)and requests made to all mental handicap hospitals throughout Wales and England to obtain a comprehensive client list. Five houses and three flats were established; all used ordinary housing, the houses being mainly large terraces for groups of between four and six residents with the flats serving one or two people.

A total of 125 clients were identified as coming from within the NIMROD catchment area; 62 living in traditional forms of residential care and 63 in the family home. Of the former 62, 22 were subsequently transferred to NIMROD staffed accommodation. No significant differences in clients' characteristics, as measured by the Social and Physical Incapacity (SPI), and Speech, Self Help and Literacy (SSL) Scales (Kushlick et al, 1973), and by the Quality of Social Interaction (QSI) Scale (Holmes et al, 1982), were evident between the group transferring to NIMROD accommodation and the total client group, indicating no bias in the selection of those for transfer. According to the SPI and SSL Scales, the vast majority could walk (95 per cent) and were continent (86 per cent). Almost half had speech (45 per cent) and were competent in the skills of feeding, washing and dressing (41 per cent). Around a quarter were rated as severely behaviour disordered (27 per cent) and 14 per cent were literate. According to the QSI Scale, nearly two-thirds were said to interact appropriately to varying degrees, while a third were said to be socially impaired.

The Andover territory (also approximately 60,000 total population) was subdivided to give distinct catchment areas for each of two houses provided. They served all adults with the most severe or profound learning disabilities, who required a residential service. Checks of service rolls and also of the Wessex Register, which had a historical file dating back to the survey undertaken in 1963 (Kushlick and Cox, 1973), together with a new survey of everyone in residential care within Wessex and contiguous counties were conducted to ensure full identification. Twenty-seven adults were identified who had next-of-kin in the territory, had a severe learning disability and met the behavioural disability criteria.

Ten of the 13 people already in residential care moved into the houses on their opening (the three who remained in their previously available residential situation did so for reasons independent of their behaviour or severity of handicap). Four people moved in from their family homes, giving a total of 14 adults who lived in the two houses at some time during the research period. According to the SPI/SSL Scales, all were Ambulant, seven (50 per cent) had Severe Behaviour Disorder, one (7 per cent) was Severely Incontinent Only and six (43 per cent) were rated as Continent, Ambulant and with No Behaviour Disorder (CAN) but with No Self Help. In terms of the SSL Scale alone, one person was rated as having Self Help Only, four as having Speech Only and the remaining nine (64 per cent) as having No Speech, Self Help or Literacy. Five were assessed as having the triad of social impairments and seven as being socially impaired (Wing and Gould, 1979). Three adults had been transferred to the houses directly from locked hospital wards where, between them, they had spent about seventy years.

The presence of challenging behaviour

In addition to the SPI classification already given above, the challenging behaviour of all NIMROD and Andover residents was measured using the Disability Assessment Schedule (Holmes et al, 1982). A way of classifying almost all (12) of the problem behaviour items included in that schedule as either constituting a severe or moderate level of challenge was devised (see Felce et al, in press for greater detail) by using the results of a survey which was undertaken by MacDonald and Barton (1986) to discover how direct-care staff ranked the relative severities of the items contained in Part Two of the Adaptive Behavior Scale (Nihira et al, 1974). By this method, physical aggression, self-injury and destructiveness are considered severely challenging if they occur at all, ie at any frequency. Temper tantrums, wandering off, anti-social acts and inappropriate sexual behaviours are considered severely challenging behaviours if they occur at a marked frequency; while objectionable personal habits, attention-seeking, overactivity, disturbing noises and stereotyped behaviour are considered as moderately challenging, even if occurring frequently.

Among the 36 residents of both schemes combined, 23 (64 per cent) presented behaviours of a type or of a frequency to be rated as severely challenging; 14 (39 per cent) for reasons of being physically aggressive, nine (25 per cent) for being destructive, 14 (39 per cent) for being self-injurious, seven (19 per cent) for having temper tantrums, four (11 per cent) for wandering off and four (11 per cent) for having other seriously anti-social behaviours. In addition, moderately challenging behaviours were reported for 19 individuals comprising overactivity, attention-seeking, making disturbing noises or having other objectionable personal habits and engaging in stereotypic behaviours. Only nine people (25 per cent) had neither a severely nor moderately challenging behaviour included in this classification system, and one of these had been admitted with the extreme weight loss and behavioural regression typical of anorexia nervosa.

Indeed, individuals had multiple challenging behaviours. Eight residents were rated as having two severely challenging behaviours, five were rated as having three, one as having four and two as having five. Those classified as having at least one severely challenging behaviour had, on average, 3.5 different types of severely or moderately challenging behaviour each (range, 1 - 8).

Discussion

In relation to the question of the feasibility of ordinary housing provision, both services unquestionably admitted people with multiple severely challenging behaviours. Not all those eligible were admitted, although coverage was almost total in the more restricted Andover sample. However, no decisions were made to exclude individuals on the basis of their challenging behaviour and the groups served were representative of the total samples in critical respects. Both groups had a higher representation of people classified according to the Kushlick, Blunden and Cox (1973) method as having Severe Behaviour Disorder (27 per cent and 50 per cent for NIMROD and Andover respectively) than the 17 per cent average found nationally in the 1970 hospital census (DHSS, 1972). In the decade since the first houses opened, one person has moved from NIMROD accommodation to the locked ward of the local mental handicap hospital because of an inability to cope with his challenging behaviour. None of the people admitted to the two Andover houses have returned to more restrictive settings.

With one exception, therefore, all people with challenging behaviours admitted to ordinary housing services in two parts of the country have been maintained in the community. In many ways, this achievement is equal to what is known about the 'specialist' hospitals. Arguments in favour of the continuing need for hospital provision do not appeal, in our experience, to evidence that clients improve in or benefit from hospital care. The case for continuation mainly rests on the fact that many people with the most severely challenging behaviours currently reside in hospital and that the feasibility of alternative service models is yet to be demonstrated. Using a criterion of ability to cope, the NIMROD and Andover housing developments have demonstrated over a substantial period that ordinary housing services can cater for the great majority of individuals with severe learning disabilities and challenging behaviour. Services of similar ethos could be capable of achieving similar results. If this is achieved, only a handful of individuals in any district or region may pose a level of problem which might call for a particularly different solution. Even in this eventuality, the experience of the University of Kent Special Development Team suggests that such solutions may involve the provision of ordinary community housing (see Emerson, 1990, McGill and Mansell, Chapter 9).

THE EFFECTIVENESS QUESTION: DO ORDINARY HOUSING SERVICES PROVIDE BETTER OUTCOMES AND A BETTER QUALITY OF LIFE?

Change in challenging behaviour over time

The DAS assessment was repeated for each of the NIMROD residents at approximately six-monthly intervals over five years (Footnote 3) and staff were asked to assess the severity of management problem reported behaviours posed. Challenging behaviours were not found to diminish, quite the reverse. Significantly more challenging behaviours were reported for the NIMROD accommodation group following admission and the passage of time (Lowe et al, in press) and more were seen by staff as presenting more severe management problems by the end of the evaluation period. Table 1 shows the proportions of the NIMROD group who were assessed at the beginning and the end of the study as having the various severely or moderately challenging behaviours considered above.

Change in skills and quality of life

Nonetheless, significant increases in skills as registered by the Adaptive

Table 1   Proportion of NIMROD accommodation residents with severely and moderately challenging behaviours at T1 and T8.

	T1		T8	
	n	(%)	n	(%)
Severely Challenging Behaviours				
Physical aggression	8	(36)	11	(50)
Destructiveness	5	(23)	9	(41)
Self-injury	8	(36)	9	(41)
Temper tantrums	3	(14)	13	(59)
Wandering off	3	(14)	1	(5)
Anti-social	3	(14)	5	(23)
Inappropriate sexual	0	(0)	3	(14)
Moderately Challenging Behaviours				
Overactivity	1	(5)	5	(23)
Attention seeking	3	(14)	4	(18)
Disturbing noises	1	(5)	12	(55)
Objectionable personal habits	5	(23)	16	(73)
Stereotypies	6	(27)	2	(9)

Behavior Scale Part One (Nihira et al, 1974) and the Pathways to Independence Checklist (Jeffree and Cheseldine, 1982) occurred for the NIMROD group compared to those remaining in hospital (Lowe et al, in press). Progress was particularly found in the areas of responsibility, domestic activity, economic activity and community skills. Similar evidence of greater progress for those living in ordinary housing compared to those remaining in hospitals was found in the research on the Andover houses (Felce et al, 1986). Improvements were found particularly in the domestic activity, self-direction and independent functioning domains of the Adaptive Behavior Scale.

Other aspects of improved lifestyle on which the two research projects are consistent concern greater contact with the community and increased frequency of friendship or family contact (de Kock et al, 1988, Lowe and de Paiva, 1991b). In addition, several studies, conducted mainly in the Andover houses but also using a data set gained from NIMROD, compared the opportunities for activity and the level of participation residents had with (a) those which residents had had previously in institutional settings, (b) those which similar residents in institutions had, and (c) those which similar residents in larger community units had (see Felce and Repp, 1992 for a summary). Significantly greater levels of opportunity and participation were found in the ordinary houses. Each resident spent, on average, about half of their time meaningfully occupied in a domestic, leisure, personal care or social pursuit compared to residents with similar disabilities in institutional or large community unit settings who spent three-quarters, nine-tenths and even nineteen-twentieths of their time either doing nothing or exhibiting challenging behaviour. The improved levels of opportunity and participation were related to the quantity and quality of interaction between staff and residents in the houses (Felce and Repp, 1992).

Discussion

Addressing the benefits to client welfare, it is clear that individuals living in these ordinary houses had a greater level of participation in activities typical of daily living, enjoyed a better social life and more frequent family contact and gained skills at a faster rate than would have been the case had they received a hospital or, indeed, a larger community unit service. Both resident and family consumer views gained on the NIMROD service support this impression of improvement (Lowe, 1992). Living in ordinary housing then is not just an issue of principle but one which can be demonstrated to be in the person's better interests. However, the hope that these improvements would also be reflected in a lessening of behavioural challenge was not borne out. For those who moved from hospital to NIMROD accommodation, the data showed a tendency for challenging behaviours to be reported at a higher level at the first data collection point following transfer and to continue at that or a higher level subsequently.

It is difficult to know whether there was an actual increase in difficult behaviour of residents as some response to the characteristics of the ordinary housing service or whether the difference lay in the reporting of behaviour. It is interesting that an upward trend in the reporting of challenging behaviour and of the management problems it caused was found over time not only in the NIMROD houses but also in the hospital and family homes studied. This may reflect changing expectations generally of what should be achieved. However, despite these difficulties of interpretation, it is clear that some level of challenging behaviour continued within the ordinary housing services or else staff would not have reported it. This is consistent with evidence on the chronicity of challenging behaviour in institutional and community environments (Eyman et al, 1981, Hill and Bruininks, 1984). It is also consistent with the diversity in possible causation of challenging behaviours (see Baumeister, 1989). Change in setting may have only an indirect effect on behaviours stemming from non-environmental causes. Moreover, it would be overly optimistic to suppose that environmental conditions maintaining challenging behaviour such as inappropriately timed attention or an absence of stimulation would never occur in ordinary housing services. A greater presence of some environmental conditions such as demands may even occasion a higher level of challenging behaviour.

CONCLUSIONS

The arguments in favour of ordinary housing for people with severely challenging behaviour are, of course, similar to those for people without such behaviours. If residents are to engage in and develop skills relevant to a broad range of normal activities, they must be exposed to a corresponding range of normal opportunities. As has been concluded earlier, the NIMROD and Andover developments demonstrate that it is feasible to extend such opportunities to people with severe learning disabilities and challenging behaviour. However, generalisation of the results of the research should be restricted to services which are similar in operational ethos.

Ordinary housing is only a shorthand for the expected standards concerned with the scale, design, furnishings and level of appointments or equipment in the residential environment. The focus on constructive activity within the goals of ordinary living, development and social and community integration implies that good service design will ensure a well equipped home and an adequate material environment of a level which the majority of people take for granted. The smallness of scale of ordinary housing may more easily promote service individualisation and the occurrence of small/staff resident working groups, which are conducive to staff/resident interaction and resident participation in activity (Felce et al, 1991, Harris et al, 1974).

The ordinary housing metaphor may also be taken to extend to community location, implying proximity to immediate family and any existing wider friendship networks, as well as proximity to the community amenities of the town or suburban centre. Such locational characteristics may be seen as important determinants of the opportunity for integration of all kinds. Again, given the goals of ordinary living, the ordinary housing model of provision may be seen as necessary to service effectiveness. However, a distinction must be drawn between necessary and sufficient conditions for an effective service. Figure 1 illustrates three dimensions of service design in relation to meeting ordinary life goals. The use of ordinary housing secures a major aspect of the environmental context which is required for an effective service. It does not, however, guarantee that good arrangements will be made with respect to the other two dimensions in Figure 1 - 'getting organised' and 'delivering quality'.

Figure 1   Ordinary housing: service design for an ordinary life

An ordinary context	**Getting organised**	**Delivering quality**
Small size	**Clear outcomes** everyday activities use of community relationships choice	**Rate of interaction**
Nature of housing		**Quality of support** everyday activities use of community relationships choice
Building design	**Working methods:**	
Location	IP Review Activity planning Staff: resident groupings Individual programmes Routine interaction Monitoring success	**Quality of motivation** everyday activities use of community relationships choice
Support staff		**Effective teaching** everyday activities use of community relationships choice
Autonomy	**Job descriptions**	
	Methods of quality assurance	**Effective behaviour change**
		Effective treatment

These dimensions refer to the orientation, working methods and day to day (or even minute by minute) functioning of an effective residential setting. The key issue is how to design the setting so that opportunity, support to engage in typical daily living activities, skill-teaching and behavioural development are established as central. The opportunities inherent in the ordinary housing model must not be taken for granted and nor must the kinds of outcome gains found in the NIMROD and Andover research. Conspicuous attention was given in both services to backing clear statements of aims and operational policy with procedural guides to cover individual planning, skills-teaching, activity planning, staff support and motivation of residents, and the monitoring of achievement (see Mansell et al, 1987, Felce 1993, for a full discussion of the approaches involved). The results of the NIMROD and Andover research should not be taken to apply to all ordinary housing services but only those which have given similar attention to procedural and operational details.

The other major conclusion of these studies is that challenging behaviour is not a product of institutional environments, cured by transfer to the community. If challenging behaviour is not going to decrease as a natural result of the provision of better community housing, then it must be addressed directly. Skills of behavioural analysis and programme design need to be represented within the service system. Methods for the implementation of individual teaching and behaviour change within an overall context of everyday activity and routine staff support and motivation of appropriate engagement need to be built into service functioning (see Figure 1 and also Felce, 1993). Such an attention to establishing competence within senior and front-line staff of mainstream housing services does not replace professional roles. Rather, the attainment of a general understanding and basic competence in goal planning, behavioural development and other therapeutic approaches creates a well informed and high quality workforce that is more receptive to and can better use professional advice.

FOOTNOTES

1. Estimates from recent studies suggest that between 10 per cent and 38 per cent of people with severe learning disabilities may engage in aggressive and destructive behaviours, between 6 per cent and 40 per cent may engage in self-injurious behaviours, and between 40 per cent and 60 per cent may engage in stereotypic behaviours (Borthwick et al, 1981, Corbett and Campbell, 1981, Harris and Russell, 1989, Jacobson,

1982, Kiernan and Qureshi, Chapter 1, Oliver et al, 1987).

2. NIMROD personnel had access to the results of a prevalence survey of the city conducted as a prelude to the research.

3. Data were collected on the Andover sample using the Adaptive Behavior Scale Part Two but low reliability of assessment rendered them uninterpretable.

REFERENCES

BAUMEISTER A A (1989). Causes of severe maladaptive behaviour in persons with severe mental retardation : A review of hypotheses. Presentation given to the National Institutes of Health, Bethesda, Maryland.

BORTHWICK S A, MYERS C E AND EYMAN R K (1981). Comparative adaptive and maladaptive behaviour of mentally retarded clients of five residential settings in three western states. IN R H Bruininks, C E Myers, B B Sigford and K C Lakin (Eds) *Deinstitutionalization and Community Adjustment of Mentally Retarded People.* Washington DC: American Association on Mental Deficiency.

CAMPBELL V, SMITH R AND WOOL R (1982). Adaptive Behavior Scale differences in scores of mentally retarded individuals referred for institutionalization and those never referred. *American Journal of Mental Deficiency, 86,* 425-428.

CORBETT J A AND CAMPBELL H J (1981). Causes of self-injurious behaviour. IN P Mittler (Ed) *Frontiers of Knowledge in Mental Retardation: Volume 2. Biomedical Aspects.* Baltimore, Md: University Park Press.

DE KOCK U, SAXBY H, THOMAS M AND FELCE D (1988). Community and family contact : An evaluation of small community homes for adults. *Mental Handicap Research, 1,* 127-140.

DEPARTMENT OF HEALTH AND SOCIAL SECURITY (1971). *Better Services for the Mentally Handicapped.* London: HMSO.

DEPARTMENT OF HEALTH AND SOCIAL SECURITY (1972). *Census of Mentally Handicapped Patients in Hospital in England and Wales at the end of 1970.* London: HMSO.

DEPARTMENT OF HEALTH (1989). *Needs and responses : Services for adults with mental handicap who are mentally ill, who have behaviour problems or who offend.* London: HMSO.

DURAND V M AND KISHI G (1987). Reducing severe problem behavior among persons with dual sensory impairments: an evaluation of a technical assistance model. *Journal of the Association for Persons with Severe Handicaps, 12,* 2-10.

EMERSON E (1990). Designing individualised community-based placements as an alternative to institutions for people with a severe mental handicap and severe behaviour problem. IN W Fraser (Ed) *Key Issues in Mental Retardation Research.* London: Routledge.

EMERSON E, BEASLEY F, OFFORD G AND MANSELL J (1992). An evaluation of hospital-based specialised staffed housing for people with seriously challenging behaviours. *Journal of Intellectual Disability Research, 36,* 291-307.

EYMAN R K, BORTHWICK S A AND MILLER C (1981). Trends in maladaptive behavior of mentally retarded persons placed in community and institutional settings. *American Journal of Mental Deficiency, 85,* 473-477.

FELCE D (1989). *The Andover Project: Staffed Housing for Adults with Severe or Profound Mental Handicaps.* Clevedon, Bristol: BIMH Publications.

FELCE D (1993) Ordinary housing: a necessary context for meeting service philosophy and providing an effective therapeutic environment. IN R Jones and C Eayrs (Eds) *Challenging behaviour and Intellectual Disabilty: A psychological perspective.* Clevedon, Bristol: BILD Publications.

FELCE D, DE KOCK U, THOMAS M AND SAXBY H (1986). Change in adaptive behaviour of severely and profoundly mentally handicapped adults in different residential settings. *British Journal of Psychology, 77,* 489-501.

FELCE D, LOWE K AND DE PAIVA S(in press). Ordinary housing for people with severe learning disabilities and challenging behaviours. IN E Emerson, P McGill and J Mansell (Eds) *Severe Learning Disabilities and Challenging Behaviours: Designing high quality services.* London: Chapman and Hall.

FELCE D AND REPP A C (1992). Behavioral and social climate of community residences. *Research in Developmental Disabilities, 13,* 27-42.

FELCE D, REPP A C, THOMAS M, AGER A AND BLUNDEN R (1991). The relationship of staff:client ratios, interactions and residential placement. *Research in Developmental Disabilities, 12,* 315-331.

HARRIS P AND RUSSELL O (1989). The prevalence of aggressive behaviour among people with learning difficulties (mental handicap) in a single health district : Interim report. Bristol, University of Bristol : Norah Fry Research Centre.

HARRIS J M, VEIT S W, ALLEN G J AND CHINSKY J M (1974). Aide-resident ratio and ward population density as mediators of social interaction. *American Journal of Mental Deficiency, 79,* 320-326.

HEMMING H (1982). Mentally handicapped adults returned to large institutions after transfers to new small units. *British Journal of Mental Subnormality, 28,* 13-28.

HILL B K AND BRUININKS R H (1984). Maladaptive behaviour of mentally retarded individuals in residential facilities. *American Journal of Mental Deficiency, 88,* 380-387.

HOLMES N, SHAH A AND WING L (1982). The Disability Assessment Schedule : A brief screening device for use with the mentally retarded. *Psychological Medicine, 12,* 879-890.

JACOBSON J W (1982). Problem behavior and psychiatric impairment within a developmentally disabled population: Behavior frequency. *Applied Research in Mental Retardation, 3,* 121-139.

JEFFREE D AND CHESELDINE S (1982). *Pathways to Independence.* Sevenoaks: Hodder and Stoughton Educational.

KUSHLICK A, BLUNDEN R AND COX G R (1973). A method of rating behaviour characteristics for use in large scale surveys of mental handicap. *Psychological Medicine, 3,* 466 - 478.

KUSHLICK A AND COX G R (1973). The epidemiology of mental handicap. *Developmental Medicine and Child Neurology, 15,* 748-759.

LOWE K (1992). Community-based service - what consumers think. *British Journal of Mental Subnormality, 38,* 6-14.

LOWE K AND DE PAIVA S (1991a). *NIMROD: An overview.* London: HMSO.

LOWE K AND DE PAIVA S (1991b). Clients' community and social contacts: results of a five year longitudinal study. *Journal of Mental Deficiency Research, 35,* 308-323.

LOWE K, DE PAIVA S AND FELCE D (in press). Effects of a community-based service on adaptive and maladaptive behaviours: A longitudinal study. *Journal of Intellectual Disability Research.*

LOWE K, FELCE D AND ORLOWSKA D (in press). Evaluating services for people with challenging behaviour. IN I Fleming and B Stenfert-Kroese (Eds) *People with Severe Learning Difficulties Who Also Display Challenging Behaviour.* Manchester: Manchester University Press.

McDONALD L AND BARTON L E (1986). Measuring severity of behavior : A revision of Part II of the Adaptive Behavior Scale. *American Journal of Mental Deficiency, 90,* 418-424.

MANSELL J, FELCE D, JENKINS J, DE KOCK U AND TOOGOOD A (1987). *Developing Staffed Housing for People with Mental Handicaps.* Tunbridge Wells: Costello.

NIHIRA K, FOSTER R, SHELLHAUS M AND LELAND H (1974). *AAMD Adaptive Behaviour Scale.* Washington DC: American Association on Mental Deficiency.

O'BRIEN J (1987). A guide to life-style planning. IN B Wilcox and G T Bellamy (Eds) *The Activities Catalog: An alternative curriculum for youth and adults with severe disabilities.* Baltimore: Paul H Brookes Publishing Co.

OLIVER C, MURPHY G H AND CORBETT J A (1987). Self-injurious behaviour in people with mental handicap : a total population study. *Journal of Mental Deficiency Research, 31,* 147-162.

PAGEL S E AND WHITLING C A (1978). Readmissions to a state hospital for mentally retarded persons : reasons for community placement failure. *Mental Retardation, 16,* 164-166.

SHERMAN B R (1988). Predictors of the decision to place developmentally disabled family members in residential care. *American Journal on Mental Retardation, 92,* 344-351.

SUTTER P, MAYEDA T, CALL T, YANAGI G AND YEE S (1980). Comparison of successful and unsuccessful community-placed mentally retarded persons. *American Journal of Mental Deficiency, 85,* 262-267.

WELSH OFFICE (1983). *The All Wales Strategy for the Development of Services for Mentally Handicapped People.* Cardiff: Welsh Office.

WING L AND GOULD J (1979). Severe impairments of social interaction and associated abnormalities in children : Epidemiology and classification. *Journal of Autism and Developmental Disorders, 9,* 11-29.

CHAPTER 9

THE SPECIAL DEVELOPMENT TEAM*

Peter McGill and Jim Mansell

* Sections of this paper are adapted from McGill, Hawkins and Hughes (1991), Emerson and McGill (in press), and McGill, Emerson and Mansell (in press).

INTRODUCTION

The Special Development Team was created in 1985 as part of South East Thames Regional Health Authority's programme to replace large mental handicap hospitals in the South East (Korman and Glennerster, 1985, 1990). The Team comprised a Team Leader and five Team Members, all selected because of their experience in work with people with challenging behaviour and in practice drawn from a range of backgrounds. The Team was based at the University of Kent in what is now the Centre for the Applied Psychology of Social Care, where the Regional Health Authority also funded other work on the development of learning disability services (see Mansell, Brown et al, 1987).

The Team was set up to help local service agencies develop individualised services for people with severe and profound learning disabilities who had the most serious challenging behaviour. In particular, the Team was expected to help enable districts to resettle people from the closing hospitals who were often said to be impossible to care for in community services, and for whom Regional policy had originally proposed building new institutions (South East Thames Regional Health Authority (SETRHA), 1979, 1985). Formally the team's aims were defined as: (1) the provision of practical assistance to local Health, Educational, and Social Services in the design and implementation of individualised model services for people with a severe learning disability and seriously challenging behaviours; and (2) the provision of advice and information on a consultative basis to local services within the SETRHA area regarding the development of services for this client group (Emerson, Barrett et al, 1987).

The strategy of setting up the Special Development Team was intended to fulfil a number of purposes. First, by focusing upon the 'most challenging' individuals within the Region it was intended to provide additional practical support to local agencies in developing community based services for their most difficult-to-serve clients, at a time when local services faced many pressures due to the pace of the deinstitutionalization programme. Second, it was hoped that these local projects, as a result of the additional input, would serve as demonstration projects through which local services would have the opportunity to develop policies, procedures and competencies which would be applicable to other services for people with severe disabilities within their own area. That is, it was hoped that the lessons learned from these demonstration projects would generalise across settings within localities. Third, the strategy had an implicit objective of helping to demonstrate to local and national policy makers that well planned community services provided the best option for **all** people with severe learning disabilities, including the most seriously behaviourally disordered.

In terms of the individual placements set up with the Team's help, it was not expected that each person's challenging behaviour would be successfully treated or resolved before they moved to community settings (not least because one of the reasons for replacing the hospitals was their failure to meet such complex and highly individualised needs), nor that it would necessarily disappear once they had moved (since there is evidence from other projects, eg Lowe and de Paiva, 1991, and good reasons to predict that this will not happen, McGill et al, in press). Rather, the goal was to manage and treat challenging behaviour as far as was possible, given the constraints of lack of knowledge as well as practical considerations, in what would be better resourced and better organised placements; and to enable the individuals concerned to experience a good quality of life **in spite** of any continuing challenging behaviour.

THE TEAM'S MODEL OF WORK

The Special Development Team used a four stage process involving case identification (Emerson, Toogood et al, 1987), the development of an individual service plan (Toogood et al, 1988), support in commissioning services (Cummings et al, 1989) and, finally, providing additional support to new services during their initial years of operation (Emerson, Cummings et al, 1989, McCool et al, 1989).

Case identification

Each District Health Authority in the Region was allocated two to four places on the Team caseload. Typically a 'short-list' of eight to ten potential service users were identified who were screened by the Team and final decisions made in conjunction with local staff. The main criteria for acceptance onto the Team's caseload were level of ability (having a 'severe' learning disability) and severity of the challenging behaviour. The main reasons for actively seeking identified individuals, rather than operating an open referral system, were the number of referrals which such a system would generate, the time it would take to screen out inappropriate referrals and, most importantly, the desire to foster a sense of ownership among local senior managers and professionals by having them play a central role in identifying the service users with whom the Team would work. By the end of

1990 the Team had accepted 35 referrals to develop services for service users in 14 separate District Health Authorities: 10 District Health Authorities have taken lead responsibility for 24 service users; three Local Authorities for nine service users; and one voluntary organisation (a housing association supported by the local authority) has taken responsibility for two service users.

Individual service planning

Following acceptance of a service user on to the Team's caseload a written individual service plan was developed as a collaborative venture between the Team, managers, and professional staff in the receiving services and relatives, friends or advocates who could speak on behalf of the service user themselves. The serious disabilities of the service users precluded their effective contribution to such an abstract process although on many occasions they were present at meetings convened to develop this plan. The individual service plan itself contained a detailed specification, including estimates of revenue and capital costs, of the support required to provide a high quality community based service for the service user. The main compromise made in these plans was the use of group living arrangements to reduce staff costs. In most cases the plan was for one person with seriously challenging behaviours to live with one to three other people with learning disabilities but without either challenging behaviours or complex medical needs which might require the immediate attention of staff. In addition to the Team's help, local agencies could access pump-priming monies (£45,000 per service user at 1990 prices), in addition to any 'dowry' money, and some capital resources.

Commissioning new services

If the responsible local agencies agreed with the proposals submitted in the form of an individual service plan, or negotiated a variation upon the plan with the Team then the Team would provide additional support to the local agency in commissioning the new service. The tasks undertaken by the Team at this stage included working with local managers and professionals in order to: identify and purchase new property; recruit and train new staff; develop policies and procedures for the new service; and help prepare the service user for their move (Cummings et al, 1989). By April 1992, of the 33 plans submitted, 22 had resulted in services being established by the Team in conjunction with 10 local agencies. The number of services established per year was: 1987(1), 1988(9), 1989(5), 1990(1) and 1991(6).

Supporting services

The Team provided additional professional support to the services during the first one to two years of their lives. Initially, support was very intensive (often the equivalent of all of one team member's time), the aim being to gradually reduce Team support as the local agency gained in experience and confidence. While it varied across services, the types of support undertaken included advising upon the implementation of agreed policies and procedures, providing specialist advice concerning the analysis and treatment of the service user's seriously challenging behaviours, staff training, progress chasing within the local agency and providing information as well as practical and emotional support to local staff. At all times the new service was managed by the local agency and therefore fitted in with local management arrangements. Usually a Project Co-ordinating Group was set up to review progress and ensure that any special arrangements needed in the placement were protected from decay or inadvertent destruction.

THE MODEL OF RESIDENTIAL CARE

Most services had detailed operational policies based on guidelines developed by the Team (Special Development Team, 1988). Typical policies stressed, explicitly or implicitly, a number of themes which could be considered to be the defining features of the way in which the placement was intended to operate:

Normalisation

Service operation was explicitly based on normalisation with the aims of the service usually being expressed in terms of the five accomplishments (O'Brien, 1987) and attention being given to the image created and maintained of service users, eg through the maintenance of the physical environment, the advertisements used to recruit staff, the involvement of service users in decision making, and so on.

Individualisation

It was intended that the operation as well as the planning of the placement be based on the continued use of an individual planning process to select activities and achieve goals appropriate to individual needs.

Integration

Placements were expected to ensure that service users were not only physically present in their local community but also actively took part in community activities that brought them into regular contact with ordinary, non-handicapped people. Although subsumed in normalisation, integration was emphasised as a theme in its own right especially in terms of the use of the community and of generic services.

Structured involvement of service users in activities

All policies stressed the importance of engaging service users in a wide range of appropriate housework, occupational and recreational activities through a structured process of planning and staff deployment.

Staff development

Considerable stress was laid on the promotion of staff knowledge and skill through their experience in the service and additional training, and on the constructive deployment and use of this resource by the provider agency.

Basic service operation, therefore, was intended to involve the structured enrichment of the service user's social and physical environment in a manner similar to that developed in the Andover Project (Mansell, Felce et al, 1987, Felce, 1989). Primary attention was to be given to the modification of those features of the environment assumed to be associated with challenging behaviour and the construction of adaptive behaviour which could theoretically replace service user challenging behaviour (Goldiamond, 1974). In most cases more specific procedures were also developed before the services opened around the management and recording of service user behaviour, the promotion and recording of service user activities, and the deployment of staff. There was, of course, considerable variation between services in the degree to which they successfully implemented these principles of placement organisation.

By April 1992, the provision of services was as follows:

* Twenty two services have been set up, all in ordinary houses or flats, close to community facilities.

* Fifteen people still live in their new homes. Three people were moved back to hospital, of whom one has returned to a new house; two

people have been moved to a new (larger) staffed house to save money; and two people have died of natural causes.

* One person lives on her own; five people live with one other person and nine people live with two to four others.

* Staff establishments range from seven to 15 whole time equivalent (often including waking night staff)

IMPACT OF THE SERVICES

1. An individual case study

There are of course lessons to be learned from both the successes and the failures in this project: this case study is one of the successes. 'Sue Thompson' (not her real name) was born in 1954 in the South of England. Her mother reports that abnormal development began at the age of three, shortly after a bout of pneumonia. Sue lost the little speech that she had attained, and her development seemed to cease in all respects other than physical growth.

Her mother reports that Sue's behaviour gradually became socially inappropriate, she began tearing clothes and soft furnishings and showed little interest in other people. Sue's parents consulted numerous specialists, hoping for a definitive explanation of what was wrong with her, and were eventually told that she was 'autistic'. They did not feel, however, that they had been given an adequate explanation of what this actually meant. By the time she was aged six, Sue had grown to a size at which her parents were unable to continue to meet the challenge presented by her tendency to destroy furniture. Sue was therefore admitted to the children's section of a large NHS mental handicap hospital within the South East Thames Region.

Sue spent the next 27 years in this hospital. By 1987 most of the residents had been moved out, as the hospital was scheduled for closure by the end of 1988. Sue was still there and many were pessimistic about the chances of her succeeding in a community service. She had originated from outside of the hospital's usual catchment area and was initially classified as being 'stateless'. Such individuals were divided between the catchment District Health Authorities (DHAs) and, given the apparent difficulties in providing a service for her, the responsible DHA referred Sue to the Special Development Team.

The Team and the DHA started preliminary planning of an individualised service for Sue. In late 1987, however, Sue's parents asked if she could be resettled in their local area. By late 1988 the local DHA had agreed to take responsibility for resettling her, and the planning process recommenced with the Team.

This was too late, however, to allow Sue to move directly into her new house. The hospital that had been her home for so long closed in late 1988, and Sue was moved (via a small hospital and a large hostel) to a house for women with seriously challenging behaviour on the periphery of the Region's other large mental handicap hospital.

During early 1989, the Team spent time observing and interacting with Sue, interviewing staff and examining records, so that by late 1989 an Individual Service Plan (ISP) was presented to the DHA. The ISP process reviewed the behaviours that Sue currently exhibited that would be likely to severely challenge a future service:

> "..these include assault of others (pulling hair, pinching, scratching), manual evacuation and smearing of faeces, removing and tearing her clothes, eating inappropriate objects (eg, torn clothing), throwing objects and stealing food. These behaviours occur on at least a daily basis if she has the opportunity. Aggression occurs regularly and persistently whenever she is approached. She currently spends the majority of her day sitting or lying under a blanket in the corner of the ward. The combination of faecal smearing and aggression on others approaching has led to her being avoided by staff unless it is absolutely necessary to approach her....in general she is a very challenging young woman who will respond with unpleasant aggression (faeces smeared hand in the victim's hair) if approached."

While this was a formidable picture, the plan proposed staffing and other arrangements that would allow Sue to live in an ordinary four bedroomed house with three other people. The DHA accepted the plan and started preparing for the type of service that the Team had recommended. By November 1989 a suitable house had been identified and, shortly afterwards, the first staff (Team Leader and Deputy) took up post.

During early 1990 the house was renovated, decorated and furnished, and three co-tenants (with mild learning disabilities and without seriously challenging behaviour) were identified. By March 1990, a complete establishment (seven whole time equivalent) of support workers had been recruited. The managing agency and the Team jointly organised and ran two weeks of induction training for the support workers and Sue and her co-tenants moved into their new house in July 1990. Sue was now aged 35 and had been in various institutions since the age of six.

Data collected over the course of the Team's involvement with Sue (Mansell and Beasley, in press) allows comparison of her lifestyle and behaviour across three different settings: her original hospital; the hospital house; and her current placement.

As has been found typical of client experience in the large hospitals, Sue received very little contact from staff (an average of 3.5 per cent) in the large hospital (Figure 1). Marginally increased contact of 6 per cent (despite a one-to-one staff ratio) was found in the second setting. Only in her current placement has this significantly increased to an average of 46 per cent.

A significant proportion of this staff contact consists of assistance to Sue to participate in purposeful activities. While such assistance occurred 1 per cent and 2 per cent, respectively, of the time in the two institutional settings, it has averaged 25 per cent in her current placement.

Figure 1   'Sue Thompson': staff contact in three settings

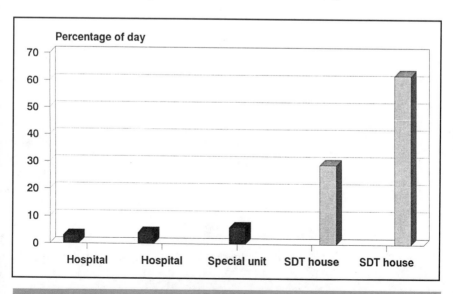

There is little doubt that this increasing level of assistance is responsible for Sue's increasing engagement in purposeful activity from 3 per cent and 7 per cent in her previous settings to 20 per cent currently (Figure 2).

At the same time, however, there have been more variable outcomes in her challenging behaviours. While stereotyped behaviour has declined there have been small but significant increases in aggressive and noncompliant behaviour. While these increases probably reflect the new level of 'demand' and social contact in Sue's life they appear to have stabilised while contact, assistance and engagement continue to increase (Figure 3). Further, the character of her aggression is much less unpleasant. While she still grabs staff and pulls their hair, attention to her toileting and physical needs has led to her no longer wearing incontinence pads and to her using the toilet appropriately, with help. As a result faecal smearing happens very rarely.

Sue's service has not been without its problems. In its early days a deliberately 'relaxed' regime was associated with great difficulties in managing Sue's behaviour. As structure (a balanced day's activities, clear guidelines for staff on how to work with Sue, opportunity planning, shift planning, recording of participation and behaviour) were added in, Sue's behaviour became more manageable and her participation in purposeful

Figure 2   'Sue Thompson': engagement in three settings

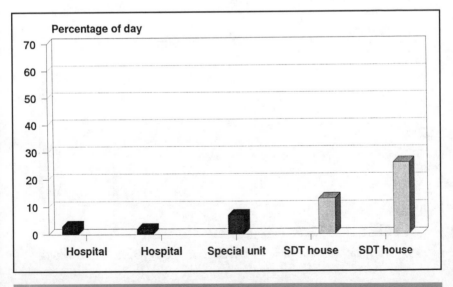

Figure 3   'Sue Thompson': challenging behaviour in three settings

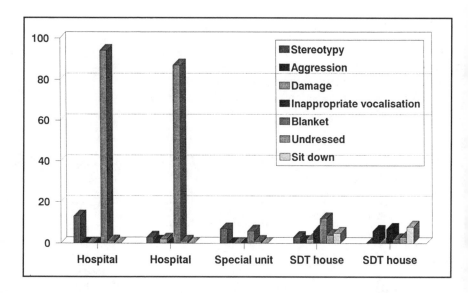

activity increased. The following year, Sue had a stay in a general hospital marked by confused medical management. This was a period of great stress for the staff and it took some months for their morale and organisation to recover.

Despite the difficulties there is no doubt that Sue's lifestyle has changed markedly for the better. Photographs taken by staff show her walking on the beach, loading the washing machine, drinking tea in a cafe, pouring milk on her Weetabix, and participating in many other ordinary, everyday activities (Di Terlizzi et al, 1992). She is fully dressed and looks healthy; previously thin and almost emaciated, she has put on two and a half stones since coming out of hospital. When asked to comment on the changes her father wrote:

> "if it is possible, with only nine months' love, and home care, to see such improvement in health and behaviour, then I have only one question - why did it take 27 years of torment in an institution to achieve this?"

IMPACT OF THE SERVICES

2. The evaluation study

Eleven of the 22 people who have moved (together with seven yet to move) have participated in an evaluation of activity patterns and interaction in the services set up with the help of the Special Development Team. Figure 4 shows the percentage of the day spent engaged in constructive activity before and after transfer to small staffed houses in the community.

Figure 4   Percentage of day spent engaged in constructive activity before and after transfer to small staffed houses.

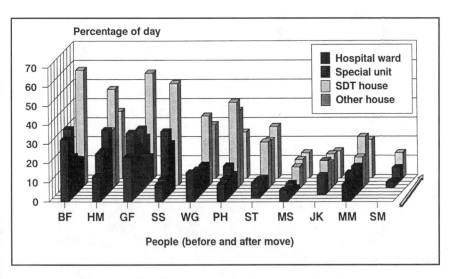

Averaging the observations in each condition, the group almost doubled their level of participation in meaningful activity, from 16 per cent to 28 per cent. One person whose placement broke down (WG) moved to a large institution and then to a small private home at the last datapoint, where her level of participation shows some decrement (this person has since moved back to her local area). Similarly, three people in houses (MM, HM and PH) show declining levels of participation following initial increases after their moves. The people who have not yet moved out of hospital showed no clear trend in their level of participation in meaningful activity, strengthening the case for attributing changes in 'movers' to their new community services rather than passage of time or general improvement in all services. More detailed analysis shows that these increases consist of participation in practical housework tasks, including assisted use of relatively complex equipment like irons and microwaves, and longer mealtimes.

Minor problem behaviours (mainly self-stimulation) showed an inverse relationship with engagement for everyone except MS (Figure 5). This suggests that self-stimulation can often be competed out by engagement in purposeful activities. Serious problem behaviour (Figure 6) decreased overall in nine cases after transfer to community settings, although this data should be interpreted with caution because it is highly variable; reduction does not always coincide with transfer and momentary time-sampling does not necessarily detect infrequent but very serious problems. Nevertheless, it does appear possible to conclude at least that the higher levels of participation in meaningful activity were achieved without problem behaviour happening more often.

Figure 5   Percentage of day spent showing minor problem behaviour before and after transfer to small staffed houses.

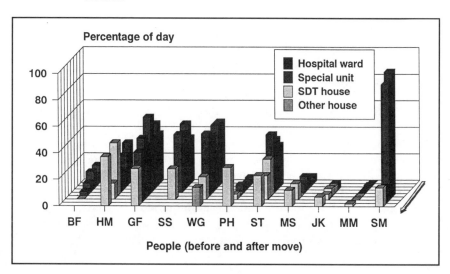

In terms of social contact received from other people, individuals in hospitals and special units received contact from staff for a relatively small proportion of the day (Figure 7). The total contact received was 7 per cent in hospital and 9 per cent in special units (ie equivalent to 46 minutes and

Figure 6 Percentage of day spent showing major problem behaviour before and after transfer to small staffed houses.

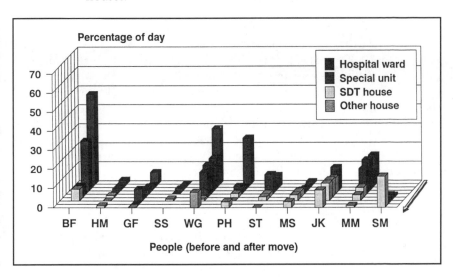

59 minutes respectively in an 11 hour day). In the houses supported by the Special Development Team total contact received was 26 per cent (172 minutes). Although the fact that for three-quarters of the day people in these houses are still not receiving contact is at first sight rather dispiriting, data from another study (Hughes and Mansell, 1990) of 'mainstream' community houses shows only 11 per cent contact, indicating that the houses set up with the Team's help are performing much better than some other community-based services. It is also important that in the houses set up with the help of the Special Development Team 42 per cent of the contact was in the form of assistance rather' than conversation (compared with 29 per cent in hospital and 18 per cent in special units). These houses therefore delivered much more contact and more of the contact was directly therapeutic (ie 72 minutes of assistance in the day in the houses compared with 13 minutes in the hospital and 11 minutes in the special units).

DISCUSSION

The best placements have generally been those that have had organisational structures in place to define what clients should be doing; when, where, and

Figure 7   Amount and type of contact received.

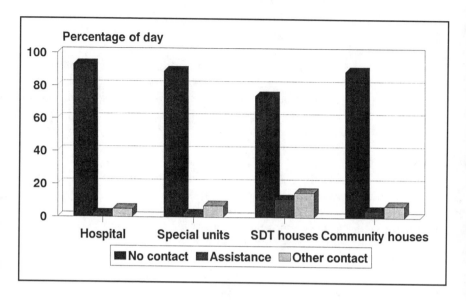

with whom they should be doing it; what support they need to do it; and have kept reliable records of what they have done. While such structures were set up in almost all placements at the beginning (and were intended to be set up in all), in many they have decayed and no longer play the central role intended for them. This factor is probably one of the main causes of variable outcomes between placements and of decay in quality of some placements over time, and it was probably also an important factor in two of the three placement breakdowns arising from the client's challenging behaviour.

In the first 18-24 months of each placement's existence Team involvement has often substituted for a vacuum of effective local management and support. Thus home leaders have often turned to the Team for supervision and technical support around the management of challenging behaviour and the organisation of the service. Sometimes there has simply been a lack of the necessary resources (eg, clinical psychologists) locally. In other cases there has been a lack of commitment, or even outright antipathy, from middle managers in the learning disability service (not usually the same people who planned the service with the Special Development Team because of turnover). As community services have grown this problem has worsened with management and support resources becoming more stretched and, often, less competent. This is particularly important given that many of these placements have faced crises arising as a result of the client's behaviour or the failure of the placement to support the client effectively. Sometimes these crises have been handled constructively and the placement has been maintained, though perhaps in a different form. In other cases the crisis has not been managed and the placement has broken down. Generally there is evidence of a lack of understanding of crisis and its management and a very reactive (and reactionary) approach when crises occur. Weak external management and support is then also likely to be a crucial factor in placement decay and breakdown.

The Special Development Team has focused on developing services for a small number of individuals (those attributed to be the 'most challenging') on the grounds that Districts could deal on their own with the others (the less challenging). By operating on this basis it has been possible to demonstrate the virtual comprehensiveness of the community placement model. In the meantime, however, Districts have been showing that they are capable of much less comprehensiveness than originally assumed. In many Districts many clients are in expensive private placements of dubious quality because local providers cannot yet serve them or their attempts have failed. This process of excluding the less challenging while providing for the most challenging is one of the most ironic outcomes of the Region's strategy. Clearly, then, mainstream community services must become more competent at dealing with challenging behaviour - it is a mistake to see the 'problem' of challenging behaviour as being one of a small, 'nameable' group. This carries the further implication that interventions designed to develop mainstream service capability are likely to be directed at the service system rather than the individual placement.

IMPLICATIONS FOR SERVICES

In summary, the major implications of the work reported above include:

POLICY

* community-based services are clearly feasible for people with severe learning disabilities and the most seriously challenging behaviour - the decision as to whether to provide them is essentially one of judging costs and benefits

. * even specialist institutional provision continues to provide a very poor quality of life for clients despite the resources which have been invested in it

MANAGEMENT

* the success of community care depends on adequate local management and professional support. There are clear signs of this becoming very stretched as community services expand

* if placement breakdowns are to be avoided, expertise must be developed in the management of crises

* the success of community services for people with challenging behaviour depends not only on specialist services but also on mainstream services becoming more competent at managing moderate levels of challenge

CLINICAL PRACTICE

* evidence that challenging behaviour reduces in many placements suggests that as much attention be given to the organisation of placements as to individual clinical treatment

* more generally the work supports the clinical investigation of relationships between challenging behaviour and the characteristics of service settings

* systemic interventions are likely to be useful in improving the capability of service systems to effectively manage challenging behaviour

RESEARCH

* evidence of decay following initial improvements shows the importance of long-term follow-ups which track placement performance and its impact on client behaviour

* the considerable body of literature on individual clinical intervention needs to be supplemented by research on the effectiveness of more systemic interventions

* the evidence on the relationship of challenging behaviour to setting variables (eg institution versus community) remains confused and much work is needed to clarify the effects and modes of operation of such variables.

REFERENCES

CUMMINGS R, EMERSON E, BARRETT S, McCOOL C, TOOGOOD A AND HUGHES H (1989). Challenging behaviour and community services. 4. Establishing services. *Mental Handicap, 17,* 13-17.

DI TERLIZZI M, BUSBY B AND McGILL P (1992). Inside-out: Life before, during and after institutionalisation. Poster presented at British Institute of Mental Handicap Annual Conference, Edinburgh.

EMERSON E, BARRETT S, BELL C, CUMMINGS R, McCOOL C, TOOGOOD A, AND MANSELL J (1987). Developing services for people with severe learning difficulties and challenging behaviours. Canterbury: Institute of Social and Applied Psychology.

EMERSON E, CUMMINGS R, HUGHES H, TOOGOOD A, McCOOL C, AND BARRETT S (1989). Challenging behaviour and community services: Evaluation and overview. *Mental Handicap, 17,* 104-107.

EMERSON E and McGILL P (in press). Developing services for people with severe learning disabilities and seriously challenging behaviours: South East Thames Regional Health) Authority, 1985-1991, IN I Fleming & B Stenfert Kroese (Eds) *People with Severe Learning Difficulties who also Display Challenging Behaviour.* Manchester: Manchester University Press.

EMERSON E, TOOGOOD A, MANSELL J, BARRETT S, BELL C, CUMMINGS R AND McCOOL C (1987). Challenging Behaviour and community services: 1. Introduction and overview. *Mental Handicap, 15,* 166-169.

FELCE D (1989). *The Andover project: Staffed housing for adults with severe or profound mental handicaps.* Clevedon, Bristol: BIMH Publications.

GOLDIAMOND I (1974). Towards a constructional approach to social problems. *Behaviorism, 2,* 1-84.

HUGHES H M AND MANSELL J (1990). Consultation to Camberwell Health Authority Learning Difficulties Care Group: Evaluation Report. Canterbury: Centre for the Applied Psychology of Social Care.

KORMAN N AND GLENNERSTER H (1985). *Closing a hospital: The Darenth Park project.* London: Bedford Square Press.

KORMAN N AND GLENNERSTER H (1990). *Hospital closure.* Milton Keynes: Open University Press.

LOWE K AND DE PAIVA S (1991). *NIMROD: An overview. A summary report of a year research study of community based service provision for people with learning difficulties.* London: HMSO.

MANSELL J AND BEASLEY F (In press). Small staffed houses for people with a severe mental handicap and challenging behaviour. *British Journal of Social Work.*

MANSELL J, BROWN H, McGILL P, HOSKIN S, LINDLEY P AND EMERSON E (1987). Bringing people back home: A staff training initiative in mental handicap. Bristol and Bexhill: National Health Service Training Authority and South East Thames Regional Health Authority.

MANSELL J, FELCE D, JENKINS J, DE KOCK U AND TOOGOOD A (1987). *Developing Staffed Housing for People with Mental Handicaps.* Tunbridge Wells: Costello.

McCOOL C, BARRETT S, EMERSON E, TOOGOOD A, HUGHES H AND CUMMINGS R (1989). Challenging behaviour and community services. 5. Structuring staff and client activity. *Mental Handicap, 17,* 60-64.

McGILL P, EMERSON E, AND MANSELL J (in press). Individually designed residential provision for people with seriously challenging behaviours. IN Emerson, P McGill and J Mansell (Eds) *Severe learning disabilities and challenging behaviour: Designing high-quality services.* London: Chapman and Hall.

McGILL P, HAWKINS C AND HUGHES H (1991). The Special Development Team, South East Thames. IN D Allen, R Banks & S Staite (Eds) *Meeting the challenge: Some U.K. perspectives on community services for people with learning difficulties and challenging behaviour* (pp. 7-13). London: King's Fund.

O'BRIEN J (1987). A guide to personal futures planning. IN G T Bellamy & B Wilcox (Eds) *A comprehensive guide to the Activities Catalog: An alternative curriculum for youths and adults with severe disabilities.* Baltimore: Paul H Brookes.

SOUTH EAST THAMES REGIONAL HEALTH AUTHORITY (1979). Strategies and guidelines for the development of services for mentally handicapped people. South East Thames Regional Health Authority.

SOUTH EAST THAMES REGIONAL HEALTH AUTHORITY (1985). Mental handicap special services. South East Thames Regional Health Authority.

SPECIAL DEVELOPMENT TEAM (1988). Annual Report 1987. Canterbury: Centre for the Applied Psychology of Social Care.

TOOGOOD A, EMERSON E, HUGHES H, BARRETT S, CUMMINGS R AND McCOOL C (1988). Challenging behaviour and community services: 3. Planning individualised services. *Mental Handicap, 16,* 70-74.

CHAPTER 10

COMMUNITY SUPPORT TEAMS FOR PEOPLE WITH LEARNING DISABILITIES AND CHALLENGING BEHAVIOURS

Eric Emerson
Paul Cambridge, Jane Forrest and Jim Mansell

This paper examines some key organisational aspects of an increasingly popular approach to the provision of specialised support for people with learning disabilities and challenging behaviours, that of the locally based peripatetic community support team (Community Support Team). We will pay particular attention to the identification of key issues in relation to performance and organisational durability.

BACKGROUND

The last five years have witnessed the rapid emergence of community support teams as a key component in the range of community based services provided to people with learning disabilities. The Community Support Team model, while having similarities to existing systems of professional support (eg clinical psychology services, community mental handicap teams and the outreach services of specialist treatment units), is distinctive in being:

* targeted to the support of people with challenging behaviour (and in many cases their carers or supporters)

* predominantly peripatetic in operation, and

* generally multi-disciplinary or trans-disciplinary in composition.

The growth in popularity of Community Support Teams has been encouraged by a number of factors, including the consistency of the Community Support Team model with 'ordinary life' principles of service design (Allen et al, 1991, Blunden and Allen, 1987, Emerson et al, 1991), dissatisfaction with existing models of specialised support, particularly the perceived failure of specialist treatment units (eg Newman and Emerson, 1991); the low intensity of support available to families (eg Qureshi, 1990 and Chapter 5), the entrepreneurial drives of non-medical professions, especially Clinical Psychology, dehospitalisation and the development of community services and the development of needs-led and case managed approaches to community care. The implementation of the current community care reforms (National Health Service and Community Care Act, 1990) have also helped create the impetus for organisational change and, in some local instances, the funding conditions for facilitating the opportunistic development of Community Support Teams. A redefined focus on joint working through community care planning has also helped the planned development of Community Support Teams as a way to plug gaps in local service provision resulting from the traditional separation of health and social care.

These various factors have combined to establish Community Support Teams as the preferred service option in many localities. Thus, for example, 17 of the 19 bids by District Health Authorities for North Western Regional Health Authority funds earmarked for challenging behaviour in 1990 involved the establishment or development of some variant of the Community Support Team model. While the model in its broad aspects has clearly gained rapid acceptance, existing and planned Community Support Teams in the UK display a wide diversity of organisation and structure. These include service objectives and client level aims, sources and styles of funding, inter-agency working, macro organisation accountability and devolved authority, team management and staffing arrangements and the emphasis placed on a co-ordinated and case managed approach to resources and support.

As yet, little is known about the conditions under which such teams most effectively develop and operate. Research investigating the effectiveness of Community Support Teams would ideally need to take account of organisational process and context and provide information concerning the quality and cost of client level interventions. Such work is currently underway at the Centre for the Applied Psychology of Social Care (University of Kent at Canterbury) and the Hester Adrian Research Centre (University of Manchester). This joint project involves the collection of information on the costs of the services provided by Community Support Teams and their impact on the quality of life of six users from each team. Close links have been established between the project and a similar project being undertaken at the Mental Handicap in Wales Applied Research Unit (see Lowe et al, in press).

THE CHARACTERISTICS OF COMMUNITY SUPPORT TEAMS

To provide some context to this work, a national survey was undertaken in 1991/2 to identify specialist services available for people with challenging behaviour and learning disabilities. The survey involved the distribution of a brief postal questionnaire to all 211 Departments of Clinical Psychology in England, Wales and Scotland. Sixty nine questionnaires were returned, giving a disappointingly low response rate of 33%. The resulting data must therefore be interpreted with caution, although some broad trends emerged. These will be considered below in the context of an analysis of the components of a comprehensive local service strategy for challenging behaviour and our current knowledge concerning the epidemiology, etiology and treatment of challenging behaviours.

A Comprehensive Local Service Strategy for Challenging Behaviours

A comprehensive local strategy for challenging behaviours is likely to comprise a number of interrelated and interdependent components, including (1) prevention; (2) early intervention; (3) the provision of technical and practical support, including at times of crises; and (4) the development of alternative placements (Mansell et al, in press a, b).

Prevention has a number of specific components whose aim would be to reduce the incidence of challenging behaviours. These would include targeting high quality services for those individuals most at risk of developing challenging behaviours, thus reversing a tradition of marginalisation and exclusion (cf Emerson et al, in press). This would involve deploying resources to ensure that individuals with more severe learning disabilities, people with additional sensory impairments or impaired expressive or receptive communication and people with some specific syndromes (cf Murphy, in press) are supported in developing socially appropriate ways of influencing the behaviours of carers and exercising control over important aspects of their environments (Dunlap et al, 1990). In addition, it is important to ensure that those most at risk of developing challenging behaviours are at least risk of being exposed to conditions which may facilitate the development of challenging behaviour, eg unpredictable or uncontrollable stress, social and material deprivation and physical and sexual abuse.

Early intervention requires the use of information systems to identify the emergence of challenging behaviour at the earliest possible stage and the timely provision of sufficiently intense practical and technical support to effect changes in the person's behaviour.

The provision of technical and practical support of sufficient intensity to bring about changes in a person's challenging behaviour involves a number of components. These include: detailed assessment; the implementation of agreed interventions; and the provision of practical, informational and emotional support to carers, including at times of crises. Thus intervention may involve such diverse components as developing the skills of carers, implementing technical intervention strategies or providing carers with additional support in the form of respite or counselling. It will also require the development of systems for effectively preventing and managing crises (Mansell et al, in press b). The essential aim of such support is to enable carers to work in appropriate and sustainable ways with people with challenging behaviours.

Placement development. Whatever the effectiveness of the preceding measures it will, at times, prove necessary for agencies to develop alternative long term residential, educational or vocational placements for individuals which reflect the special needs of the individual with challenging behaviour. Person centred planning, which has provided a cornerstone of recent developments in community care policies (Department of Health, 1989; Social Services Inspectorate, 1991), would appear to be of particular importance to the development of placements for people with challenging behaviour given the accumulating evidence regarding the chronicity of such behaviours (Qureshi, in press).

In the following sections we will use information collected from the survey described above, as well as information drawn from the emerging literature on Community Support Teams, to highlight some of the potential strengths and weaknesses of the service model. In particular we will discuss the potential roles of Community Support Teams within the strategic context outlined above and the likely effectiveness of such teams in achieving their stated aims.

As noted in the introduction, peripatetic Community Support Teams specifically targeted at challenging behaviour are a relatively recent development, although they have clear links to other forms of service provision. Thus, of the 17 Community Support Teams identified in the survey for whom data was available, only three had been established for over three years (the year of establishment of both Community Support Teams and the 14 Specialised Treatment Units identified in the survey is given in Table 1). Twenty seven respondents indicated that local agencies were currently planning for the development of specialised services, approximately 60 per cent of which consisted of Community Support Teams.

In general, the Community Support Teams identified in the survey and described elsewhere (eg Burchess, 1991, Bromley and Emerson, in press, Hill-Tout et al, 1991, Lowe et al, in press, Maughan, 1991, McBrien, in press, Staite, 1991, Toogood et al, in press) are small, typically employing between

Table 1   Year of Establishment of Specialised Services

	Community Support Teams	Specialised Treatment Units
1982	—	2
1983	—	—
1984	—	—
1985	—	—
1986	—	—
1987	1	1
1988	2	6
1989	4	1
1990	5	1
1991	3	2
1992	2	1
Total	17	14

three and five whole time equivalent staff. The model underlying the operation of Community Support Teams is that the provision of intensive support to people in their natural settings over the short to medium term should be effective in bringing about changes in the behaviours of the person with learning disabilities and their carers so that the successes of intervention may be maintained, or indeed built upon, over time.

In most other aspects Community Support Teams are characterised by their diversity. Thus, for example, the teams identified represent a range of staffing models. Staffing models for professional staff within Community Support Teams include:

* uni-disciplinary teams in which team members are drawn from the same profession, often nursing, but occasionally social work;

* multi-disciplinary teams in which team posts are allocated to different professions, a pattern of provision similar to Community Mental Handicap Teams;

* trans-disciplinary teams in which team members are members of a profession but team posts are not allocated to specific professions, ie all posts have the same job description and selection is based upon the competency of individual applicants.

In addition, a number of the Community Support Teams identified in the survey employed staff without professional qualifications, often at the care assistant or assistant psychologist level, whose primary role was to work under the direction of one or more qualified team members in the implementation of intervention plans. Funding for the Community Support Teams identified in the survey was primarily provided by District Health Authorities and Trusts (87 per cent); the remaining three teams were joint funded in that two or more agencies each contributed greater than or equal to 20 per cent of the teams ongoing revenue funding.

Case management arrangements within services for people with learning disabilities and challenging behaviours deserve special attention because of the particular complexities of casework and support in this area and the likelihood that service packages will be relatively expensive (Department of Health, 1989, para 3.3.2). Many users supported by Community Support Teams have also moved between care systems or providers, or have been involved in Care in the Community programmes, giving case management a vital co-ordinating role (Cambridge, 1992a). Some are also effectively local experimental services, subject to close scrutiny and review and without long term financial guarantees. Such services have to think carefully about targeting resources and achieving positive user outcomes, making case management an implicit if not explicit requirement (Knapp et al, 1992). Moreover, the reason for the existance of Community Support Teams is to intervene in service and client level processes and to affect positive changes in both domains. Case management provides a mechanism for affecting change by providing a process or series of core tasks, centred upon the needs of the individual service user. The Community Support Team service model seeks to perform most if not all the core tasks of case management (Challis and Davies, 1986):

Case finding (targeting) and referral

Assessment screening and selection

Care planning and service packaging

Monitoring and review (reassessment)

Case closure

While primarily utilising a team approach, the composition of the team will largely depend on the agencies involved (see Cambridge 1992a for a typology) and may involve shared care tasks arrangements with other providers (Social Services Inspectorate, 1991). A particularly difficult task for any community service is the narrowing and refinement of targeting criteria (Cambridge 1992b). This is particularly acute in Community Support Teams because of limited capacity and the specialist nature of services. Attention therefore also needs to be focused on referral arrangements which in turn can be influenced by inter agency working.

The majority of teams in the survey operated an open referral system with 64 per cent accepting referrals from multiple sources, 33 per cent of teams accepted more than two thirds of their referrals from Local Authority Social Services Departments, just one team accepted more than two thirds of its referrals from Health Authority sources. Open referral systems mean that assessment and screening arrangements for intake need to be especially tight. With regards to the clients served, four per cent of the teams identified in the survey only served children, 48 per cent only served adults, the remaining 48 per cent serving both children and adults. Teams vary considerably with regard to the existence and nature of procedures for assessment and screening, care planning, monitoring and review. These range from highly detailed operating procedures specifying the exact processes involved in assessment (eg Burchess, 1991) to a traditional 'professional' model characterised by the virtual absence of formal operating procedures on the assumption that decisions are best guided by the 'clinical experience' of team members. Anecdotally a considerable number of teams have reported difficulties with regards to case closure, although such difficulties are clearly not inevitable (cf, McBrien, in press).

The critical consideration for the effective performance of the core tasks of case management is not only the degree to which a case-managed rationale has been developed but the authority and power to negotiate and affect significant and lasting change within the service system. While the ideal may be for Community Support Teams to lead case management for the individuals with which they work, and for their case management responsibilities to be meshed with wider arrangements in the agencies and other services involved, the political and operational reality appears somewhat different as the inability of many teams to affect effective case closure procedures illustrates. Few teams also appear to be effectively armed with the sorts of case management devices, such as devolved budgets and authority, which would allow them to more effectively pursue a case-managed rationale.

Community Support Teams and the prevention of challenging behaviours

A number of Community Support Teams report involvement in staff and carer training as a preventative activity. In all instances, however, such activities appear somewhat peripheral to the essential mission of the teams - the provision of additional or specialised support to people with challenging behaviour. Not surprisingly the investment of resources by teams in this area of activity is low. No other types of preventative activities are described by Community Support Teams.

Community Support Teams and early intervention

Community Support Teams as currently organised within the UK **devote few resources to issues of early intervention.** As noted earlier, 48 per cent of the teams identified in the survey only served adults. In addition, the majority of teams with explicit operational policies employ the severity of the person's challenging behaviour as one of the major criteria for prioritising referrals.

Community Support Teams and the provision of practical and technical support

As noted above, the central aim of Community Support Teams is the enhancement of the client's quality of life through the provision of intensive short/medium term support in the person's natural setting. Four issues regarding the potential strengths and weaknesses of Community Support Teams in this area are discussed below.

1. The limited information available regarding the chronicity of challenging behaviours and the effectiveness of intervention suggests that (at least seriously) challenging behaviours are highly persistent over time and may show only temporary amelioration in response to intervention (Qureshi, in press). These observations highlight the potential difficulty of maintaining throughput in short to medium term intervention services such as Community Support Teams and, indeed, Specialised Treatment Units (Newman and Emerson, 1991), underlining the need for an effective approach to case management which ensures effective targeting, intake, case review and closure. In addition, however, evidence that challenging behaviours may be highly persistent indicates that intervention oriented services may need to pay more serious attention to the prevention of the harmful physical and social

consequences of challenging behaviours as they occur over periods of years or even decades. These may include, for example, procedures for the safe and effective management of episodes of aggression and self-injury, preventative approaches including the use of prosthetic environments and (at times) mechanical restraint, and procedures to support carers to sustain appropriate working practices with people with challenging behaviour. That is, more attention may need to be given to the prevention of additional physical impairments and social handicaps arising from possibly intractable behavioural disabilities. Such pessimistic predictions may also, of course, reflect inadequate access to appropriate treatment.

2.   Current knowledge concerning the effectiveness of different approaches to intervention clearly indicates that behavioural and psychopharmacological approaches must, at present, be considered the approaches of choice (Baumeister and Sevin, 1990, Oliver and Head, 1990, Murphy, in press, Repp and Singh, 1990). Indeed, both approaches may need to be incorporated in programmes of a sufficient intensity and duration to bring about widespread and/or lasting changes in targeted behaviours. This observation contrasts sharply with the therapeutic orientation of Community Support Teams. While a considerable diversity exists with regards to the perceived utility of behavioural approaches compared with 'alternative' or 'creative' therapies, very few teams indeed appear to embrace biologically based interventions within their remit.

3.   The majority of Community Support Teams seek to provide a mix of technical and practical support to clients and their carers. Temporary practical support is included within the Community Support Team 'package' on the assumption that such provision may be essential, either indirectly (eg through providing respite for carers) or directly for the effective implementation of an intervention plan. Indeed, some preliminary results suggest that it is the provision of practical support by Community Support Teams that is most valued by carers (Bromley and Emerson, in press). Such a strategy may prove problematic, however, if the provision of external resources serves to significantly reduce demands on carers to develop new ways of working with the client. In such circumstances the withdrawal of the external support may be

associated with the re-emergence of the challenging behaviour, a phenomena familiar in Specialised Treatment Units upon client discharge (Newman and Emerson, 1991).

4. While many Community Support Teams possess some capacity for providing practical support, few have sufficient resources to respond effectively to crises requiring the injection of significant amounts of additional support in a setting. Indeed, many Community Support Teams do not consider crisis management to fall within their remit, rather crises are perceived as significant distractions from more 'proactive' activities.

Community Support Teams and placement development

While the activities of Community Support Teams may identify the inappropriateness of placements, few appear to be centrally involved in the actual processes of designing, commissioning and establishing alternatives. This would appear to largely reflect the marginalisation of Community Support Teams within service purchasing and providing organisations. Thus, while Community Support Teams may have specific operational links with other service components, these are primarily with other professional services, eg clinical psychology, Community Mental Handicap Teams, specialist treatment units.

CONCLUSIONS

The importance of organisational context

The analysis provided above suggests that while Community Support Teams may be effective in providing technical advice and practical support with regards to the implementation of interventions, a local comprehensive strategy for meeting the 'challenge' of challenging behaviour requires intervention on a number of fronts. Furthermore, unless local services are themselves efficient in the areas of prevention, early intervention, crisis management and placement development, Community Support Teams are likely to find that their effectiveness in their target areas will be significantly diminished. Thus, for example, in the absence of effective agency and systems-wide approaches to crisis identification and management, individually based interventions are likely to be undermined. Unless effective systems for developing alternative placements exist, the activities of

Community Support Teams may be restricted in many instances to identifying the deficiencies of existing placements and/or lead to teams devoting disproportionate resources to supporting intrinsically inappropriate placements or coping with placement breakdown, which itself will have implications for the perceived success of the service model. At a more local level deficiencies in service infrastructure for effectively managing staff performance in residential and day settings have considerable implications for the intensity and duration of agreed programmes of intervention.

In reality, of course, the organisational contexts framing team activities tend to be characterised by scarcity of resources, including skilled human resources, inflexibility in team working, structure and management, poorly developed service review and inadequate mechanisms for matching resources to individual needs. In short, the infrastructure lacks robustness in the critical areas of the early identification of emerging problems, systems for planning and monitoring staff and client activity, effective training strategies, devolved budgets and authority and a comprehensive approach to assessment and individual service planning.

These observations have a number of important implications. In particular they point to the constraining features of organisational context and operational remit upon the success of the Community Support Team model. Potentially there is scope to ensure the organisational model adopted fits with broader aspects of macro-organisation, such as service lead responsibilities (Knapp et al, 1992). Most Community Support Teams reflect unitary or lead agency arrangements, although there are some examples of semi-independent arrangements. If the potential benefits of Community Support Team services are to be maximised, it will be necessary for local planners, managers and funders to ensure that services are capable of effectively implementing agreed procedures within the context of a local strategy for challenging behaviour. The Community Support Team must be seen as just one component of such a strategy, with its organisational location and form designed to facilitate the efficient and effective achievement of its client level aims and service level goals. This necessitates an operational and functional mesh with other services and agencies and an appropriate repertoire of management and resource devices at the team level.

REFERENCES

ALLEN D, BANKS R AND STAITE S (Eds) (1991). *Meeting the Challenge: Some Perspectives On Community Services for People with Learning Difficulties and Challenging Behaviour.* London: King's Fund.

BAUMEISTER A A AND SEVIN J A (1990). Pharmacologic control of aberrant behaviour in the mentally retarded: Toward a more rational approach. *Neuroscience & Biobehavioral Reviews, 14,* 253- 262.

BLUNDEN R AND ALLEN D (Eds) (1987). *Facing the Challenge: An ordinary life for people with learning difficulties and challenging behaviours.* London: King's Fund.

BROMLEY J AND EMERSON E (in press). *Rising to the Challenge? Services Responses to Challenging Behaviour.* Manchester: Hester Adrian Research Centre.

BURCHESS I (1991). The Intensive Support Team, Kidderminster. IN D Allen, R Banks & S Staite (Eds) *Meeting the Challenge.* London: King's Fund.

CAMBRIDGE P(1992a). Questions for Case Management II. IN S Onyet & P Cambridge (Eds) *Case Management: Issues for Practice.* Canterbury: CAPSC/PSSRU, University of Kent at Canterbury.

CAMBRIDGE P (1992b). Case Management in Community Services: Organisational Responses, *British Journal of Social Work, 22,* 495-517

CHALLIS D AND DAVIES B (1986). *Case Management in Community Care.* Aldershot: Gower.

DEPARTMENT OF HEALTH (1989). *Caring for People.* London: HMSO.

DUNLAP G, JOHNSON L F AND ROBBINS F R (1990). Preventing serious behaviour problems through skill development and early interventions. In A C Repp & N N Singh (Eds) *Perspectives on the Use of Nonaversive and Aversive Interventions for Persons with Developmental Disabilities.* Sycamore, Illinois: Sycamore Publishing Company.

EMERSON E, CAMBRIDGE P AND HARRIS P (1991). *Evaluating the Challenge.* London: King's Fund.

EMERSON E, McGILL P AND MANSELL J (Eds) (in press). *Severe Learning Disabilities and Challenging Behaviours: Designing high quality services.* London: Chapman & Hall.

HILL-TOUT J, DOYLE T AND ALLEN D (1991). Challenging Behaviour Service, South Glamorgan. IN D Allen, R Banks & S Staite (Eds) *Meeting the Challenge.* London: King's Fund.

KNAPP M, CAMBRIDGE P, THOMPSON C, BEECHAM J, ALLEN C AND DARTON R (1992). *Care in the Community: Challenge and Demonstration.* Aldershot: PSSRU/Ashgate.

LOWE K, FELCE D AND ORLOWSKA D (in press). Evaluating services for people with challenging behaviour. IN I Flemming & B Stenfert-Kroese (Eds) *People with Severe Learning Difficulties who also Display Challenging Behaviours.* Manchester: Manchester University Press.

MANSELL J, McGILL P AND EMERSON E (in press, a). Conceptualising service provision. IN E Emerson, P McGill & J Mansell (Eds) *Severe Learning Disabilities and Challenging Behaviours: Designing high quality services.* London: Chapman & Hall.

MANSELL J, HUGHES H AND McGILL P(in press, b). Maintaining local residential placements. IN E Emerson, P McGill & J Mansell (Eds) *Severe Learning Disabilities and Challenging Behaviours: Designing high quality services.* London: Chapman & Hall.

MAUGHAN J (1991). The Family Support Team. IN D Allen, R Banks & S Staite (Eds) *Meeting the Challenge.* London: King's Fund.

McBRIEN J (in press). The Behavioural Support Team. IN E Emerson, P McGill & J Mansell (Eds) *Severe Learning Disabilities and Challenging Behaviours: Designing high quality services.* London: Chapman & Hall.

MURPHY G (in press). Understanding challenging behaviour. IN E Emerson, P McGill & J Mansell (Eds) *Severe Learning Disabilities and Challenging Behaviours: Designing high quality services.* London: Chapman & Hall.

NEWMAN I AND EMERSON E (1991). Specialist treatment units for people with challenging behaviours. *Mental Handicap, 19,* 113-119.

OLIVER C AND HEAD D (1990). Self-injurious behaviour in people with learning disabilities: determinants and interventions. *International Review of Psychiatry, 2,* 101-116.

QURESHI H (1990). Parents Caring for Young Adults with Mental Handicap and Behaviour Problems. Hester Adrian Research Centre: Manchester.

QURESHI H(in press). The size of the problem. IN E Emerson, P McGill & J Mansell (Eds) *Severe Learning Disabilities and Challenging Behaviours: Designing High Quality Services.* London: Chapman & Hall.

REPP A C AND SINGH N N (Eds) (1990). *Perspectives on the Use of Nonaversive and Aversive Interventions for Persons with Developmental Disabilities.* Sycamore, Illinois: Sycamore Publishing Company.

SOCIAL SERVICES INSPECTORATE (1991). *Care Management and Assessment: Managers Guide.* London: HMSO.

STAITE S (1991). The support team for people with challenging behaviour, Southmead Health Authority, Bristol. IN D Allen, R Banks & S Staite (Eds) *Meeting the Challenge.* London: King's Fund.

TOOGOOD S, BELL A, JACQUES H, LEWIS S AND SINCLAIR C (in press). Meeting the challenge in Clwyd: The first 30 months. *Mental Handicap:*

CHAPTER 11

SERVICE PROVISION FOR PEOPLE WITH MILD LEARNING DISABILITY AND CHALLENGING BEHAVIOURS: THE MIETS EVALUATION

Julie Dockrell, George Gaskell, Hamid Rehman and Charles Normand

INTRODUCTION

The closure of long-stay mental handicap hospitals has resulted in a range of new initiatives to cater for client needs (Kings Fund, 1980). The Mental Impairment Evaluation and Treatment Service (MIETS) was established by South East Thames Regional Health Authority (SETRHA) in 1987 to assist in the community placement of clients with mild learning disability and challenging behaviours. MIETS, serving the 15 Districts in SETRHA, complements the Special Development Team which provides services for clients with severe learning disability and challenging behaviour (see Emerson et al 1987, McGill and Mansell, Chapter 9).

MIETS is a ward, with 13 beds, situated at the Bethlem Royal Hospital. A multidisciplinary team offers psychiatric, clinical psychology, occupational therapy, social work and nursing inputs. The service was set up with the following aims and objectives:

(1) To provide a psychiatric assessment and treatment service for adults who have a mild learning disability and have serious behavioural and/or psychiatric disorders.

(2) To provide clinical information about clients in order to help local District Teams enable the person to participate as fully as possible in all aspects of daily life.

(3) Where appropriate to commence treatment or advise on the management of specific behavioural problems.

(4) Through contacts with the local teams during a client's admission, provide guidance and support which will allow the team to develop new expertise and knowledge.

THE EVALUATION

With the stated range of objectives covering Regional, District and individual needs, we adopted a systems perspective in the design of the evaluation. The need for such an approach, which views MIETS as part of a process, is highlighted by the position of MIETS in the intervention cycle as shown in Figure 1.

Districts referring a client to MIETS are required to set out specific questions concerning the client which they would like the Unit to

Figure 1   The Intervention cycle

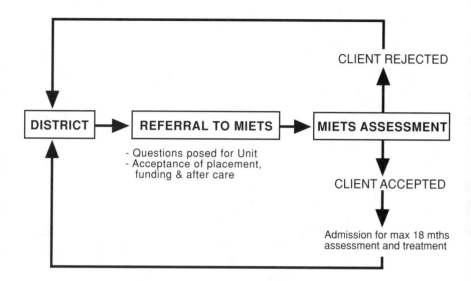

investigate. After a preliminary assessment of the client a quasi-contractual arrangement is agreed by the District Health Authority and MIETS. The client is admitted for a maximum stay of 18 months during which time MIETS investigates the agreed set of questions, the District funds the service and accepts responsibility for providing care following discharge.

The Unit's recommendations about the type of placement after discharge are advisory; it is the District Teams who decide on the actual placement. It is important to note that there are substantial differences across the Districts in SETRHA, in terms of their philosophy and provision of care, that influence both use of MIETS and the type of placements provided for clients following discharge from the Unit. Given that MIETS is part of a system, its activities must be put into the context of the other key elements within the system. This led to the formulation of three broad research questions:

i)   Is the MIETS unit meeting its own aims and objectives?

ii)   Is such a specialist service required by the Districts?

iii)   How successful is MIETS in contribution towards community placements for its clients?

To answer these questions the evaluation builds on a number of interrelated perspectives in four categories.

(1) The service users' views of MIETS
   * Interviews with District managers and senior clinicians (N=70).
   * Survey of direct care staff in Districts (N=213).
   * Interviews with clients (N=64).

(2) Changes in clients' behaviour and placements
   * Structured interviews with key workers.
   * Standard psychological tests (Vineland and ABS).

(3) In-house special services
   * Documentation of assessments and interventions in Unit.
   * Behavioural observations.

(4) Financial analysis
   * The cost of the MIETS services and other placements for the client group.

In addition to the analysis of levels one to four above, we have constructed some exemplary case studies and, by way of a synthesis of the above perspectives, an economic and policy analysis, which brings together the various elements of the evaluation to lead to policy implications.

CHALLENGING BEHAVIOUR

A definition

The King's Fund Report, *Facing the Challenge* (1987), quotes the Special Development Team's definition of challenging behaviour. For the SDT:

> "Severely challenging behaviour refers to behaviour of such intensity, frequency or duration that the physical safety of the person or others is likely to be placed in serious jeopardy, or behaviour which is likely to seriously limit or delay access to and frequent use of ordinary community facilities".

The first clause of this definition is quite specific, instancing "physical safety ... in serious jeopardy". The second clause is more general and open to a variety of interpretations.

It was apparent from the interviews with senior managers and clinicians in the Districts that the term covers a wide range of behaviours and that what is deemed to be challenging behaviour depends on a variety of factors such as the state of service development, eg staff skills and availability of local facilities in the District. When we interviewed managers and senior professionals in the Districts only a minority (11 per cent) of the interviewees found the term helpful. While the term challenging behaviour may define a problem, it does not articulate service needs or related provisions in a constructive or specific way.

In the survey of direct care staff in the District Teams, we looked to see if there was any agreement as to what constitutes challenging behaviour. The behaviours included in the questionnaire were derived from the District interviews, reports from MIETS staff and a review of the relevant literature (eg Harris and Russell, 1989). There were 24 items and respondents were asked the frequency and level of difficulty posed by each behaviour.

The analysis of the responses indicates that challenging behaviour covers two quite different types of behaviour. This leads us to propose a distinction between 'problem' and 'dangerous' behaviours. Table 1 presents the key results.

Table 1   Problem and Dangerous Behaviours

PROBLEM BEHAVIOURS	DANGEROUS BEHAVIOURS
• Frequent • Posing few serious problems	• Infrequent • Posing serious problems • Often within purview of the Criminal Justice System
EXAMPLES	**EXAMPLES**
• Verbal Abuse • Pestering • Defecating/Smearing • Throwing Things • Exposing Self	• Physical Violence • SIB • Arson • Sexual Abuse • Attempts at Suicide

As the Table illustrates problem behaviours tend to be frequently experienced but pose few serious difficulties. Dangerous behaviours are qualitatively different and fit into the first clause of the SDT's definition. These behaviours pose serious difficulties for the Districts but are relatively infrequent. Many such dangerous behaviours come within the purview of the criminal justice system and, as such, reflect a societal and consensual definition of the unacceptable. Seventy percent of the clients included in the MIETS evaluation were referred for some form of dangerous behaviour; only 12 per cent were referred for problem behaviour (88 per cent of the clients had two or more referral questions posed).

The extent of the problem

An initial focus of our study was to determine (1) the extent to which people with such challenging behaviours pose problems for the District Teams, and (2) whether there was a need for a MIETS type service. We pursued three lines of inquiry into the scope of the problem facing the Districts. Firstly, we looked at the pattern of admissions to see whether they were drawn from a cross section of Districts or whether, perhaps, MIETS was serving only a minority of the Districts. In terms of referrals, 13 of the 15 Districts had at least one client admitted to MIETS suggesting that the Unit is meeting a common problem facing the greater majority of the District Teams.

The second approach to assessing the scope of the problem involved a postal survey to each of the District Health Authorities. We asked a senior manager or a clinician for the number of clients fitting the MIETS criteria who were resident within District facilities and the number in out-of-District placements. In addition to this we also obtained details from the Regional mental handicap hospital of the number of clients with mild learning disabilities and challenging behaviours resident there and awaiting discharge to the Districts.

All the Districts responded to our request but it was necessary to exclude two of the 15 Districts from this analysis because they were unable to supply figures differentiating between mild and severe learning disabilities. In responding many of the other Districts alluded to problems with the questions posed due to lack of information and the uncertainties regarding the definition of challenging behaviour. We also found that some Districts were not aware of their clients in the Regional mental handicap hospital.

During the period July to September 1990 there were 11 clients in MIETS; 122 clients in the care of DHAs, consortium agreements or Social Services;

18 in the Regional mental handicap hospital not acknowledged by Districts and 52 in facilities outside the Districts. Of the 52 clients outside the Districts many were in private hospitals. From the District reports we estimate that, in each District, there was an average of 9.3 clients fitting the MIETS criteria within local facilities, excluding MIETS but including the Regional mental handicap hospital, and there were 5.2 clients in out-of - District placements.

Whilst this survey was not intended to be an epidemiological study, but rather an indication of the extent of the problem presented by challenging behaviour, it has established the gap between the capabilities of the Districts and the demands placed upon their resources.

Thirdly we asked Districts about their need for challenging behaviour services for this client group. Nearly 50 per cent noted a gap in providing services for this client group; they acknowledged both a lack of expertise and a lack of trained staff as being critical factors. Moreover, many reported that referrals to MIETS reflected the lack of local provisions to cater for individual needs. Many emphasised that MIETS was a useful service with which to have access.

Thus we have established that clients with mild learning disability and challenging behaviour are presenting problems for the majority of Districts; that the MIETS service is used by almost all the Districts in SETRHA; and that the majority of the clients are referred for dangerous behaviours. To this extent SETRHA, in setting up MIETS, was responding to a common problem beyond the capabilities of the District Teams.

THE MIETS UNIT

In our initial interviews it became clear that MIETS fulfils a range of service functions for the Districts within SETRHA (Dockrell et al, 1990). Recent referrals to the Unit suggest that many Districts still continue to require some form of specialist input for clients exhibiting dangerous behaviours. In this section we describe the types of services offered by the MIETS unit.

Assessments and interventions in the Unit

Detailed information from the clients' files was collected to identify assessments and interventions carried out in the Unit. Just under a half of the clients who enter MIETS are given a specific series of assessments. The

Unit's experiences highlighted the need to assess for the presence of mental illness, to establish the extent of the learning disability and identify future placement needs.

Figure 2   Assessments provided at MIETS

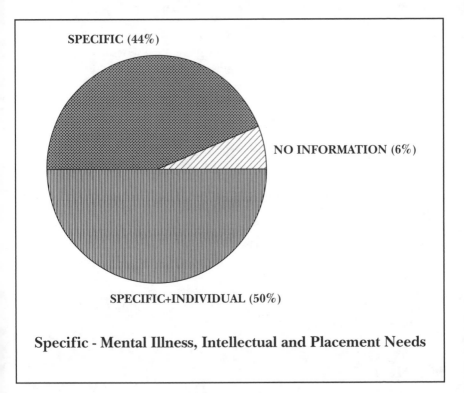

SPECIFIC (44%)

NO INFORMATION (6%)

SPECIFIC+INDIVIDUAL (50%)

Specific - Mental Illness, Intellectual and Placement Needs

As Figure 2 shows, 44 per cent of clients received this special assessment. Some 50 per cent of clients have the special package plus individually tailored assessments. Such assessments include sexual knowledge and interests, or fire-setting or the level of dangerousness. It is of note that 65 per cent of the clients were assessed as mentally ill; thus many clients experience both a learning disability and a mental illness.

Figure 3 shows the types of interventions conducted by the Unit. These interventions are directed towards the problems identified during assessment.

Figure 3   Interventions provided at MIETS

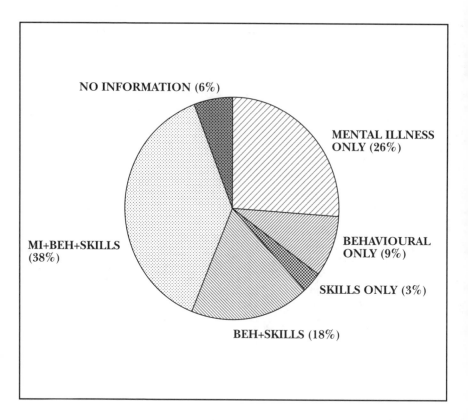

The clients daily routine at MIETS

To establish the nature of the client activities and interactions in the Unit a selected group of clients were observed over an eight hour blocked session. The eight hours (8am - 4pm) were spread over four consecutive days. A computerized technique (Beasley et al, 1989) was modified to meet the needs of the MIETS population. Clients' behaviour was recorded at 30 second intervals. Three broad categories of behaviour were observed and recorded at each observation point; activities, social interaction and challenging behaviour. The categories were further subdivided into target behaviours and the presence of each behaviour recorded at the 30 second interval. In addition to the above, the numbers of staff and other clients in the presence of the observed client were noted at every five minute interval.

Figure 4   Daily Activities - Average of eight client observations (8am - 4pm)

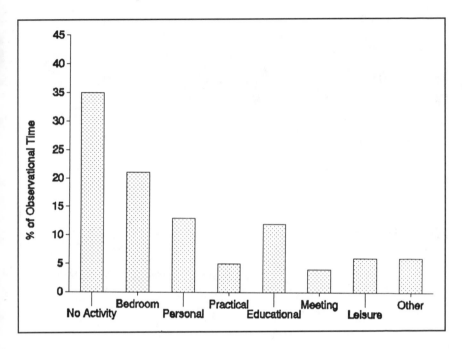

As Figure 4 demonstrates, the majority of clients' time is spent either not actively engaged or in their bedroom. So despite the intense level of assessments and interventions described previously, only 16 per cent of the average clients' time is spent on therapeutic activities (education and meetings).

Although clients are not engaged in any formal activity for a large proportion of the day, it may be the case that social interaction with staff, or the mere presence of staff, may act in a therapeutic manner. The results, however, do not indicate a high level of interaction.

Figure 5 shows that staff/client interaction occurs for 31 per cent of the time whilst client/client interaction occurs for only 11 per cent of the time. For 67 per cent of the time on the Unit clients have no verbal contact with either staff or other clients. When we look at the presence of staff we find that staff are in the company of clients for only 43 per cent of the time.

Figure 5   Social Interaction
               Mean percentage time for eight clients

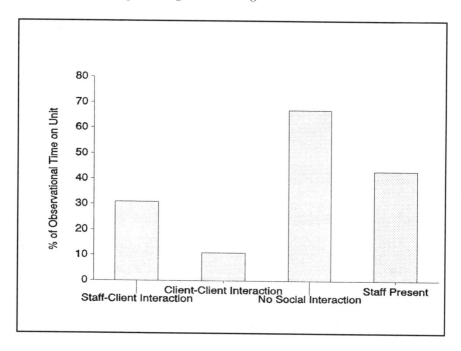

The above findings were rather surprising for us given the very high staff/client ratio within the Unit. We thought it might be the case that the minimal social interaction occurring between staff and clients may be occurring when the client is not actively occupied in any constructive activity. In other words if most of the social interaction occurs when the clients are not actively engaged it could be argued that the client's day is partly filled with activities and partly with interaction with staff which could be of equal therapeutic value. However, Figure 6 does not support this hypothesis.

Looking at the no activity period we find that social interaction between staff and clients occurs for only 26 per cent of the time. For the greater majority of the period of no activity there is no social engagement.

These behavioural observations do not depict an environment of intensive engagement and involvement. Rather they reflect what might be observed in a typical ward situation. For the majority of the day clients are on their own in an unstructured and unfocussed environment.

Figure 6   Social Interaction During No Activity
Mean percentage time for eight clients

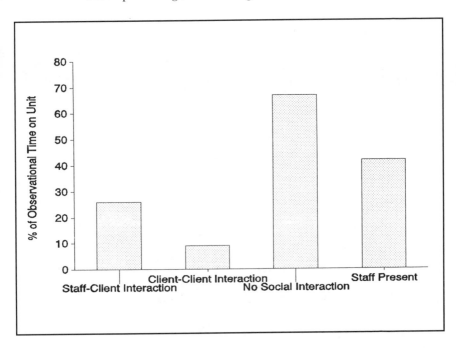

Our personal experience of the Unit leads us to conclude that the staff's involvement with clients revolves around three main areas: routine activities, eg feeding, giving out medication; programme implementation; and crisis intervention. Outside of these three areas, during the day at least, staff do not generally initiate social contact with clients. This, as we demonstrated above, leads to clients being isolated for much of the day.

Length of stay at MIETS

When MIETS was set up, a maximum admission of 18 months was built into the contracts with the Districts. We find that the duration of admission has decreased over the life of the Unit. The mean length of stay has declined from 14.2 months for the first 12 referrals to 13.7 months for the next 11 and to 12.4 months for the final 11. This progressive reduction reflects both the development of skills within the Unit and the speed with which the Districts find placements for those ready for discharge. However, some clients have spent much longer in the Unit, often due to the failure of Districts to set up appropriate placements.

WHAT MIETS ACHIEVED: THE VIEW FROM THE DISTRICTS

In our interviews with District Managers and senior clinical staff, we asked them to comment on the effectiveness of MIETS drawing upon their experience of discharged clients. MIETS is widely recognised for its professionalism and concentration of specialist services that many Districts lack. Over 50 per cent thought that the clients' behaviour had improved; 66 per cent felt that the problem behaviours were better understood; 50 per cent thought they were better able to manage the difficult behaviour; 46 per cent considered that the prospects for community living were better. Having said this, there are criticisms of MIETS. There is a view that the Unit is similar to an institution and thereby very removed from community services. This leads to concerns about the generalizability to community settings of the work done in the Unit. But in practice, when asked to reflect on specific clients, the senior District staff were on the whole positive about outcomes.

We followed up these assessments with a series of more specific questions in the survey of direct care staff. Figures 7 and 8 present the results.

Figure 7   The Impact of MIETS Assessments and Interventions Districts' views of MIETS provisions

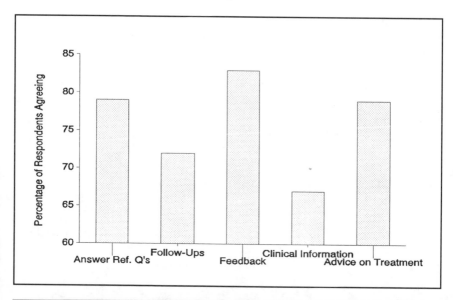

Figure 8   Implementing MIETS Recommendations - Districts' views

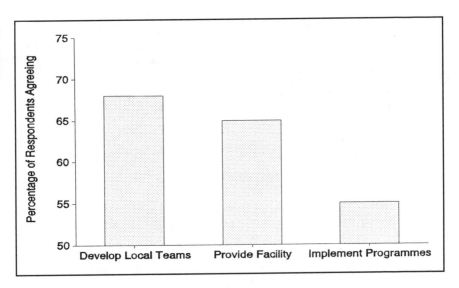

These figures, drawing on only those with experience of a client discharged from MIETS, are necessarily based on small numbers. However, they do convey a generally positive assessment of the work of the Unit. Thus investigating the referral questions, giving clinical information, advice on treatment and feedback during admission, helping the local teams develop skills and following up on the clients after discharge, are perceived to have been achieved by a substantial majority. Of note however, is that only 55 per cent thought they were able to implement the programmes recommended by MIETS and 65 per cent that they were able to provide the type of facility that was recommended for the client. In some respects, these latter two aspects demonstrate the gap between the specialist services offered by MIETS and the capacities of the Districts to carry through the work following the discharge of the client.

DOES MIETS CONTRIBUTE TO COMMUNITY PLACEMENTS FOR CLIENTS?

A range of residential options exist for individuals with learning disabilities and challenging behaviour. In this section we consider the different types of living opportunities offered to clients in SETRHA. We have details of pre-admission placements (origins) and placements at three and six months post discharge from MIETS (destinations) for 34 clients. The destination at six months post-discharge is our final point of contact with the client and the care worker.

There are three types of local facilities currently used in SETRHA:

*   Hospital homes - small to medium sized units in the grounds of an NHS hospital.

*   Campus homes - homes for about six clients located in centres for community learning disability services.

*   Community homes - homes for three to four clients in residential streets.

Table 2 sets out the origins and destinations of the 34 clients. In terms of origins it can be seen that clients come from a range of establishments varying in levels of security.

Table 2   Origin and Destination of Clients

Origin	Destination (at 6 months)						
	Prison	Private/ Special Hospital	Hospital	Hospital Home	Campus Home	Commu -nity Home	Own/ Parental Home
Prison (7)	1	1	1		2	2	
Private/Special Hospital (9)		3	1		2	3	
NHS Hospital (13)		1	1	3	2	2	4
Breakdown Campus/ Community/Own/ Parental Home (5)		2			1	1	1
	1	7	3	3	7	8	5
		11		3		20	

As can be seen, 20 out of 34 clients referred to MIETS achieved a community placement maintained for at least six months post-discharge. Thus 59 per cent of the clients were successfully integrated into community placements.

Some further comments on this table of origins and destinations are of relevance. Seven of the 14 clients who were not discharged into community placements went to placements which were not recommended by MIETS. In four cases they went to NHS hospitals or to private hospitals because the Districts were unable to provide suitable community placements. In a further three cases, all in one District, and not withstanding a recommendation for a community placement, clients went to a hospital home, presumably a policy decision in the District. To this extent the effectiveness of the Unit in terms of facilitating community placements is in part dependent on the ability and willingness of the Districts to provide such facilities. But we must reflect a view expressed by some District managers. MIETS recommendations were occasionally seen as unrealistic if the placement specified was not available or the programmes developed in the Unit difficult to implement in the community. If these Districts had been able to make community placements available, the rate of integration of MIETS clients into the community would have been almost 80 per cent.

VARIETIES OF COMMUNITY CARE AND QUALITY OF LIFE OPPORTUNITIES.

A stated objective of MIETS is to help District Teams enable a client to participate as fully as possible in daily life. For 32 out of 34 clients, ie 94 per cent, MIETS recommended a high service intensity community placement. But, as has been seen in the analysis of origins and destinations, how this recommendation is acted upon depends on the District's priorities, skills and the facilities available.

There is at present no consensus on a clear definition of quality of life (Landesman, 1986). However we have taken a few measures which we feel are indicative of an ordinary life. Using information taken from the interviews with key workers and details of the staffing from the financial questionnaire, we scored each placement type on six quality of life criteria.

The criteria were:

  * Personal privacy - own or shared bedroom;

* Choice/autonomy - free access to facilities in the establishment;

* Participation in domestic activities - cooking, cleaning, etc;

* Freedom - whether establishment locked or not, freedom to make visits outside;

* Access to neighbourhood - proximity to local shopping area;

* Use of community facilities - frequency of use of cinemas, swimming pools, etc.

A comparative scaling approach allowed us to categorise low, medium or high on each of the measures. Scores of low, medium or high and the staff/client ratios for the daytime are shown in Table 3. From the table it can be seen that, within our criteria for quality of life opportunities, the community home comes closest to 'an ordinary life' with the provision of greater privacy, freedom and access to neighbourhood.

A financial analysis of these care strategies was conducted using the 1989/90 accounts and a detailed questionnaire covering all aspects of capital and revenue expenditure. As far as possible our calculations included all elements in the cost structures to ensure that a 'level playing field' was

Table 3   Quality of Life Opportunities

	COMMUNITY PLACEMENTS		
QUALITY OF LIFE CRITERIA	Hospital Home	Campus Home	Community Home
Day time staff/client ratio	0.3:1	0.45:1	0.75:1
Personal Privacy	LOW	LOW	HIGH
Choice/Autonomy	MEDIUM	HIGH	HIGH
Participation in Domestic Activities	MEDIUM	HIGH	HIGH
Freedom/Level of Security	MEDIUM	MEDIUM	HIGH
Access to Neighbourhood	LOW	MEDIUM	HIGH
Use of Community Facilities	LOW	HIGH	HIGH

established for comparative purposes. As can be seen in Table 4 below, the cost per client/year in hospital, campus and community homes is £27,000, £36,000 and £64,000 respectively.

Table 4   Cost (per client year) and Quality of Life

Hospital Home **£27,000**	**Campus Home** **£36,000**	**Community Home** **£64,000**
PROVIDES	BUYS MORE	BUYS MORE
- Little Personal Privacy - Little Access to Neighbourhood - Little Use of Community Facilities - Medium Level of Choice/Autonomy - Medium Level of Participation in Domestic Activities - Medium Level of Freedom	- Staff - Choice/Autonomy - Participation in Domestic Activities - Access to Neighbourhood - Use of Community Facilities	- Staff - Privacy - Freedom - Access to Neighbourhood

These costs are based on two examples of hospital homes, two community homes and one campus home. Each example was catering specifically for individuals with learning disabilities and challenging behaviour. Since the annual cost and quality of life are closely associated Table 4 also shows what extra opportunities are purchased with the £9,000 moving from hospital to campus homes and with the additional £28,000 moving from the campus to community home.

It is evident from these cost figures that implementing the idea of community care for this client group involves high service intensity and commensurately high costs. The major element in these additional sums is the higher staff/client ratios which provide the wherewithal for these clients to pursue an increasing range of 'ordinary life' type activities and for care staff to give more individual programme planning.

In the campus home there are a number of reasons why costs are lower than in the community home. For example the former, by virtue of their location, have ready access to specialist learning disability services which are more expensive to provide in a community home setting. Such considerations might point to the campus home as an acceptable trade-off between cost and quality of life. However, if clients are to adjust to a life in the community, it may be both necessary and desirable to start with a high intensity service, progressively reducing the staff/client ratio as the client becomes more socially competent. While a campus home may prepare clients only for a campus life, the community home may prepare clients for either low service intensity support or eventual 'discharge' from the District's services.

FINANCIAL ANALYSIS

We have established that, of the 34 clients of MIETS, 20 were discharged to community placements and three to a hospital home. Of the remaining 11, one went to prison and 10 to NHS, private or special hospitals. We have also seen that the high service intensity environment of the community home is, as would be expected, associated with high costs. The next question to be considered concerns the financial implications of the MIETS service. What is the aggregate level of expenditure involved for the clients as a group and how does this compare with alternative provisions? Let us consider three models.

Model I. MIETS plus achieved destination

As we have argued, MIETS is not an end in itself but rather a means to a desirable end, that of achieving, where feasible, community placements for clients. As such, MIETS can be viewed as an investment on the part of the Districts (with support from SETRHA), an intensive and high cost short term intervention designed to achieve a better quality of life for clients. For this analysis the costs have been calculated over a six year period; a little over a year in assessment and intervention at MIETS and about five years in post-MIETS placement. On this basis, we can estimate the total expenditure for the 34 clients; an average of 13 months in MIETS, plus four years 11 months in their achieved destinations. On this basis the total cost is £9,200,000.

Model II. Continuing care in the original placements.

A basis for comparison requires us to make certain assumptions. A parsimonious approach is to take the original placements of the clients, where they were at the time of referral to MIETS, and to calculate the costs for a six year period. In other words, had MIETS not existed, then this comparison figure is based on the assumption that clients would have stayed where they were. For the 34 clients this amounts to £7,300,000.

Overall, it can be seen that the expenditure involved in Model I at £9,200,000 is some 25 per cent more than the cost of maintaining the clients in their original placements in Model II. Our choice of a six year comparison period is somewhat arbitrary. MIETS, at a cost of £80,000 per client for 13 months, adds considerably to the costs of the achieved placements. This can be seen in table 5, which looks at average costs per client.

Table 5   Average Costs of Different Care Packages

MODEL I	Investment in 13 months stay in MIETS - cost £80,000	Post MIETS placement cost - £38,700 per client year
MODEL II	No investment in interventions - cost £35,000	Continuing in original placement - cost £35,000 per client year

This shows that, while MIETS is a high cost service, on discharge the average cost of clients per year is within an additional 10 per cent per annum of their original placements.

Model III. Other alternatives to MIETS.

Given that many clients were referred to MIETS as a result of a breakdown in their original placement, a breakdown that was often described as a crisis, the assumption underlying Model II, that the clients would have stayed for six years in this placement, is questionable. For some clients we ascertained what alternatives the District Teams had considered but we have insufficient information to cover the sample. We therefore offer Model III which shows at 1989/90 prices the costs of various placements used or considered by the Districts for people with dangerous behaviours.

For our sample a treatment in MIETS plus the remainder of the six years in the achieved destinations amounts to £45,100 per client per year, a figure which, while more costly than prison or an NHS hospital, is about the same

Table 6   Alternatives to a MIETS Placement - Cost per client year

Private Hospital	£52,000
Special Hospital	£44,300
NHS Hospital	£32,000
Prison	£25,000

as a special hospital and about £7,000 less than the private sector hospitals. It is of note that during the course of this evaluation the private sector expanded considerably suggesting that Districts are making greater use of this option as the availability of NHS hospital beds declined. NHS hospitals are unlikely to be a long term option given their planned closure.

Returning to the original basis for comparison we can draw some conclusions about the financial implications of a specialist service such as MIETS. Overall, the achieved placements are more costly than the previous packages. For approximately 25 per cent additional expenditure, 22 out of 34 clients moved to less constrained placements and a further three who had been referred following a breakdown in a community placement were subsequently discharged to the community. Such achievements in terms of improved quality of life for many clients appear to us to justify the extra expenditure but, of course, this is a subjective assessment. What can be said with confidence is that MIETS achieved a better quality of life for clients at a great cost. If community care is to be implemented as a policy, it is necessary to recognise the financial implications.

OVERVIEW AND IMPLICATIONS

Our overview of this evaluation of the MIETS unit is divided into three sections:

* An assessment of the MIETS unit;
* The viability of community care;
* Policy implications.

The MIETS Unit

The MIETS unit is widely acknowledged for its sophistication in the assessment and treatment of clients with mild learning disabilities and serious challenging behaviour. Those Districts that have referred clients to the Unit are positive about the work done with clients. Following a period at MIETS, almost 60 per cent of clients achieved a community placement that was maintained for at least six months. Sixty five per cent of clients moved to a less constrained placement and a further nine per cent were returned to community placements following a referral after breakdown.

However, there are some qualifications to this generally positive assessment. If the Unit is to collaborate effectively with the Districts to help clients its recommendations about placements and service levels must be realistic in terms of what is achievable. Secondly, while the average length of admission has declined, is an average of thirteen months necessary? We know that many of the longer admissions were due to the failure of some Districts to make available appropriate placements. In such circumstances, the MIETS professionals have been prepared to extend the period of admission rather than see clients move to unsuitable placements. An alternative strategy would be to set a more stringent admission period. The provision of more intensive evaluations and treatments would have to be combined with a greater willingness in some Districts to make available appropriate placements. In part we base this recommendation to shorten the length of admission on the results of the behavioural observations. Clients are not sufficiently engaged in therapeutic activities, nor is staff/client interaction at a high level of intensity. During the working day, when staff/client ratios are at the highest, more could be done to prepare many clients for the requirements of care in the community and to offset the problems of generalizability from an institutional setting to community placements. But if what we have observed at MIETS is almost an inevitable consequence of an institutional setting it raises the question as to whether other approaches would be more successful. Should specialist services be located in a hospital at all? Would a more community or campus based unit promote an organisational ethos of a different and more desirable kind?

The viability of community care

With the closure of the long stay mental handicap hospitals, MIETS was set up to provide a specialist service to facilitate community placements for a group of clients who presented considerable difficulties for the District Teams. It is likely that, without the specialist services offered by MIETS, many of its clients would have ended up, or remained, in prison or in special or private hospitals. The Unit and the District Teams have demonstrated that community care is a viable option for many people with challenging behaviours which are dangerous.

With stabilization of medication and individually tailored packages for the management of behavioural problems, the Unit has demonstrated success in achieving discharges into community care. But, at the same time, some clients have presented challenges that defeated the experts in the Unit. There are a small number of clients who will need long term, probably secure care.

One of the more surprising findings to emerge from the monitoring of the post-MIETS placements is that five clients were living 'at home' with families supported by local services six months after discharge. This finding is not so remarkable when we consider the practices in one District in SETRHA. Here clients referred to the District Team are given a short term crisis intervention package. Where the package is successful, the clients are then found sheltered work supervised by trained staff and regularly monitored by the clinical professionals. A market garden was set up for such employment and the clients paid a reasonable wage drawing on both "profits" and government sources. Real work is seen as a part of the therapeutic process, building up clients' self esteem; an approach which is well supported by social psychological analyses of work and unemployment. Some clients have further progressed to lodgings in the community or returned to their homes. Thus, for some clients, this is a feasible option, one which is clearly supported by the data on post-MIETS placements. This again argues for a range of service provisions tailored to the capabilities of the clients. Of course, sheltered work settings are not easy to establish, particularly in difficult economic times. But, given the range of costs of community care facilities, it would seem to be justified for Districts to explore such opportunities on both economic and therapeutic grounds.

Policy implications

The key question is whether specialist services continue to be required for people with mild learning disability and dangerous behaviours. Our evidence strongly suggests that many of the Districts in SETRHA are not in a position to achieve community care placements for some in this client group without additional specialist inputs. The Districts are still referring clients to MIETS and are sending clients into private sector hospitals. Furthermore, the profile of the client group is changing. Increasingly, clients are coming, not from NHS hospitals, but from various community settings, including the Courts. The client group will continue to pose many problems for the District Teams and, without specialist inputs, the likelihood of achieving community placements is small. There is also the small number of clients for whom MIETS could do little to help them progress to local services. Thus the issue becomes: what are the options for the provision of short to medium term specialist services to support the District Teams? The requirements common to a number of Districts but not necessarily shared by all are for:

* specialist psychiatric inputs,

* specialist psychological inputs,

* a safe environment,

* highly trained staff,

* links to District Teams,

* fast response to crises,

* a task force function.

In principle, such services could be organised at either the Regional level, eg a MIETS type unit with developments, or as a unit shared between three or four Districts or within each District. Some of the Districts in our survey favoured the latter solution but, rather than opt for one particular model, we recommend the development of a range of provisions. It seems unlikely that every District could justify the expenditure to cover the required services and indeed the availability of professional staff is problematic. At an entirely Regional level it is hard to see how the Districts' needs could be catered for adequately. A mix of service provisions responsive to the District's requirements and ready to adapt to developments in the Districts and in the client group seems the most desirable option.

The second issue concerns the provision of longer term community placements. We have seen that there is a trade off between the quality of life achieved and the cost involved. Hospital homes are cheaper than campus homes and campus homes are cheaper than community homes, but the more costly the placement the more it is likely to offer greater opportunities to pursue an ordinary life. Experience with community homes for this client group is relatively limited; it is possible that, over time, clients will require lower service intensity; an issue for further research.

CONCLUSION

This evaluation has shown that with the help of specialist services, such as those brought together in the MIETS unit, the District Teams can move many clients with mild learning disabilities and serious challenging behaviours into community placements. This is undoubtedly a substantial achievement. But we have identified some weaknesses in both the 'special unit' approach and in the Districts themselves. For this system to operate more effectively and to maximise 'ordinary life' opportunities for this client group, there is a need for comprehensive policies at District and supra-District levels.

REFERENCES

BEASLEY F, HEWSON S AND MANSELL J (1989). MTS: Handbook for observers. University of Kent at Canterbury, Centre for the Applied Psychology of Social Care.

EMERSON E, BARRETT S, BELL C, CUMMINGS R, TOOGOOD A AND MANSELL J (1987). Developing services for people with severe learning difficulties and challenging behaviours. University of Kent at Canterbury, Institute of Social and Applied Psychology.

DOCKRELL J, GASKELL G AND REHMAN H (1990). Challenging behaviours: problems, provisions and 'solutions'. IN Dosen A, Van Gennep A, Zwanikken G J (Eds) (1990) *Treatment of mental illness and behavioural disorder in the mentally retarded*. Leiden, the Netherlands: Logon Publications.

HARRIS P AND RUSSELL O (1989). The prevalence of aggressive behaviour among people with learning difficulties (mental handicap) in a single health authority: Interim report. University of Bristol: Norah Fry Research Centre.

KING'S FUND CENTRE (1980). *An Ordinary Life: comprehensive locally-based residential services for mentally handicapped people.* London: King's Fund.

KING'S FUND CENTRE (1987). *Facing the Challenge: An ordinary life for people with learning difficulties and challenging behaviour.* London: King's Fund.

LANDESMAN S (1986). Quality of life and personal life satisfaction: Definition and measurement issues. *Mental Retardation, 24,* 141-143.

PART 5

STAFF TRAINING

CHAPTER 12

WORKING WITH PARENTS: THE MANAGEMENT OF SLEEP DISTURBANCE IN CHILDREN WITH LEARNING DISABILITIES

Lyn Quine

INTRODUCTION

Sleep disturbance is a widespread form of challenging behaviour which affects families bringing up both handicapped and non-handicapped children. Many children have disturbed sleeping patterns (Richman, 1981a). Studies have estimated that up to 20 per cent of two year old children and 14 per cent of three year old children wake regularly during the night (Richman et al, 1975, Jenkins et al, 1980, Jenkins, Owen et al, 1984). In the Isle of Wight survey, Rutter et al, (1970) found that even at ten to 12 years old up to 20 per cent of children are regarded by their parents as having problems of this nature. Night-time difficulties are known to be associated with maternal distress and with daytime behavioural difficulties (Richman, 1981a, 1981b).

Young people with severe learning disabilities seem to be particularly likely to present sleep problems (Bartlett et al, 1985, Clements et al, 1986, Quine, 1991). Bartlett et al (1985), in a study of 214 children with severe learning disabilities under 16 years of age, found that 86 per cent of those under six years old, 81 per cent of six to 11 year olds, and 77 per cent of the 12 to 16 year olds were reported by parents as having sleep problems: 56 per cent woke on average once a night, 53 per cent had difficulty getting the child to go to bed and 56 per cent in settling the child.

An earlier study by the author (Quine, 1991) found in a first interview that 51 per cent of a sample of children with severe learning disabilities (aged 0-16) had night settling problems, 67 per cent had night waking problems, and 32 per cent of parents reported that they did not get enough sleep. At a second interview three years later it was found that all three problems were remarkably persistent. Of the children who had settling problems, almost half still had problems three years later, while of the children who had waking problems over two thirds still had them. The children who were most likely to present sleep problems were those with poor communication skills. Mothers of such children showed high levels of stress. They were also more likely to engage in certain behavioural patterns towards their child at night. We called these 'maternal responsiveness'. Such mothers were more likely to attend to the child immediately at night by offering drinks, cuddles and attention. They were less likely to allow the child to cry for a few minutes, to play music to help settle the child, or to read him/her a bedtime story. We speculated that maternal responsiveness might have the effect of initially encouraging and then maintaining sleep problems, while limited communication skills might make it harder for parents to train such children to present more appropriate bedtime behaviour.

Our next step was to consider methods of treatment for sleep problems. Although widely used, night sedation appears to be of limited value for managing sleep problems in children with severe learning disabilities, and there is some evidence that hypnotic drugs may actually be inappropriate since their use is associated with REM sleep suppression, which has been found to be already impoverished in this particular group (Kales, Allen et al, 1970, Kales, Kales et al, 1975, Clausen et al, 1977, Grubar, 1983). However, we had come across a number of studies in the literature that suggested that the use of behavioural approaches offered promise in the management of sleep disturbance, and that parents could be effective teachers of their own children at home (Jones and Verduyn, 1983, Cunningham, 1985, Hewitt, 1985, Richman, Douglas et al, 1985, Bidder et al, 1986). We therefore considered training health professionals who regularly have contact with young children in behavioural approaches to sleep disturbance. We decided to develop and test a cascade model of training that would make efficient use of scarce professional resources and would recognize the important role of parents as co-therapists and teachers. The approach makes the assumption that parental involvement in therapy will benefit both child and parents, either directly as a result of enhancing parental management, teaching and interactive skills, or indirectly by improving family functioning through support and counselling (Cunningham, 1985).

AIMS OF THE STUDY

The aims of the study were twofold:

1. to develop and evaluate a three day training course for health professionals in the use of behavioural approaches to the management of sleep disturbance

2. to set up an intervention trial with 25 families to assess whether training health professionals to teach behavioural techniques to parents is effective in reducing children's sleep disturbance.

DESIGN AND METHODOLOGY

Evaluating the effectiveness of training health professionals to teach parents behavioural approaches to the management of sleep disturbance was therefore carried out in two stages:

i) the development and evaluation of a three day course in behavioural approaches to sleep disturbance for health professionals.

ii) an intervention trial in which 12 trained health visitors and community nurses worked with a group of 25 families who had a child with both learning disabilities and sleep disturbance.

Procedures for organising and evaluating the training course

The study was carried out with the full co-operation and active support of Medway District Health Authority. Twelve health professionals - seven health visitors, one community nurse, two district nurses and two school nurses - from various areas of the health district were seconded to the research team for the course of the study. The anticipation was that the professionals would be relieved of at least part of their normal workload. The selected staff had not had professional contact with any of the families before, so all families started from the same base. The researchers worked closely alongside the health visitors/community nurses, supervising, advising and monitoring the parents' training programme.

Training staff in behavioural approaches to sleep disturbance

The 12 health professionals attended an introductory course on behavioural approaches to sleep disturbance which was held one day a week for three weeks at the University. The course was staggered for two reasons; firstly to facilitate assimilation and learning and secondly for practical purposes, since it was difficult for professionals to be absent from their normal work for three full days in one week. A further day was convened one week after the end of the course for the details of the intervention trial to be discussed and the research materials and sleep diaries handed out. The course was taught by an educational and a social psychologist, both of whom were qualified teachers, and a clinical psychologist. Details of the course units and exercises can be obtained from the researchers.

During the course the health professionals built up a personal reference manual. Each professional was given a hard backed ring binder containing transparent envelopes. For each component of the course or group activity a card containing the main points of teaching and space for notes, comments and answers was provided which could be slipped into one of the plastic envelopes. In addition, for the evaluation trial, health professionals were supplied with standard format interview schedules for carrying out the initial behavioural interview with parents, progress assessment sheets, sleep diaries and sleep management contract forms on which the agreed sleep programme could be summarised and signed by parents and health professionals.

The course was evaluated by administration of a pre and post course test of Knowledge of Behavioural Principles as Applied to Children (KBPAC) (O'Dell et al, 1979).

Procedures for organising and evaluating the intervention trial

Sample selection

The intervention trial took place in the Medway health district. All the Medway schools, social education centres, and child assessment and care centres that ran playgroups for pre-school children with learning disabilities were approached and asked to send a letter home to parents (examples of all documentation can be found in Quine and Wade, 1991). The letter contained details of the study and offered places on the programme to parents. Forty families initially expressed interest in taking part in the study, and 25 families (63 per cent) completed programmes. These families formed the experimental group. All fulfilled the criteria we had selected for eligibility for inclusion in the study. These were one of the following: night settling problems - usually three or more times a week; night waking - usually three or more times a week; limited hours' sleep - usually three or more times a week. Table 1 shows the dropout from the study.

The children who finally received treatment were a highly selected group. It is quite possible that there was a bias in the families who expressed interest initially, and of those, 65 per cent entered treatment. This compares with 50 per cent in the study of non-handicapped children by Richman et al (1985). Although our previous studies found no sex differences in the prevalence of sleep problems, almost twice as many boys as girls entered the programme. In addition, there was considerable marital unhappiness and maternal irritability in the treatment group. It is interesting to speculate whether factors relating to marital unhappiness and maternal irritability were influential in the parents' decision to seek treatment for the child.

Design

A single-case experimental design with multiple baseline across subjects was

Table 1   Dropout from study

DROPOUT FROM STUDY

40 families expressed interest

- ■ 25 (63%) completed programmes
- ■ 1 dropped out during programme
- ■ 14 dropped out before intervention began
  - ● 3 had family problems
  - ● 1 child went into residential care
  - ● 1 child went into phased care
  - ● 1 child went into foster care
  - ● 2 felt programme offered would not help
  - ● 1 failed to keep initial appointment and to respond to further letters
  - ● 5 no longer had a sleep problem

---

chosen. In this type of study, by convention, the letter A is used to designate a baseline (no treatment) condition, the letter B to designate treatment. In the A/B design, the initial period of observation involves the repeated measurement of the natural frequency of occurrence of the target behaviour under study. This period is defined as the baseline, or A phase, of the study. The primary purpose of baseline measurement is to have a standard against which to evaluate the effectiveness of the subsequent experimental intervention. The B phase of the study is the introduction of treatment. A treatment effect is demonstrated by showing that performance differs from one phase to the next. In a multiple baseline across subjects, a treatment is applied **in sequence** to a single targeted behaviour across a number of subjects exposed to similar environmental conditions. Baseline measurements continue to be collected for the rest of the group. The controlling effect of the treatment is inferred from the rate change in the treated subject(s) against their own baseline and against the rate for the (as yet) untreated subjects in the group - who should remain unchanged.

Teaching parents the techniques

An initial visit by the health professionals to each of the families in the experimental group took place. At this meeting the sleeping problem was clearly specified, and parents were asked to keep baseline recordings of their son or daughter's sleeping patterns for a two week period using a sleep diary. A sleep diary provides an accurate record of the child's sleep patterns and provides feedback to both parents and health professional about the initial severity of the problem and the progress the child is making. Difficulty in settling to sleep, frequency and duration of episodes of night waking, sleeping in the parents' bed and repeated coming downstairs were recorded. Background information about the management techniques parents had already tried, the child's behaviour, and mental and physical impairments were also collected. The child's doctor was consulted to confirm that there were no medical reasons why a sleep management programme should not be implemented. On the second visit, a week later, the baseline data were examined, and a treatment/training programme tailored to individual family needs was negotiated with the parents and young person (where possible). This was written up on a chart, and the parents were requested to continue recording the child's sleep patterns in the diary throughout the trial.

Four techniques were taught. The first involved setting the scene for the desired behaviour or introducing positive routines. Many children with sleep problems do not have a regular bedtime routine, so they do not associate going to bed with going to sleep. Introducing a routine provides the child with a clear, unequivocal cue that bedtime is approaching. The child should then be settled in bed and left to sleep. The second technique involved removing incentives for sleep disturbance by not attending to the child when he or she cries or makes a fuss. This method is called extinction, and can achieve dramatic results in a short time. However, it involves leaving the child to cry and many parents find this very stressful. The method usually results in an initial increase in frequency and intensity of the problem behaviour, and so its use is only to be recommended for parents who feel strong enough to cope or those who require very fast results. The third technique is a variation of extinction and is much easier to use. It involves a step approach to the problem. Instead of leaving the child to cry, the parent gradually distances herself from the child's room. First she sits by the bed, holding the child's hand or stroking him. Then when the child settles without fuss, she gradually moves her chair step by step from the room on subsequent evenings until she sits first by the door, and then outside the room. During these steps she should have as little interaction as possible with her child. The final technique that was taught is called positive reinforcement, and can be used in conjunction with the other techniques. It involves rewarding the child for appropriate night-time behaviour, for example, settling to sleep promptly or sleeping through the night.

Reinforcers can be anything the child enjoys, such as praise, sweets or toys. One child we worked with enjoyed a musical light show toy and this was used as an effective reinforcer. Reinforcers can be given intermittently or faded when the desired behaviour is established.

Parents were advised to avoid prolonged routines and overstimulation, and were taught about the importance of being consistent in their approach. They were warned that their progress might initially be slow. Progress was monitored on a regular weekly basis by the health visitor. Frequency of initial home visiting was agreed between parent and health visitor.

When an outcome that was regarded as satisfactory was reached, advice on maintaining the improvement was given. Follow-up took place after three months to check that progress had been maintained.

Although the techniques were relatively straightforward, a range of modifications to the programmes were necessary to suit individual parenting styles and family coping resources. Some parents were extremely reluctant to consider alternatives to well established but unconstructive coping strategies which were sometimes having the effect of maintaining the sleep problem. Such cases required tact and sensitivity on the part of the health visitor and a degree of flexibility in the techniques to be applied.

Evaluating the effectiveness of the intervention

The study resolves into four questions: Can staff without previous training be taught behavioural approaches to managing sleeplessness? Can parents learn the techniques? Do the techniques work? Do other changes in maternal attitudes and behaviour occur? Appropriate checks were built into the study at each level. They included a test of knowledge of behavioural principles to health visitors; a questionnaire about the programme; a short test for parents to establish how well they had understood the procedures; and data on the success and maintenance of the treatment outcome. After three months we carried out a follow-up in which parents were requested to fill in a two week diary so that we could check that progress had been maintained.

We hypothesised that if the intervention was successful and the children's sleep patterns improved, other changes might occur within the family. These were most likely to be in the mother's behaviour towards the child, and in her perceptions of herself, her child and her partner. Accordingly, mothers in the experimental group were interviewed before and after the intervention. Measures of attitudes and behaviour and satisfaction with settling and waking patterns were taken, and the pre and post intervention means were compared by use of matched paired t-test.

FINDINGS

Evaluation of the training course

As we noted, the 50 item Knowledge of Behavioural Principles as Applied to Children Test (O'Dell et al, 1979) was administered to the health professionals before and after the course. All the health professionals signicantly improved in their knowledge of behavioural principles during the course (Figure 1). The mean knowledge score was 25.8 (sd 7.0) at Time 1 and 37.0 (sd 6.6) at Time 2 (t = 7.8, df = 11, p < 0.001).

Figure 1   Training course: Results for KBPAC

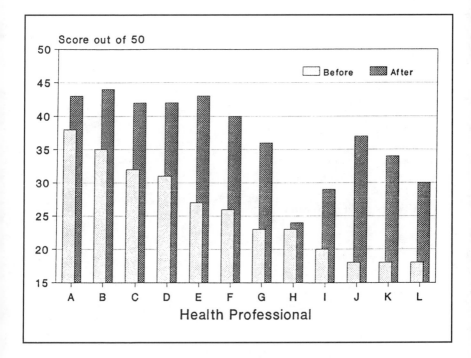

Description of the treatment group

The treatment group consisted of 25 children, 17 of whom were boys and eight girls. Eight children were the only child, six the eldest child, three the middle child and eight the youngest child of the family. Twenty two came from two parent families and three from single parent families. One child was adopted, but the rest lived with at least one natural parent. Twenty two mothers were married, and one mother was divorced, one separated and one single. Eight mothers had full or part time paid employment. Twenty fathers were employed and two were unemployed.

The children's skills, abilities and behaviour were assessed using the Behaviour Problem Index (Cunningham et al, 1986). The Behaviour Problem Index is a structured interview designed to elicit from parents and

Table 2   Charesteristics of sample

Mobile		19	(76%)
Not Mobile		6	(24%)
Continence During Day			
	Does not wet	10	(40%)
	Does not soil	11	(44%)
Can feed self without help		13	(52%)
Can wash self without help		3	(12%)
Can dress self without help		2	(8%)
Vision	Poor or blind	3	(12%)
Hearing	Poor or deaf	7	(28%)
Understanding Communication			
	Poor	14	(56%)
	Fair	5	(20%)
	Good	3	(12%)
Using Communication			
	Poor	12	(48%)
	Fair	6	(24%)
	Good	3	(12%)

care staff details of the child's physical and developmental skills, communication skills, sensory impairments, medical conditions and behaviour problems.

Table 2 shows the children's skills and abilities. Over three-quarters of children were mobile, about 40 per cent were continent during the day, and about half could feed themselves without help. Three children had poor vision and seven poor hearing. About half had poor understanding and use of communication.

Improvement in parental knowledge of behavioural principles

In order to test whether the **parents** had been able to learn the principles of behavioural management, we gave them a short test before and after the intervention. We used a shortened version of the Knowledge of Behavioural Principles as Applied to Children test (KBPAC) (O'Dell et al, 1979). This instrument was adapted by Furtkamp et al, (1982) and is a ten-item test of knowledge. Figure 2 shows a significant improvement between the pre and post test means in the parents' knowledge scores, confirmed by a matched

Figure 2   Results for Knowledge Test for parents

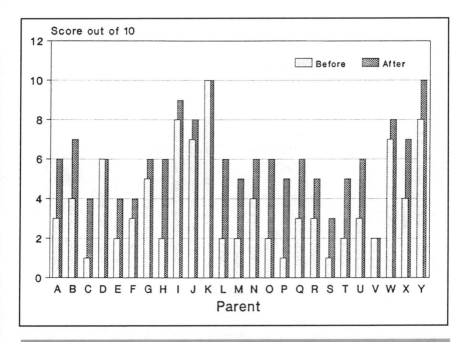

paired t-test. The mean knowledge score was 3.8 (sd 2.5) at Time 1 and 6.0 (sd 2.0) at Time 2 (t = 8.5, df = 24, p < 0.001). This shows clearly that parents had learned principles of behavioural management.

Results using the multiple baseline design

We present below the results of two trials of four children using the multiple baseline design. In single case designs both experimental and therapeutic criteria can be used to evaluate the data (Risley, 1970). The experimental criterion refers to the way in which data are evaluated to determine whether the intervention has had a reliable effect on behaviour. The therapeutic criterion refers to whether the effects of the intervention have achieved an important change in the subject's everyday functioning. Visual inspection is the most commonly used method of evaluating the experimental criterion and consists of examination of a graphic display of the data. A method of evaluating the therapeutic criterion is to have relatives of the subject evaluate the change in the subject's behaviour (Barlow and Hersen, 1984).

In a multiple baseline design, baseline measurements of the occurrence of the target behaviour start to be collected from all subjects at the same time. Then one by one the children begin treatment. Figure 3 shows that while each child with settling problems treated sequentially improved considerably from his or her baseline position, the baselines of the children awaiting treatment remained relatively stable. Figure 4 shows the same for waking problems. The children began to improve on their baseline positions as soon as treatment started, while the baselines of the other children for whom treatment had not yet begun did not change. Follow-up data on the charts show that the improvement was, by and large, maintained after three months.

A disadvantage of the classical multiple baseline design is that it requires the completion of many weeks of diaries by parents of children who have not yet started treatment. Many of the parents in our study were tired out and short of energy because of the difficulties of caring for a child who sleeps badly. We did not think it ethical to insist on laborious filling in of diaries for weeks on end before treatment could begin. For the remainder of the sample, therefore, we decided to ask for a two week baseline period only. The experimental criterion was demonstrated by showing that each child improved from his or her own baseline position while the baselines of untreated children remained stable over the two week period. Summary tables for settling and waking problems follow.

Figure 3   Settling Time Multiple Baseline Design

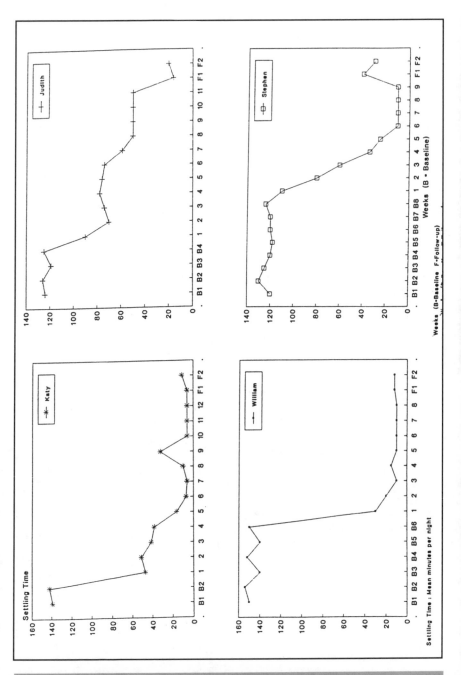

Figure 4   Awake Frequency Multiple Baseline Design

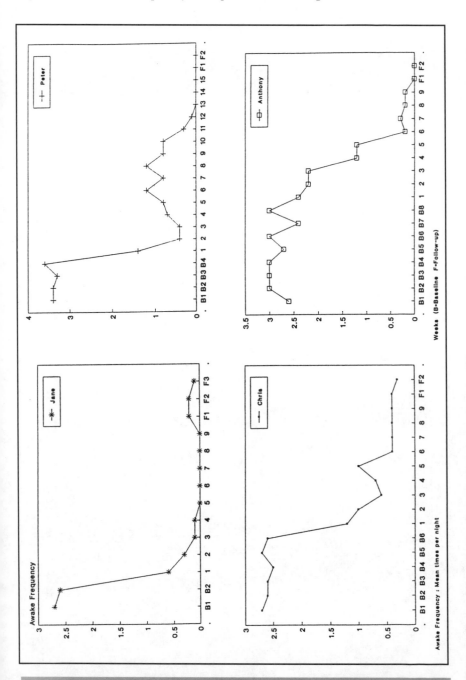

Improvement in sleep patterns

The results show that the intervention had a reliable effect on the children's settling and waking patterns. Each child improved in his/her settling or waking patterns.

The improvement in the children's **settling** problems was marked. Table 3 presents a summary of the progress of the 15 children with settling problems. It can be seen that the children took from 45 to 180 minutes (mean 111 minutes) to settle to sleep before the intervention, and between 5 and 60 minutes (mean 20.4) to settle after the intervention.

Table 3   Settling problems: Summary Table

	Time taken to settle at night (average minutes per night)		
	Baseline	Post-Treatment	Improvement
Mark	180	5	175
Laura+	150	56	94
Katy	140	5	135
William	140	10	130
Timothy*	130	10	120
Judith	120	45	75
Patrick*	120	5	115
Robert	120	60	60
Stephen+	120	10	110
Peter	100	25	75
Lucy	95	25	70
Simon	75	10	65
Ben	70	5	65
Mary+	70	25	45
Jonathan	45	10	35

* Falls asleep downstairs
+ Repeatedly comes downstairs

The children's **waking** patterns improved dramatically too. Table 4 presents a summary of the progress of the 15 children with waking problems. We have calculated both the number of times per night the child woke (awake frequency) and the mean minutes per night of time the child was awake (awake duration). This allows us to take account of both the child who wakes infrequently but for a long time each waking, and the child who wakes frequently for a short time. Frequently, too, children did not sleep in their own beds at night, choosing either to sleep in the parents' bed, to bed-hop between parent, relative or sibling, or to exchange beds with one parent at some time during the night. The Table shows that before the intervention,

Table 4   Waking problems: Summary Table

	Awake Frequency (per night)		Awake Duration (per night)		Does not sleep in own bed (per week)	
	Pre	Post	Pre	Post	Pre	Post
Adam	4	1.3	-	-	5	0
Anthony*	3	0.3	27	5	-	-
Ben	3.5	1	60	5	-	-
Christopher	2.5	0.5	110	5	7	0
Edward	4	0	-	-	5	0
Jane	2.7	0	90	0	-	-
Jenny*	2.5	0	120	0	-	-
Jonathan	2.6	0.4	-	-	6	0
Katy	3	0	-	-	4	0
Martin	2.2	0	50	0	-	-
Matthew	3.5	0	50	0	6	0
Peter	3	0	90	0	-	-
Robert	3	1	-	-	6	1
Ryan	3	0	30	2	6	0
Simon	3	0.3	75	15	-	-

* Mother lies down with child

the average number of times per night the children woke up ranged from 2.2 to 4.0 times (mean 3.1), and the average duration of time awake ranged from 30 to 120 minutes (mean 70.2 minutes). After the intervention the average number of wakings per night was from 0 to 1.3 (mean 0.3) and the average duration per night of time awake was from 0 to 15 minutes (mean 3.2).

Parents were asked to stop recording when the child settled off easily to sleep and no longer woke at night, or when the parents' sleep was less disrupted, or when an outcome that they regarded as satisfactory was reached. The health professionals worked towards goals that had been agreed with parents. Parents varied in their beliefs about what was a suitable bedtime or settling time for their child and this is reflected in the results. Some parents were quite happy for a child to take half an hour or so to settle as long as the child was reasonably quiet and stayed in his or her own bed, leaving the parents to enjoy their evening. At the end of the intervention one or two children, such as Laura and Robert, still took quite a long time to settle to sleep, but Laura had stopped coming downstairs repeatedly and began to settle without fuss, and Robert, a child with severe physical disability, learned to settle in his own bed at a reasonable bedtime every night.

Each child was given a 'clinical' rating by the two research psychologists. A rating of 1 indicated slight improvement; 2 indicated moderate improvement; 3 indicated marked improvement and 4 indicated that the target for settling or waking had been reached. The ratings were made on the basis of detailed knowledge of each of the cases, scrutiny of the sleep diaries, and information provided by the health visitors; and agreement between the two psychologists was 23/25 (92 per cent). Thus calculated, the overall success rate (those with complete or marked improvement) was 80 per cent.

Maternal satisfaction with settling and waking patterns

We used mothers' reports of satisfaction with sleep patterns to invoke the therapeutic criterion. Most mothers were delighted with the results of the intervention. They were asked to rate their satisfaction with the child's settling and waking patterns on a seven point scale from '1' not satisfied to '7' satisfied. Figures 5 and 6 show that there was a significant difference between the pre and post intervention maternal satisfaction scores for both settling and waking patterns. The mean score for satisfaction with settling at Time 1 was 2.2 (sd 1.7) and at Time 2 it was 6.3 (sd 1.1) (t = 1.5, df = 24, p < 0.001). The mean score for satisfaction with waking at Time 1 was 2.2 (s.d. 1.9) and at Time 2 it was 6.2 (sd 1.4) (t = 7.4, df = 24, p < 0.001). Only one mother was not satisfied with her child's current settling pattern. This was a mother who had chosen to implement programmes for settling and waking separately and had not yet moved on to a settling programme. Only one mother was not satisfied with the child's current waking pattern, and for the same reason. The waking programme was to be implemented after the programme for settling. These programmes are now under way. Lucy's mother was neither satisfied nor dissatisfied with her child's settling patterns. The health visitor had worked on her settling patterns, which improved greatly during the programme. However, by the time of the post intervention interview, Lucy had spent a period of time in hospital. When she came home her behaviour had deteriorated, and she developed a waking problem and began to demand attention during the night. She was referred back to the health visitor.

Three month follow-up

Three months after each child's programme was completed, we asked mothers to fill in a two week sleep diary to check whether progress had been

Figure 5   Satisfaction with settling

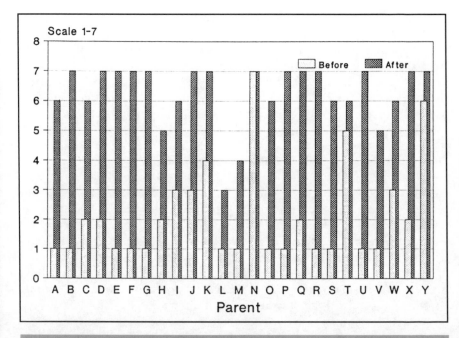

Figure 6   Satisfaction with waking

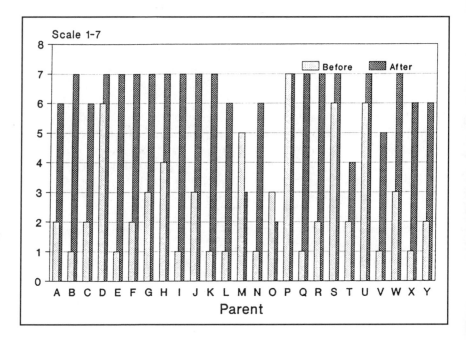

maintained. Two families had not completed the three month period, and three families have so far not responded to requests to fill in sleep diaries, so these results are based on 20 families. Of the 12 children with settling problems, all but one had maintained the progress made and some had improved upon it. Stephen was now taking about 40 minutes to settle, but this was not a problem for his mother since he now played quietly in his bedroom without disturbing the family. His mother thought that it was a great improvement on the two hours of noisy behaviour she had been used to.

Ten out of twelve children had maintained their progress with waking patterns. Simon and Robert's waking patterns seemed to have deteriorated slightly since the final two weeks of the programme. Simon is a multiply handicapped child who had had very severe settling and waking problems accompanied by severe headbanging. Now, although he wakes, his parents are able to check on him and to go straight back to bed. His headbanging has decreased dramatically and his mother is satisfied that the improvement in his behaviour has been maintained. Robert is also multiple handicapped. His mother found it very hard to be consistent in her appraoch to his sleep problems. She was not well herself, and her husband is being treated for depression. Both she and her husband are very anxious about Robert and this sometimes leads her to be very responsive to his cries and demands for attention. However, there has been a dramatic improvement in his sleeping patterns overall, as examination of the baseline rates of sleep problems documented in his diary shows. All the children now slept in their own beds through the night.

Overall, 17 of the 20 children (85 per cent) had maintained progress or improved, while Robert and Simon had maintained their progress with settling but had deteriorated slightly from the last two weeks of the programme, and Stephen now took a little longer to settle but no longer came downstairs. However, even these children's sleeping patterns had improved dramatically from their baseline positions.

Changes in maternal behaviour

As we mentioned earlier, we wanted to investigate whether improving the children's sleep patterns would result in other changes too - particularly in the mothers' behaviour towards their children and in their maternal stress and attitudes towards themselves, their child and their partner.

Irritability and smacking: In order to examine differences in maternal behaviour before and after the intervention, mothers were asked to indicate on five point scales how frequently they were irritable with the child, and how frequently they smacked the child. The ratings were scored from 1 - never, 2 - once per week or less, 3 - 2-6 times per week, 4 - daily, to 5 - more than daily. Also on a five point scale, mothers were asked to indicate how frequently they were worried about losing control. This scale was scored for 0 - no loss of control feared; 2 - sometimes fears losing control; 3 - frequently fears losing control; 4 - occasionally loses control; to 5 - frequently loses control.

At the end of the intervention mothers reported less irritability with their children. Figure 7 shows that they also smacked their children less frequently and were less afraid of losing control and punishing their child too severely. The differences in pre and post intervention scores were all statistically significant. For irritability the mean score at Time 1 was 2.5 (sd 1.0) and at Time 2 it was 1.8 (sd 0.9) (t = 5.3, df = 24, p < 0.001). For smacking the mean score at Time 1 was 1.6 (sd 1.1) and at Time 2 it was 0.6 (sd 1.0) (t = 5.3, df = 24, p < 0.001), and for feared loss of control the mean score at Time 1 was 0.9 (sd 0.9) and at Time 2 it was 0.3 (sd 0.5) (t = 2.8, df = 24, p < 0.01). This is an important finding since it suggests that behavioural training may be a feasible approach to the prevention of parenting difficulties and, perhaps, child abuse.

Figure 7   Irritability and smacking

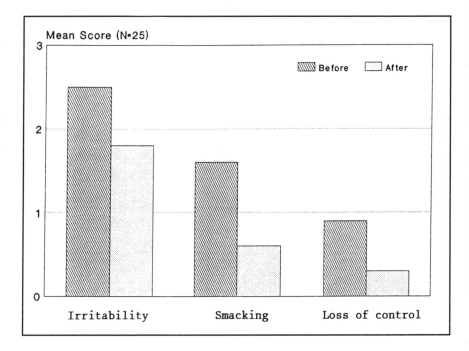

Changes in maternal attitudes

Mother's perceptions of self: Given our early argument concerning the value of intervention for family adaptation, we wanted to explore possible changes in the **attitudes** of mothers in our experimental group towards family relationships. We therefore used a number of rating scales to explore the mother's perceptions of herself, her child and her relationship with her partner. These were sets of bi-polar items separated by seven point scales which we adapted from the work of Davis, Booth and Rushton (1988). The value of seven refers to the pole indicated in Table 5.

There were 20 items describing the mother's feelings about herself. These were summed to form a total score of positiveness. Table 5 shows that there

Table 5 Results of pre- and post-intervention interview with Child's mother: description of self

Mother's description of self	Pre		Post		t. value		d.f.
	Mean	s.d.	Mean	s.d.			
Affectionate	5.2	0.9	6.4	1.1	4.6	***	24
Not irritable	3.8	1.5	4.7	2.1	2.5	**	24
Flexible	5.2	0.9	6.3	1.3	3.8	***	24
In control	4.8	1.3	6.3	0.9	6.2	***	24
Patient	4.2	2.1	5.0	1.8	2.6	**	24
Understanding	5.0	1.3	6.6	1.2	8.5	***	24
Reliable	6.2	1.2	6.1	1.5	0.3	N/S	24
Happy	4.8	0.9	5.8	1.7	4.5	***	24
Competent	5.1	0.6	6.0	1.2	4.0	***	24
Relaxed	3.8	1.5	5.0	2.0	4.3	***	24
Friendly	6.2	1.3	5.8	1.6	1.1	N/S	24
Lots of energy	4.0	1.6	4.9	2.0	2.2	*	24
Have sense of humour	5.3	0.6	6.0	1.7	2.3	*	24
Not lonely	4.6	1.4	5.6	1.9	2.6	**	24
Confident	4.8	1.7	6.0	1.1	3.7	***	24
Provide support	5.9	1.4	5.7	1.3	0.6	N/S	24
Healthy	5.3	1.5	5.6	1.1	1.1	N/S	24
Not depressed	3.9	1.6	4.8	1.9	3.4	**	24
A good person	5.1	0.8	5.9	1.6	2.8	**	24
Not shy	4.4	2.2	4.4	2.0	0.0	N/S	24
Positiveness	**97.4**	**14.2**	**113.1**	**16.7**	**7.4**	***	**24**

*p< 0.05   **p< 0.01   **p< 0.001

was a significant difference between pre and post intervention means, indicating that mothers had a more favourable view of themselves at the end of the intervention. A number of individual items contributed to the change. Mothers felt themselves to be more affectionate, flexible, in control, patient, understanding, happy, competent, relaxed, energetic, good-humoured and confident. They felt less irritable, lonely and depressed. This suggests that involvement in the children's sleep programmes had quite far-reaching effects, not only achieving improvement in the children but also enhancing the mothers' perceptions of self. This might make mothers more able to cope with the care of the handicapped child, and less likely to succumb to the effects of stress. This is particularly important since it is well known that mothers caring for a handicapped child are particularly vulnerable to stress (Quine and Pahl, 1985).

Mother's relationship with child

There were 14 items describing the mother's perceptions of her child. These were summed to produce a total score of positiveness. Table 6 shows that mothers had developed a much more favourable view of the child by the end of the intervention: they viewed the child as happier, having less of a temper, having better concentration, being more able to manage alone and to communicate needs, being more interested in his or her surroundings, more affectionate, more obedient and more easy to handle.

Mother's relationship with partner

There were 16 items describing the mother's feelings for her partner. Again there were significant differences between pre and post intervention scores (see Table 7). By the end of the intervention mothers had a more positive view of their feelings about their partner. They saw themselves as more loving and affectionate and happier towards them, spending more time talking to them and being able to confide in them, more able to understand them, more helpful and more joyful towards them. They felt more relaxed with them, less critical and more able to make decisions with them.

CONCLUSIONS

The purpose of the study was to determine whether health professionals such as health visitors and community nurses could learn and apply behavioural techniques to help parents manage their children's sleep

Table 6   Results of pre- and post-intervention interview with
Child's mother: mother's relationship with child

Mother's relationship with child	Pre Mean	s.d.	Post Mean	s.d.	t. value		d.f.
Happy	5.4	0.6	6.2	1.6	2.6	**	24
Hasn't a temper	3.0	1.7	3.0	2.4	3.0	**	24
Not timid	4.5	1.6	3.4	1.9	1.9	N/S	24
Concentrates well	3.0	1.6	3.8	2.0	2.5	*	24
Healthy	5.5	1.6	5.8	1.5	1.0	N/S	24
Manages on own	3.0	1.7	3.8	2.0	2.5	*	24
Likes people	5.9	1.4	6.0	1.5	0.3	N/S	24
Communicates needs	4.0	1.6	5.0	2.2	3.3	**	24
Doesn't have problems	2.5	1.3	3.0	1.7	1.3	N/S	24
Interested in surroundings	5.2	1.0	5.9	1.8	2.2	*	24
Affectionate	5.6	0.6	6.5	1.3	4.5	***	24
Determined	6.0	1.4	5.7	1.3	1.0	N/S	24
Obedient	3.1	1.5	4.0	2.0	2.4	*	24
Easy to handle	2.9	1.0	4.0	1.9	3.1	**	24
Positiveness	**65.4**	**8.8**	**72.6**	**9.9**	**4.2**	*****	**24**

*p< 0.05   **p< 0.01   **p< 0.001

disturbance. The study showed that health visitors and community nurses improved their knowledge of behavioural principles during training. Parents, too, improved in their knowledge after being taught by health professionals. This indicates that the training course was successful in training health professionals in behavioural principles and that they in turn were able to pass on their knowledge to parents.

Table 7   Results of pre- and post-intervention interview with
Child's mother: relationship with partner

Mother's relationship with partner	Pre		Post				d.f.
	Mean	s.d.	Mean	s.d.	t. value		
Love	5.5	0.7	6.6	1.0	4.2	***	21
Proud of	6.0	1.5	6.0	1.4	0.2	N/S	21
Spend time talking to	4.7	1.4	6.5	1.2	6.5	***	21
Not jealous of	6.2	1.1	6.1	1.6	0.2	N/S	21
Happy towards	1.9	1.2	6.0	1.4	10.1	***	21
Confide in	5.2	1.2	6.3	1.6	4.5	***	21
Not dependent on	3.7	1.8	3.8	1.7	0.3	N/S	21
Affectionate towards	5.3	0.6	6.5	1.3	4.5	***	21
Make decisions with	4.8	1.6	5.6	2.2	2.0	*	21
Understand	5.0	1.1	6.4	1.3	5.6	***	21
Relaxed with	5.0	1.3	6.2	1.6	3.7	***	21
Do not criticise	4.3	1.2	5.5	1.9	3.7	***	21
Helpful to	5.2	1.0	6.3	1.5	3.0	**	21
Not embarrassed by	6.0	1.3	5.9	1.7	0.4	N/S	21
Protective towards	5.3	1.4	5.0	1.6	1.2	N/S	21
Joyful towards	6.9	0.9	6.3	1.2	9.7	***	21
Positiveness	**84.3**	**10.2**	**100.8**	**14.7**	**6.7**	***	**20**

*p< 0.05   **p< 0.01   **p< 0.001

The effect of the behavioural treatment was assessed by use of a single case experimental design with multiple baseline across subjects. We were able to demonstrate clearly that while the baselines showing the frequency of occurrence of sleep problems of children treated sequentially improved, the baselines of children awaiting treatment remained relatively stable. This was true for all 25 children in the treatment group. These improvements were, by and large, maintained at three month follow-up. In addition we were able to show that parental satisfaction with their child's settling and waking patterns improved significantly during the course of the intervention.

Clinical ratings of improvement by the research psychologists showed that 80 per cent (20/25) had either reached the target set at the outset of the programme or displayed a marked improvement, 16 per cent (4) showed a moderate improvement and 4 per cent (1) a slight improvement. All children showed some improvement.

Implications for practice

The findings from our study have important implications for practice. The success rate for the study compares favourably with the rates reported by other researchers. Richman et al (1985), for example, report a 77 per cent rate of success, measured similarly, while Jones and Verduyn (1983) reported success in 84 per cent of cases, and Seymour et al (1983) in 78 per cent. Each of these studies was carried out with non-handicapped children and used experienced clinical psychologists or child psychiatrists as therapists. These professionals worked with parents who were sufficiently motivated to attend a series of clinic appointments. The implication of our research, which used a home-based service, and trained health visitors to teach behavioural techniques to parents of children with severe learning disabilities who often have additional physical handicaps, suggests that nothing is lost by using such a cascade model of training. There is much to be gained. The cascade model of training allows service managers to make efficient use of scarce specialised professional resources. It allows important skills to be acquired by larger groups of health and social services professionals and to be passed on to parents within a partnership that enhances parental management and interactive and teaching skills, and leads to greater family adaptation and stability.

Children with severe learning disabilities often have limited use and understanding of language and learn at a much slower rate than do their non-handicapped peers. The greater the learning disabilities the longer the child takes to learn. Physical impairments will add to the difficulty by reducing the opportunities for learning. They can also increase the likelihood that a child will have a sleep problem. Such children often find it difficult to get comfortable at night or find it hard to change position; they may experience discomfort due to muscle spasm; they may be made uncomfortable by incontinence or by skin irritations. Children with visual or hearing impairments may not receive the cues that other children receive that bedtime is approaching. This makes the child with learning disabilities or physical impairment both more prone to sleep disturbance and more difficult to teach. Many children with severe learning disabilities also suffer from epilepsy, which in itself can disrupt the child's sleeping patterns.

The high success rate in this study shows that behavioural methods of managing night-time disturbance can be effective even with the most difficult children. The improvements result in a number of positive changes in relationships within the family. Behavioural methods are particularly valuable because they do not rely on the child's understanding of language. The child with severe learning disabilities may fail to respond not because he or she cannot but because he or she does not understand what we want him or her to do. Behavioural approaches help parents sort out and simplify the messages given to the child so that he or she has a better chance of understanding. They provide a more constructive alternative to night sedation, which has been, until recently, the most widespread method of dealing with childhood sleep problems.

Implications for policy

Sleep disturbance is one of the most widespread, persistent and stressful problems exhibited by young children with severe learning disabilities. Despite this it has not generally been identified as a severely challenging behaviour, partly because of its invisibility - it generally occurs at night, unobserved by service providers - and partly because parents often see it as an inherent part of the child's learning disability, and therefore do not report it or request help. We believe that it is time for sleep disturbance to be recognised as a severely challenging behaviour, and for strategies for helping parents to be designed and implemented. The key elements of such a policy would be:

* Clarification of the responsibilities of agencies so parents know where to turn for help.

* Regular assessment of children with learning disabilities. Such assessment should include mobility, skills and abilities, health problems, epilepsy, and behavioural and sleep problems.

* Proper assessment of need for help with sleep problems and allocation of responsibility for teaching parents and carers to manage them to trained workers in mental handicap teams.

* Partnership with parents. Parents are the "experts" on their own child. They are in a unique position to observe their child's behaviour and progress and to teach their own child.

* Staff training in behavioural approaches and techniques for managing sleep problems by psychology services.

* Practical support for parents and carers while behavioural programmes are being carried out.

However, we would emphasise that all these measures should be part of a continuous health programme for all children, which starts during the mother's pregnancy and aims at the prevention of impairment where possible, early detection of problems, and the achievement of the maximum potential of each child.

Acknowledgements

We would like to thank the Medway health professionals who carried out the intervention, and the parents and children with whom we worked.

REFERENCES

BARLOW D H AND HERSEN M (1984). *Single-case Experimental Designs: Strategies for Studying Behaviour Change.* New York: Pergamon Press.

BARTLETT L B, ROONEY V AND SPEDDING S (1985). Nocturnal difficulties in a population of mentally handicapped children. *British Journal of Mental Subnormality, 31,* 54-59.

BIDDER R T, GRAY O P, HOWELLS P M AND EATON M P (1986). Sleep problems in pre-school children: community clinics. *Child: Care, Health and Development, 12,* 325-337.

CLAUSEN J, SERSEN E A AND LIDSKY A (1977). Sleep patterns in mental retardation: Down's Syndrome. *Electroencephalography and Clinical Neurophysiology, 43,* 183-191.

CLEMENTS J, WING L AND DUNN G (1986). Sleep problems in handicapped children: a preliminary study. *Journal of Child Psychology and Psychiatry, 27,* 399-407.

CUNNINGHAM C (1985). Training and education approaches for parents of children with special needs. *British Journal of Medical Psychology, 58,* 285-305.

CUNNINGHAM C, SLOPER T, RANGECROFT A, KNUSSEN C, LENNING C, DIXON I AND REEVES D (1986). The Effects of Early Intervention on the Occurrence and Nature of Behaviour Problems in Children with Down's Syndrome. Final Report to DHSS, Hester Adrian Research Centre, University of Manchester.

DAVIS H, BOOTH A AND RUSHTON R (1988). Parent counselling and support. Paper presented at DHSS/DES/VCHC Joint Seminar on Early Intervention, Castle Priory, Wallingford, Berkshire.

FURTKAMP E, GIFFORT D AND SCHIERS W (1982). In-class evaluation of behaviour modification knowledge: parallel tests for use in applied settings. *Journal of Behaviour Therapy and Experimental Psychiatry, 13,* 2, 131-134.

GRUBAR J C (1983). Sleep and mental deficiency. *Review of Electroencephalography and Neurophysiology, 13,* 107-114.

HEWITT K (1985). Behavioural approaches to sleeplessness. *Mental Handicap, 13,* 112-114.

JENKINS S, BAX M AND HART H (1980). Behavioural problems in pre-school children. *Journal of Child Psychology and Psychiatry, 21,* 5-17.

JENKINS S, OWEN C, BAX M AND HART H (1984). Continuities of common behaviour problems in pre-school children. *Journal of Child Psychology and Psychiatry, 25,* 75-89.

JONES D P H AND VERDUYN C M (1983). Behavioural management of sleep problems. *Archives of Diseases of Childhood, 58,* 442-444.

KALES A, ALLEN C, SCHARF M B AND KALES J D (1970). Hypnotic drugs and their effectiveness. *Archives of General Psychiatry, 23,* 226-232.

KALES A, KALES J D, BIXLER E O AND SCHARF M B (1975). Effectiveness of hypnotic drugs with prolonged use: flurazepam and pentobarbital. *Clinical Pharmacological Therapy, 18,* 356-363.

O'DELL S J, TARLER-BENLOLO L AND FLYNN J M (1979). An instrument to measure knowledge and behavioural principles as applied to children. *Journal of Behaviour Therapy and Experimental Psychiatry, 10,* 29-34.

QUINE L (1991). Sleep problems in children with severe mental handicap. *Journal of Mental Deficiency Research, 35,* 4, 269-290.

QUINE L AND PAHL J (1985). Examining the causes of stress in families with severely mentally handicapped children. *British Journal of Social Work, 15,* 501-517.

QUINE L AND WADE K (1991). Sleep Problems in Children with Severe Learning Difficulties: An Investigation and an Intervention Trial. Final Report to Rowntree Foundation, University of Kent at Canterbury.

RICHMAN N (1981a). Sleep problems in young children. *Archives of Disease in Childhood, 56,* 491-493.

RICHMAN N (1981b). A community survey of characteristics of 1-2 year olds with sleep disruption. *Journal of the American Academy of Child Psychiatry*, *26*, 281-291.

RICHMAN N, DOUGLAS J, HUNT H, LANSDOWN R AND LEVERE R (1985). Behavioural methods in the treatment of sleep disorders - a pilot study. *Journal of Child Psychology and Psychiatry*, *26*, 581-590.

RICHMAN N, STEVENSON J E AND GRAHAM P J (1975). Prevalence of behaviour problems in three-year-old children: an epidemiological study in a London borough. *Journal of Child Psychology and Psychiatry*, *16*, 277-287.

RISLEY T R (1970). Behaviour modification: an experimental - therapeutic endeavour. IN L A Hamenlynck, P O Davidson and L E Acker (Eds) *Behavior Modification and Ideal Health Services*. Calgary: University of Calgary Press.

RUTTER M, TIZARD J AND WHITMORE K (1970). *Education, Health and Behaviour*. London: Longmans.

SEYMOUR F W, BAYFIELD G, BROCK P AND DURING M (1983). Management of night waking in young children. *Australian Journal of Family Therapy*, *4*, 217-222.

CHAPTER 13

TRAINING CLINICAL PRACTITIONERS

Peter McGill and E Veronica Bliss

INTRODUCTION

It is now generally recognised that people with learning disabilities are best served within the community rather than large institutions. Evidence is growing that community-based services can provide virtually comprehensively for all people no matter their degree of disability, even where they present a significant degree of challenging behaviour (eg, Felce et al, in press, Felce and Lowe, Chapter 8, McGill and Mansell, Chapter 9). Whilst there has been concern that seriously challenging behaviour may present a barrier to community placement, even here demonstration services are achieving considerable success (eg, McGill et al, in press). It is clear, however, that such success is not automatic and that it depends crucially on the degree to which staff have the necessary skills and knowledge, and services are well organised (see McGill and Mansell, Chapter 9).

These service developments have created a need for staff training in areas focusing directly on how staff work with clients. In particular, the move to community care means that clients who used to be able to make use of segregated amenities such as on-campus shops and leisure facilities now need to learn to use local shops and to gain skills necessary to live without congregate facilities. Secondly, there is the loss of large pools of staff who may be sources of support for one another. Staff who work in community services need to be able to support clients in the use of community facilities without what might be seen as the security and support of the institution. They also need to be able to work more independently to promote client development.

In carrying out this work staff need to be prepared for the occurrence of challenging behaviour. Self injury, aggression toward others, property destruction, inappropriate social behaviour, and criminal behaviour present considerable challenges to staff supporting clients in the community. Staff play a central role in the lives of clients, and, as such, can influence both acceptable and unacceptable client behaviour. In addition, the environment, which includes not only the physical aspects of the home or work setting but also characteristics of the staff, can play an important part in the development of acceptable client behaviour. Staff skill in responding to client behaviours as well as in assessing environmental variables will determine the success of the service. Services which are staffed by individuals with limited knowledge about the principles governing behaviour change, including issues of building relationships, allowing risk-taking, and identifying the functions of challenging behaviours will simply be unable to effect the desired changes in their clients.

It is, however, clear that staff are not currently making maximum use of the most effective approaches. Research findings suggest low rates of appropriate interactions between staff and clients (eg, Emerson et al, 1992). In addition, interactions which do occur are sometimes counter-productive in that they fail to either encourage appropriate behaviour or discourage inappropriate behaviour (eg, Felce, Saxby et al, 1987). Staff may not be spending very much time actually training clients (eg, Hile and Walbran, 1991) and may not be making available purposeful activities to promote appropriate behaviour (eg, Mansell, Felce et al, 1982). Where challenging behaviour presents a problem it is often not being responded to systematically or constructively (eg, Oliver et al, 1987).

If we accept that clients have the right to receive effective services which protect their community placement and enhance their community participation then we can only conclude that current staff training is not equipping staff to do their jobs. This reflects particularly on the practice of direct care staff and first line managers. To adopt a "practice leadership" role (Mansell et al, in press) the latter need to be able to make informed decisions about best practice and the expected outcomes of their staff's work, in addition to having the requisite skills in direct work with clients.

This paper describes two independently developed courses which have attempted to meet some of these training needs and comments on the experiences gained to date.

THE UNIVERSITY OF KENT DIPLOMA

The Diploma in Applied Psychology of Severe Mental Handicap (Challenging Behaviour) was set up in 1989 as a two year part-time course aimed at staff who have direct responsibilities for the provision of community-based services to people with severe learning disabilities who display challenging behaviour. Students have included home leaders, day service instructors, and peripatetic community support staff. There have been three intakes so far including a total of 30 students. Of these seven have completed successfully, nine have not completed, three have completed all teaching and have been given more time to carry out assessed work, and 11 have just started the course. Twenty four of the students have been sponsored by Health Authorities, four by Social Services Departments, and two by voluntary or not-for-profit service providing agencies. Nineteen have had nursing qualifications, two social work qualifications and nine have not possessed a professional qualification but have been working as first line managers or peripatetic support staff.

The course is organised on a workshop basis with students attending the University for a total of 50 days over the two years, usually in one week workshops. Students do not do placements but carry out a range of practical assignments with clients in their own agencies. As far as possible these assignments are integrated with their everyday work.

The Diploma's curriculum is based on the notion that challenging behaviour, no matter how bizarre, is usually functional for the individual, ie it is a powerful way for that individual to control their environment. It is therefore important that students can help the person to develop other ways of controlling their environment without needing to resort to challenging behaviour. This implies the development of the person's skills and, in particular, since it is a very powerful way of controlling the environment, their communication skills.

What skills should be developed and how should they be used? Approaches focusing on the development of skills have often seemed to imply that the whole of the person's day should be one long teaching programme. Skills are also often taught without proper attention to how they will be used. Students, therefore, need to be able to define what activities, in what settings, the person should be involved in - what should people with challenging behaviour be doing with all the time when they are not being challenging?

So students are helped to teach their clients and set up activities for them. Many of the activities set up, however, will be ones that the individuals concerned are a long way from learning to cope with independently. One option is a readiness criterion - "you can do this activity when you've learned it". However, people might, people do, wait for ever. Accordingly, it is crucial that students can help people participate in activities, even ones in which they might never become independent.

People with challenging behaviour are often resistant to carers' best efforts to teach and involve them in meaningful activities. They often have a long history of surviving in their environment through their challenging behaviour. So while the long-term investment must be in the kind of "positive programming" (La Vigna et al, 1989) describedabove, students also need to be able to do two additional things: manage incidents of challenging behaviour when they happen and try to prevent them from happening; and

and set up programmes based on an analysis of the individual's behaviour, aimed at directly weakening and reducing that behaviour.

No one can do all of the above on their own. Accordingly, students also need to attend to implementation issues - the training and support of staff, the negotiation (and orchestration) of managerial and professional support.

Finally, it is clear that services for people with learning disabilities are prone to abuse their users. It is important, therefore, that students are working in an ethically stringent manner.

The implementation of the curriculum based on the above competencies can be illustrated by focusing on one part of it in more detail - helping people participate in activities.

This material is taught in a one week workshop in which attention is given to four sets of competencies that students are expected to acquire:

*   They need to be able to directly support individuals and groups to participate in meaningful activities - accordingly students are given supervised practice (through working with consultant learners - people with learning disabilities who are paid to participate in the workshop) in supporting participation. The practical work is then used as the basis for generating some helpful rules to call on when trying to obtain participation (eg: allow the client to choose from a few available activities; have the environment prepared in advance; and so on).

*   They need to be able to train their staff in support techniques - accordingly part of the workshop reviews performance based approaches to staff training and students are able to practice being coaches in the work with consultant learners.

*   They need to be able to organise their staff and their environment in a way that ensures participation and gives them and others feedback on what is happening - the systems and structures necessary to do this are reviewed partly from students' own experience and partly from didactic teaching. Students then take part in a simulation in which they have to practice identifying the routines and rhythms of certain aspects of an ordinary life and doing shift planning (seen as being two of the necessary systems and structures) (cf. McGill & Toogood, in press).

* They need to understand what they are doing and be able to explain it to anyone who needs to understand - staff, managers, clients or their parents/advocates. Accordingly the theory underlying the approach is taught through getting them to read, make brief presentations and discuss the readings and the issues.

The assessment deriving from the workshop attempts to directly measure the desired competencies. Thus students have to:

* Make a video which demonstrates their ability to successfully engage a client in an activity or sequence of activities with a written specification of the support required by the client.

* Write a report describing their training of one member of staff to engage a client in an activity.

* Write a report reviewing and commenting on the ways in which they currently organise their staff and environment to achieve client participation.

* Write an essay which (amongst other things) discusses why it is important in working with people with challenging behaviour to support their participation in activities.

Within its own terms, this workshop has been highly successful in that students produce good quality work demonstrating the desired competencies. As yet, however, there is no data on the workshop's, or the course's, longer term impact on students' practice or on the behaviour of the clients with whom they work.

THE UNIVERSITY OF MANCHESTER DIPLOMA

The Manchester Course, Behavioural Approaches for Professionals working with Individuals who have Learning Disabilities (Kiernan and Bliss, 1992), is a full time, post-qualifying course of 37 weeks and is validated by the English National Board for Nursing, Midwifery and Health Visiting (ENB) as well as the Central Council for the Education and Training of Social Workers (CCETSW). Successful students are awarded the ENB 705 certificate. The University of Manchester has now recognised the course as a Diploma beginning with the most recent intake in September 1992. The course is run at the Hester Adrian Research Centre in the University with the support of Burnley, Pendle, and Rossendale Health Authority (Calderstones) and with support from the East Lancashire College of Nursing.

Since the first intake of students in 1989, 29 students have completed. There are 12 students on the current intake, intending to finish in June of 1993. From this total of 41 students, 30 have been from the North Western Region. The remaining 11 students have come from Northern Ireland, Wales and various parts of England. Thirty eight of the students have been Registered Nurses in Mental Handicap, with one student from Education and two from Social Services. The work backgrounds of students include a range of support and residential services for both adults and children. The course continues to attract applicants from all over the United Kingdom.

The format of the course includes five modules, all of which are mandatory. The first module is an initial block of six weeks academic work which is intended to give the student a broad, basic knowledge of topics related to effective behavioural practice. The subsequent modules, 2, 3 and 4 are practice placements which include four days practical work in a service other than their seconding service, with one day per week of continued academic input at the University. The continued academic input is intended to fine-tune the broad issues discussed during the first six weeks. The final module, module 5, is an in-depth study of one case from the third placement. Each module is described in more detail below.

The beginning stages of the first module are designed to assist the student in understanding the vast similarities between themselves and people with learning disabilities. They receive input regarding various methods of conceptualising behaviour, including very basic outlines of such theories as psychoanalysis, person-centred theory, gestalt theory, rational-emotive theory and existentialism as well as behaviourism. They think through how they might build on principles from various approaches to support co-workers, families, and people with learning disabilities, and how the principles might help them to understand their own behaviour. They are then in a good position to identify the strengths and weaknesses of the behavioural approach and to recognise how the principles of reinforcement, punishment, and conditioning work in their own lives.

The students also receive input on various means of assessment, including functional analysis, direct observation, structured interviews, and standardised assessments. They participate in discussions about how to increase and decrease behaviour using behavioural principles, such as shaping, differential reinforcement and extinction, etc. Throughout these discussions, students continue to identify and adjust their personal and professional values toward people with learning disabilities. They also try to determine the message each behavioural intervention might communicate to the client. They then design mock strategies for interacting with clients which highlight client strengths and which address the functional nature of challenging behaviour. They also receive practice in summarising and interpreting data.

Other issues which are covered during the first six week block include the dynamics of organisational change, staff stress, factors which affect staff-client interactions, basic research methodology, presentation skills and writing clear, concise reports.

The second module is a practical placement of six weeks duration. The student has an on-site supervisor who is familiar with the nature of the work required and who receives regular input from the course tutors. This module is intended to give the student practical experience with assessment methods. The student completes an assessment package, usually including an analogue assessment as well as other assessments appropriate to the client with whom they are working. Throughout the six weeks the student returns to the University for continued academic input one day a week. During this placement the academic work centres on assessment methods.

The third module is also a practical placement of six weeks duration. As with the second module there is an on-site supervisor and continued academic input one day a week. The focus of this module is intervention. Here the student gets practice designing or evaluating interventions which may be in place within the placement. Academic input centres around various types of interventions.

The fourth and fifth modules occur together. The fourth module is a practical placement which differs from the two previous modules in length, being 12 weeks long. This is the module in which the student completes their in-depth case study, module 5. Students complete assessments, design interventions, collect and analyse data, and draw conclusions regarding their input into the case. In addition, they collect and report on literature which has a bearing upon their assessment methods and intervention design and the overall success of the analysis and intervention. The academic input during this time centres upon general factors affecting service provision, from national policies to research regarding staff, client and family needs.

During modules 2, 3 and 4 students are required to conduct at least three hours of presentations regarding behavioural approaches to the staff on their placements. They also prepare a review of one or two recent pieces of literature for presentation and discussion to placement supervisors and course management team members. The ability to present information to a variety of groups is seen as very important, given that past students, upon their return to work, have spent some of their time organising and presenting training sessions to other staff.

Students are assessed throughout the course. During the first module, students complete six essays of approximately 750 - 1000 words each, as well as six exams. Students also receive marks for writing a weekly summary of how they have observed behavioural principles in practice. These marks represent 25 per cent of the overall final mark for the course.

Work on placements is evaluated on a weekly basis during meetings between the student and supervisor. The tutors make scheduled visits to the placements and are available to discuss issues as requested by the student or the supervisor. The supervisor gives a final mark out of 100 to the student, using a structured evaluation format as a guide for feedback. The student also completes a structured feedback form for the supervisor. Tutors are available to mediate should disagreements in marks occur.

Marks are also given for the presentations students give to staff and to supervisors. These marks are given along with feedback on predetermined aspects of the presentation and are based on observations of the presentation by the tutors. Marks on placements constitute 50 per cent of the overall course mark. Students must achieve a pass mark on each placement in order to pass the course.

The project, module 5, is also evaluated according to predetermined criteria and is read by two of the three course tutors. This is marked out of 100 and represents the final 25 per cent of the overall course mark.

The course has an external examiner who visits students and placement supervisors twice during the course. He also reads samples of the student's work and comments on the content of the course, the assessment procedures, and the overall quality of the experiences offered to students. Students failing any aspect of the course are offered vivas which would be attended by the external examiner, and may be offered the opportunity to re-do the failed component.

DISCUSSION

The two courses described above have many similarities. Both were developed out of a recognition that the success of community care for people with challenging behaviour depended greatly on the development of greater staff skills in understanding and responding to such behaviour. Both courses have, on the basis of existing knowledge of effective approaches to working with people with challenging behaviour, embraced a broadly behavioural approach. Both have also, however, recognised that technical behavioural skills must be accompanied by a broader understanding of the organisation of services and clarity about the values underlying different models of care (Emerson and McGill, 1989). The two courses have also met some similar difficulties. For example, the lack of widespread skill in working with people with challenging behaviour has made it very difficult to find practice supervisors who know more, or have more skills, than the students themselves. Both courses have also found Health Authorities sending far more students than Social Services Departments.

There are also numerous differences between the two courses. The most obvious is in their structure - while the Manchester Course is full-time and places students outside of their own agencies, the Kent Diploma is part-time and requires students to do practical work in their own agencies. The Manchester Course attempts to be rather broader than the Kent Diploma both in its remit (students who are working with people with any degree of learning disabilities vs. students working with people with severe learning disabilities) and in its orientation (various theoretical orientations being at least outlined vs. an attempt being made to teach a coherent behavioural orientation).

Whilst the similarities are perhaps significant in that they reflect factors likely to be important to others planning similar courses, it is difficult, at this early stage in their provision, to comment on the importance of their differences. Rationales are easy to find for the different approaches taken and it is not clear if they affect either the effectiveness or acceptability of the courses.

The Manchester Course has been strikingly more effective than the Kent Diploma in its student completion rate. This almost certainly relates to its being a full-time course and it is worth discussing in more detail the advantages and disadvantages of running full-time versus part-time courses.

There are many advantages to a full-time course. Students are likely to be better able to become a cohesive group who support each other; they are able to concentrate on the course without having to worry about their day-to-day jobs; they increase the breadth of their experience by doing placements outside of their own workplace. In addition, the use of the same placements from year to year helps to develop expertise amongst placement supervisors. Both the student who agrees to attend a full-time course and the agency which bears the cost of secondment are making a substantial, but relatively short-term, investment which may help to generate the commitment necessary to complete the course successfully. Against this, part-time courses are cheaper for seconding agencies, they may lead to less disruption in the students' lives, they allow students to do practical work of direct relevance to their everyday work (and may, therefore, promote maintenance and generalisation of the knowledge and skills that are acquired), and they force students and their employers to recognise the organisational barriers in the way of effective work.

As is widely recognised (in theory if not in practice) training is unlikely to succeed unless attention is also given to the organisational context in which students work and are expected to apply what they learn (Cullen, 1988). The two courses have, between them, attempted to incorporate a number of features which might make the organisational context more supportive:

*   Students are nominated by their agencies rather than gaining admission on a freestanding basis and then attempting to gain their agency's support.

*   Contracts are developed between the University and nominating agencies concerning funding and the amount of time that students will get to attend the course.

*   Agencies are given information about the courses and encouraged to identify ways in which students' new skills will be maintained and built upon.

*   Students are given a local supervisor (usually not their line manager) who, amongst other roles, can help them advocate for the support they require and can provide a local source of (possibly) long term support in a hostile culture.

*   Annual meetings are held to involve local supervisors, students and line managers to review organisational barriers and how (especially at the end of the course) the student's skills can best be used.

It may also be notable that, on the Kent Diploma, almost all the students have worked for agencies within the South East Thames Region where Diploma teaching staff and their colleagues have been involved in trying to set up the organisational climate within which students can use the skills learned on the Diploma (eg, through the work of the Special Development Team, see McGill and Mansell, Chapter 9).

Both courses have been successful in meeting and stimulating a demand for the training they provide. While seen as difficult to do, they have proven popular with their students who have felt the training to be of real practical value. The very success of the courses has, however, raised rather more fundamental issues about the basis on which they operate. Both courses have attempted to communicate up-to-date approaches to challenging behaviour to a relatively small number of students. Thus, students often end up conducting non-aversive lifestyle interventions with a handful of people with (often severe) challenging behaviour based on detailed functional analyses of each person's behaviour. This kind of training (and perhaps clinical) strategy can only be sustained with a small number of students. While it, hopefully, produces highly skilled practitioners it is an expensive and, to an extent, elitist approach. The needs which led to the development of the two courses can only be fully met by more widespread knowledge and implementation. Pyramidal training models (Page et al, 1982, Quine, Chapter 12) may be of relevance here but it may also be that more attention should be given to direct intervention in service environments rather than, or as well as, the kind of detailed, individualised work which both courses already promote. If we accept that a considerable amount of challenging behaviour is generated and maintained by services (Routledge, 1990) then individualised assessment and intervention will be unnecessary for many people and may be ethically questionable. Services need to change as well as individuals.

A second issue relates to the future of successful students. They enter something of a no-person's land in that they have developed advanced practitioner skills outside of the usual professional framework. They are not, for example, clinical psychologists and do not have the support and supervision structures available to such professionals, yet they may have a more detailed knowledge and practical skill base than many of their better established professional colleagues. While the Manchester Course has obtained validation from CCETSW and ENB, this does not guarantee successful students' acceptance and support as specialist professionals. At least in the short term, special measures are likely to be required such as bringing ex-students into a network where they can obtain some level of support from each other, and if resources allow, from course tutors. This has already happened spontaneously with the "graduates" of both courses.

IMPLICATIONS FOR SERVICES

In summary, the major implications of the work reported above include:

Policy

* An "ordinary life for people with challenging behaviour" can only be sustained by more widespread competence in, and use of, effective methods of preventing and managing challenging behaviour in community settings.

* Given that current funding for training comes largely from the NHS, attention needs to be given to its preservation in the face of organisational changes in the commissioning and provision of services.

Management

* Services must be organised to allow staff to both develop and use skills in the constructive management of challenging behaviour and the support of client participation and development.

* The role of the first line manager as a "practice leader" is particularly crucial to the delivery of a high quality service.

* While not sufficient on its own, investment in the development of staff skills and values is necessary for the provision of a good quality service.

Clinical/training practice

* Attention to both the management and the resolution of challenging behaviour is crucial to the comprehensive success of community services.

* There is insufficient training provision to meet staff needs and it is only easily available in certain parts of the country.

* Given the right specialist support, staff working directly with people with learning disabilities, and first line managers, can assume a more active role in the habilitation of clients

* Training staff to work more effectively with clients is only part of the answer; other approaches are also required to prevent services generating and maintaining challenging behaviour.

Research

* Evaluation of the courses described here, and other such courses, is necessary to establish and improve their effectiveness.

* Such evaluation should focus particularly on the ultimate impact of the courses on client lifestyles.

* The cost-effectiveness of future developments depends on the accurate assessment of training needs, in terms of the number of people requiring different kinds of training.

ACKNOWLEDGEMENTS

The Kent Diploma was developed by Peter McGill and Sheila Barrett with the support of Jim Mansell, South East Thames Regional Health Authority and the University of Kent. It is currently convened by Sheila Barrett with the assistance of a course team including Peter Baker, Anna Eliatamby, David Hughes, Heather Hughes, Peter McGill and Michele de Terlizzi.

The Manchester Diploma, in its current content, was developed by Vicky Bliss with the support of Chris Kiernan, Hester Adrian Research Centre, and members of the Course Management Team.

REFERENCES

CULLEN C (1988). A review of staff training: The emperor's old clothes. *Irish Journal of Psychology, 9,* 309-323.

EMERSON E, BEASLEY F, OFFORD G AND MANSELL J (1992). An evaluation of hospital-based specialized housing for people with seriously challenging behaviours. *Journal of Intellectual Disability Research, 36,* 291-307.

EMERSON E AND MCGILL P (1989). Normalisation and applied behaviour analysis: Values and technology in services for people with learning difficulties. *Behavioural Psychotherapy, 17,* 101-117.

FELCE D, LOWE K AND DE PAIVA S (in press). Ordinary housing for people with severe learning disabilities and challenging behaviours. IN E Emerson, P McGill, and J Mansell (Eds) *Severe Learning Disabilities and Challenging Behaviours: Designing High Quality Services.* London: Chapman and Hall.

FELCE D, SAXBY H, DE KOCK U, REPP A, AGER A AND BLUNDEN R (1987). To what behaviors do attending adults respond?: A replication. *American Journal of Mental Deficiency, 91,* 496-504.

HILE M G AND WALBRAN B B (1991). Observing staff-resident interactions: What staff do, what residents receive. *Mental Retardation, 29,* 35-41.

KIERNAN C AND BLISS V (1992). Preparing professionals to work with people who have learning disabilities and challenging behaviour. Paper for the RSM/BIMH Conference, Across Discipline: Innovations in Training for those working with people with learning difficulties. January, 1992.

LA VIGNA G W, WILLIS T J AND DONELLAN A M (1989). The role of positive programming in behavioral treatment. IN E Cipani (Ed) *The Treatment of Severe Behavior Disorders.* Washington, DC: American Association on Mental Retardation.

MANSELL J, FELCE D, DE KOCK U AND JENKINS J (1982). Increasing purposeful activity of severely and profoundly mentally handicapped adults. *Behaviour Research and Therapy, 20,* 593-604.

MANSELL J, HUGHES H AND McGILL P (in press). Maintaining local residential placements. IN E Emerson, P McGill and J Mansell (Eds) *Severe Learning Disabilities and Challenging Behaviours: Designing High Quality Services.* London: Chapman and Hall.

McGILL P, EMERSON E AND MANSELL J (in press). Individually designed residential provision for people with seriously challenging behaviours. IN E Emerson, P McGill and J Mansell (Eds), *Severe Learning Disabilities and Challenging Behaviours: Designing High Quality Services.* London: Chapman and Hall.

McGILL P AND TOOGOOD A (in press). Organising community placements. IN E Emerson, P McGill and J Mansell (Eds), *Severe Learning Disabilities and Challenging Behaviours: Designing High Quality Services.* London: Chapman and Hall.

OLIVER C, MURPHY G AND CORBETT J (1987). Self-injurious behaviour in people with mental handicap: a total population study. *Journal of Mental Deficiency Research, 31,* 147-162.

PAGE T J, IWATA B A AND REID D H (1982). Pyramidal training: A large-scale application with institutional staff. *Journal of Applied Behavior Analysis, 15,* 335-351.

ROUTLEDGE M (1990). Services for People with a Mental Handicap whose Behaviour is a Challenge to Services: A Review of the Policy and Service Context in the Seven Districts covered by the HARC Behaviour Problems Project. Hester Adrian Research Centre, University of Manchester.

CHAPTER 14

SOME DETERMINANTS OF STAFF FUNCTIONING IN RELATION TO BEHAVIOURAL CHALLENGES FROM PEOPLE WITH LEARNING DISABILITIES

A view from a national training and consultancy service

John Clements

INTRODUCTION

This paper represents a few personal reflections based upon past and recent experience of training and consulting with staff working with people who have learning disabilities and who present overt behavioural challenges. Applied Psychology Services (APS) provides training and consultancy across the United Kingdom. The training services are primarily in short course format with length of training ranging from one to twelve days per course and numbers attending varying from 12-100. Most participants work directly with clients and a proportion are in first line management positions. It is estimated that in excess of one thousand people per year attend APS programmes. Both clinical and training services are mainly concerned with staff in 'ordinary' specialist services for children and adults with learning disabilities. APS has limited involvement in services that designate themselves as exclusively concerned with 'challenging behaviour'.

Whilst this paper will consider the role of training it will locate training in a broad context. It will reflect upon a range of factors that influence staff performance and identify some of the major themes that emerge from extensive training and consultancy experience.

INFLUENCES UPON STAFF PERFORMANCE - RECURRING THEMES
SOCIAL CONTEXT ISSUES

The functioning of staff is not entirely determined by their knowledge and skills. The social context within which staff operate is a far more important determinant of their performance (see, for example, Georgiades and Phillimore, 1975, Reppucci, 1977, Peters, 1989). Consideration will be given to a number of features of the social context.

General social policy

Challenging behaviour reflects a wide range of personal needs, none of which are exclusive to people who behave in socially unaccepted ways. People who challenge will need access to a wide range of services that serve different purposes, only a few of which might be exclusively related to the behaviour itself. For example there will be needs for services that provide a home, a job, education, personal development, emergency support, respite, asylum, protection for the public, health care. In this context talk of 'a specialist service' for challenging behaviour and arguments about which form of specialist service is best, seem irrelevant. Policy should identify the full range of needs and related service provision being incorporated under the blanket heading of 'challenging behaviour'. The absence of such clarity at the policy level means that ordinary service providing organisations (and hence their staff) are very unclear as to what services they should and should not be providing to particular individuals. This context makes it very hard at the end of the day to identify and encourage specific staff behaviours in relation to people who challenge.

The second set of macro level policy issues follows to some extent from the first but also reflects a huge difference in the way that we provide for adults as opposed to children. For children there is an increasing range of influences that 'press' upon services and provide a framework of contingencies which, in the end, influence staff behaviour. These influences include the Children Act, the National Curriculum, andthe Education Inspectorate. There is little equivalent for adult services and not much evidence that 'contracting out' arrangements will make a major difference to this. Services for adults operate in a vacuum as regards standards and the contingencies that support them. In this context it is very difficult for services and for staff at an individual level to know what they should be doing. Many good things get done but it is difficult to sustain them. Many bad things get done but it is difficult to change them.

The impact of the mess existing at the broader social level could be mitigated if there was strong leadership at the local level. However one of the key themes to emerge from our interactions with staff around the UK is that there are important difficulties here as well. These break down into a number of specific concerns.

Local policy

Those who deliver services need a clear and shared understanding of what they are there for - who they are serving, what they are trying to achieve, why they are trying to achieve it and how they go about their work (Peters, 1989). This is the concept of a 'mission' which needs to live in the hearts and minds of staff, not on paper in a drawer. Many services, specialist or otherwise, lack a clear, living, realistic commitment to the needs of those who challenge. This has a number of damaging effects.

It leaves staff uncertain as to whether they should be working at all with those who challenge. Even if staff feel that this is their job, they lack any clear guidance as to what might constitute good quality work in the employer's eyes. This is demoralising for staff and makes it hard to break out of the cycle of crisis management, flavour of the month interventions and, often, the eventual transfer out of those who put great pressure on services. The second effect of this state of affairs is to render impossible the rational allocation of resources. The third effect is that it undermines any attempt at quality control - developing systems that might shape and influence staff behaviour in the service context. Without a mission there cannot be standards, without standards there cannot be meaningful systems to maintain and develop them.

Organisational structure and style

Having a mission and quality control is an important development but there are also issues concerning the kinds of organisations that can deliver the services envisaged. Take as an example a service that would seek to foster personal development in people with learning disabilities, including those who behave in socially unaccepted ways. Such work requires staff who are committed, who will form close and enduring relationships, who will work flexibly and show initiative and who will deploy a range of human helping skills. The fostering of such staff performances will require a particular kind of organisation. For example it will require an organisational culture which emphasises participation, mutual value and respect and innovation (King et al, 1971, Towell and Harries, 1979, Raynes et al 1979). A multi-layered hierarchical system, with tight job demarcation, relying heavily upon set working procedures and using aversive control mechanisms with staff is incompatible with such work.

However, in any organisation leadership is required and there are recurring themes about difficulties at this level.

Management practises

Those in immediate supervisory/management positions often lack the skills or availability to staff that would make them able to provide leadership and guidance in problem solving work with service users. Given that most staff in the primary caring relationships are unqualified and minimally trained the lack of competent task orientated leadership is all the more significant. It means that staff receive limited task orientated support. It also opens up a credibility gap between staff and managers which breeds cynicism and alienation; conditions not conducive to quality in any form of service.

These difficulties at the task leadership level are compounded by very strongly perceived difficulties in terms of motivational leadership. Most services lack coherent systems to support and motivate staff. The incidence of management practises such as supervision, appraisal, modelling, coaching, constructive feedback, listening and counselling is patchy to say the least. Even where present the competence of implementation varies. In a complex, high stress area of work, such deficiencies have a disastrous impact upon the quality of experience for user and provider alike. Staff become demoralised, they underfunction, they quit. A service with demoralised staff and a high turnover cannot deliver developmental work to users whose needs are often very hard to understand.

The above considerations have significant implications when it comes to training staff:

> **Unless we can create organisations with a clear brief for the client group in question, with competent leadership operating in a flat, open system, then the impact of training front line staff will be minimal.**

RESEARCH ISSUES

Staff behaviour should be influenced by the current state of research and developing knowledge of how to understand and to meet the needs of those who challenge. The gap between research and practise is often commented upon. Three of the issues relevant to this gap will be considered.

The intervention orientation of research

There is a straightforward paucity of research that seeks to understand the nature of behavioural challenges and that evaluates attempts to overcome those challenges. There is also no academic infrastructure that will make it feasible to carry out long term the kind of interdisciplinary research, involving the social, cognitive, and biological sciences, that is necessary for real advancement (Clements, 1987). No field of knowledge can advance these days without the presence of 'dedicated' research facilities. This is lacking for learning, behavioural, and emotional difficulties in the United Kingdom.

Intervention paradigms

Intervention research emanates mainly from the USA and is still primarily behavioural or pharmacological in orientation. Useful though these areas undoubtedly are, practise is actually operating in more varied ways. For example staff are having to look at how to help people cope with major life events, how to develop emotional management strategies, how to address cognitive difficulties; and systemic interventions are increasingly on the lips of those in a consultant role. There is little research to guide any of these endeavours.

Dissemination

Research will not get in to practise on its own merits. By the same token practise is much influenced by interventions which have no/limited research bases. The issue is dissemination - selling, or public relations, to put it in more accessible terminology. Unless this issue is treated seriously in its own right research will not get in to practise and practise will continue to be dogged by fashion and fraud. There is no magic to dissemination - it is perfectly feasible to get new ideas to those who need them. It requires attention to packaging, promotion and support.

The above considerations have significant implications when it comes to training staff:

> **Unless we can increase the volume of intervention research in the UK, develop an adequate academic infrastructure and put in to practise what is known about dissemination, then the content of training will not empower staff adequately to meet the challenges that they face.**

TRAINING ISSUES

A good system provides the supporting context and research contributes to the content; but there are issues which reside in the training domain itself.

Defining required competences

There is still work to be done on defining the overall competences required to deliver quality work with people who challenge. This goes back to the earlier points about clarifying what services are supposed to be delivering. There is also work to be done on defining who needs to know what - what range of jobs there are and which competences are needed for each of these jobs. The work of the NCVQ is very promising in this respect but has still to make a significant impact.

A shared conceptual framework

Services are fragmenting. Staff are recruited from many different backgrounds. Old models of professional training and employment are breaking down. However, all those involved in work with those who challenge need to be able to access and to communicate about the many influences that contribute to human cognitive, behavioural and emotional functioning. They cannot afford to be constrained by traditional academic boundaries and jealousies. They need also to work together with others in a co-ordinated way. This argues for organising knowledge and skills into a shared and accessible framework for understanding and analysing human functioning (Donellan, La Vignu et al, 1988, Zarkowska and Clements, 1988, Clements, 1992). This will in turn facilitate the training process.

Models of training

In order to influence practise, training needs to be closely linked in to actual work with clients. Didactic inputs need to be supported by practicum work with feedback (for example, Martin, 1972). Whilst this is readily acknowledged and we have excellent models for such training programmes (Quine, Chapter 12, McGill and Bliss, Chapter 13) most training is not actually constructed in this way. There are good reasons for this. Short course training, in one-off blocks, causes no disturbance to organisations and established systems, it provides staff with time away and some material comfort, and it provides trainers with powerful social and material reinforcement. From a behavioural perspective it is irresistible in terms of the reinforcement contingencies operating on all those involved. There is every reason to persist with this model even though it is clear from both research and experience that it does not effect sustained change in staff attitudes and behaviour (Martin, 1972, Georgiades and Phillimore, 1975, Reppucci, 1977). It is a powerful reminder of the lack of pressure to achieve real world change for people with learning disabilities.

This brings us full circle, back to the issues raised earlier in this chapter.

Unless these other issues are addressed, poor models of training will be supported because of the outcomes they achieve that have little to do with on the job functioning. The impact of training will remain more limited than it need be.

CONCLUSIONS

If the above analysis is correct, it indicates the need for action at a number of levels.

POLICY

* clarification of the range of services required

* creation of extrinsic frameworks that create a press towards identified service goals for adults

* local creation of realistic missions for particular services

ORGANISATION

* development of structures and styles compatible with identified service functions

MANAGEMENT

* competent implementation of practises that foster staff motivation and optimal functioning in relation to service objectives

RESEARCH

* increased priority to intervention research

* strategic development of academic infrastructure to support long term the kind of research required

* competent dissemination

TRAINING

* identifying competences needed by staff and managers to deliver particular kinds of services

* promotion of models of training likely to deliver the competences required

Many examples of caring and innovative practise exist in this country. They tend to be individual, isolated and often short lived. Ordinary people do extraordinary things. The problem arises in translating these examples in to routine service practice. This has always been the problem and the fundamental issues remain no different now to what they were 20 years ago. The issues are not unduly complicated although they are many in number. They can be addressed.

REFERENCES

CLEMENTS J (1987). *Severe Learning Disability and Psychological Handicap.* Chichester: Wiley and Sons

CLEMENTS J (1992). I can't explain... "Challenging Behaviour": towards a shared conceptual framework. *Clinical Psychology Forum, 39,* 29-37

DONNELLAN A M, LaVIGNA G W, NEGRI-SHOULTZ N, AND FASSBENDER L L (1988). *Progress without Punishment: effective approaches for learners with behaviour problems.* New York: Teachers College Press

GEORGIADES N J AND PHILLIMORE L (1975). The myth of the hero innovator and alternative strategies for organizational change. IN C C Kiernan & E P Woodford (Eds) *Behaviour Modification with the Severely Retarded.* Elsevier: Associated Scientific Publishers

KING R D, RAYNES N V, AND TIZARD J (1971). *Patterns of Residential Care: sociological studies in institutions for handicapped children.* London: Routledge and Kegan Paul

MARTIN G L (1972). Teaching operant technology to psychiatric nurses, aides and attendants. IN F Clark, D R Evans & L O Hamerlynck (Eds) *Implementing Behavioural Programs for Schools and Clinics.* Champaign, Illinois: Research Press

PETERS T (1989). *Thriving on Chaos.* London: Pan Books

RAYNES N, PRATT M W AND ROSES S (1979). *Organisational Structure and the Care of the Mentally Retarded.* London: Croom Helm

REPPUCCI N (1977). Implementation issues for the behaviour modifier as institutional change agent. *Behaviour Therapy, 8,* 594-605

TOWELL D AND HARRIES C (Eds) (1979). *Innovation in Patient Care.* London: Croom Helm

ZARKOWSKA E AND CLEMENTS J (1988). *Problem Behaviour in People with Severe Learning Disabilities.* London: Croom Helm

PART 6

NATIONAL GUIDANCE

CHAPTER 15

SERVICES FOR PEOPLE WITH LEARNING DISABILITIES AND CHALLENGING BEHAVIOUR OR MENTAL HEALTH NEEDS: THE PROJECT GROUP REPORT

Jim Mansell

This chapter is based on Mansell J (in press) Policy and policy implementation. In Emerson E, McGill P and Mansell J (Eds), Severe Learning Disabilities and Challenging Behaviour: Designing high-quality services. London: Chapman and Hall.

The purpose of this chapter is to outline some of the main themes of the recent report of a Department of Health Project Group (Department of Health, 1993). In setting up the Project Group, the Department of Health framed its task in these terms:

> "We believe that the time has come to offer health authorities and social services authorities something more specific in the way of guidance, and we propose to do this by seeking to build on the achievements of a very small number of local services we judge to be operating with some success. In essence, the aim is to analyse how four local services approach the task, and to synthesise the findings into practical guidance from which local services might be constructed elsewhere, with the likelihood that they too will be successful".
>
> (Section 1)

The four services were the Additional Support Team, Exeter (Williams et al, 1991), the Special Projects Team, Sunderland (Johnson, 1990, Johnson and Cooper, 1991), the Mental Impairment Evaluation and Treatment Service, South East Thames Region (Murphy and Clare, 1991, Murphy et al, 1991, Dockrell et al, 1990, 1992, Dockrell et al, Chapter 11); and the Special Development Team, also for the South East Thames Region (Emerson et al, 1987, McGill et al, 1991, McGill et al, in press).

The report refers only to England, the strategy for service development in learning disabilities is different in Wales (see Welsh Office, 1991). There is no comparable Scottish guidance, and, of course, the structure and organisation of services in Britain is quite different from the other countries which have set out to replace institutional care. Nevertheless, visits to services in these countries suggest that the main issues raised in the English report are probably present in all these service systems.

The Report considers the definition of the client group, their numbers and needs; describes the key elements of the exemplary services; comments on the most appropriate models of care; and then details guidance for commissioning authorities, contrasting examples of good with weak practice. Rather than summarise its content in this chapter, five themes which pervade the Report are described below.

THE SOCIAL CONTEXT OF CHALLENGING BEHAVIOUR

The Report emphasises the social construction of challenging behaviour; that it is the product of both individual factors and the circumstances in which the person lives (see Table 1, reproduced from the Report) .

Table 1   Factors contributing to challenging behaviour

The individual	Their circumstances
the degree of learning disability	history of neglect
a mental illness	history of sexual abuse
a physical disability eg epilepsy	history of physical abuse
a sensory impairement	a reputation for challenging others in the past
absence of adequate verbal communication	restrictive home or day time environment which maximises confrontations
age	surroundings which an individual dislikes
physical illness	lack of understanding of the *meaning* of non-verbal behaviour by carers
	low expectations of carers
	over-emphasis on risk reduction

One implication of this is that people with learning disabilities who have challenging behaviour form an extremely diverse group, including individuals with all levels of learning disability, many different sensory or physical impairments and presenting quite different kinds of challenges, ranging from chronic self-injury by people with profound learning disability to law-breaking by people with mild learning disability but who have mental health problems. Services themselves therefore need to be highly individualised.

In particular, the Report draws attention to the needs of people with learning disabilities who offend, and emphasises that these people have needs which must be addressed by local learning disability services too.

Although acknowledging that people have special needs, the point is made at the outset that people with challenging behaviour have the same needs as anyone else and that issues of 'double discrimination' on grounds of race and gender are likely to be particularly important. The Report also identifies the needs of carers and staff as important considerations. Noting that the failure of community services to keep pace with hospital closure is imposing a greater burden on families, and that working with people who present major challenges involves a great deal of stress, the Report says that services should not be provided by exploiting the personal commitment and dedication of carers and staff.

The other major implication of recognising that challenging behaviour is the product of a complex mix of individual and environmental factors is that an exclusive focus on the people who have the most challenging problems is not likely to be sufficient:

> "The proper role and characteristics of specialist services can only be achieved by attending to the competence of 'mainstream' learning disability services. The priority is to improve the capability of mainstream services to prevent problems arising in the first place, to manage them when they occur and to implement relatively sophisticated long-term arrangements for management, treatment and care. In so far as this can be achieved, specialist services will be able to concentrate on people with the most complex and difficult needs. At the moment, even moderate levels of challenging behaviour are not being appropriately managed in mainstream learning disability services and specialist services (including some of dubious quality) face apparently unlimited demand."
> (Covering letter: Report to Department of Health).

In this way the Report identifies the competence or capability of local 'mainstream' services for people with learning disabilities as an important factor determining the number of people defined as presenting a serious challenge:

> "Whether these services continue to get better depends in part on how they respond to challenging behaviour, not just in the small number of people who present exceptional problems at any one time, but throughout their service. If they develop the capacity to work with people who present challenges in small, local services they will keep the size of the problem to a

minimum and they will provide a good service to individuals in both their mainstream and specialised services ... If local services are not developed then a trickle of expensive out-of-area placements will become a rush as more people are excluded from mainstream community services by being defined as unmanageable in the community. Large amounts of money will be tied up in buying less good services. The policy of community care will be said to have failed." (Section 6)

IMPORTANCE OF MANAGEMENT COMMITMENT

The second strand in the Report is the belief that weakness of management commitment may be a more important limiting factor in improving services than knowledge and experience of models of service. A key observation made to the Project Group was that the senior managers of local service agencies could be classified by their intentions in relation to services for people with challenging behaviour, and that this helped explain different approaches to service development for this client group.

(i) **Removers** "do not want to develop locally the competence to serve people with challenging behaviour (perhaps because they perceive the task as too difficult, or not worth the effort). They seek instead to place people who cannot be served locally in out-of-area residential placements, often at considerable expense."

(ii) **Containers** "do seek to provide local services (perhaps because of the cost of out-of-area placements) but seek only to contain people in low-cost (and therefore poorly-staffed) settings."

(iii) **Developers** "seek to provide local services which really do address individual needs, and therefore give higher priority to funding services which, with more staff and more training and management input, are more expensive than ordinary community services." (Section 3.1)

The Report suggests that reasons for this include beliefs that nothing much can be achieved and so it is not worth spending the money, or that the numbers concerned are so small that the effort of developing services is not worth it, or that cheap, low-staffed institutional care is really providing the quality its proponents claim. It restates the reasons why priority should be given to these services:

(i) **People with challenging behaviour have the greatest needs**
"People with learning disabilities and challenging behaviour present the most complex and difficult problems, both at clinical and service organisation levels. Although their numbers may be relatively small, unless services respond well they occupy disproportionate amounts of time and money."   (Section 5.1.1)

(ii) **Good quality services achieve results**
"Current research suggests that good quality services already make a substantial difference to the quality of life of individuals with challenging behaviour, and therefore by implication to their carers and staff. If the characteristics that make these services work were more widespread and better supported by management it would be possible to apply even more of the available knowledge at the clinical level and to achieve even better results for individuals." (Section 5.1.2)

(iii) **Failure to develop services threatens the policy of community care**
"Doing nothing locally is not an option. Out-of-area placements will 'silt up' and reinstitutionalisation (through emergency admissions to psychiatric hospitals or via the prisons) will occur. Special institutions and residential homes for people with challenging behaviour will be expensive but of poor quality and will attract public criticism. Overall, the efficiency of services will decrease because of the widespread lack of competence in working with people who have challenging behaviour. Commissioners will have less control over and choice of services. Individual service users, carers and staff will be hurt and some individuals with challenging behaviour will be at increased risk of abuse. Staff will be at increased risk from the consequences of developing their own strategies and responses and managers will be held accountable where well-intentioned staff operate illegal or inappropriate procedures."   (Section 5.1.3)

This leads to the conclusion that:

"The key to the development of better services is management commitment. We are confident that there is now sufficient knowledge and practical experience to substantially improve services, given the kind of sustained commitment from policy-makers and managers that the services we studied had enjoyed.

Many people we met expressed anxiety that this commitment was diminishing. We think that the Department of Health could usefully re-emphasise the priority these services should command." (Covering letter: Report to Department of Health).

THE SERVICE DEVELOPMENT PROCESS

The Project Group faced the problem of how to respond to demands for clarity in dividing responsibility between health and social services authorities and in choosing between community or institution-based models of long-term care, given the constraints of wider national policy. The main vehicle it uses to address these problems is the idea that the development of services is a process in which different arrangements might be justified at different stages.

Constrained by the wider framework of defining needs as either health or social care responsibilities, the Report does not attempt to define a boundary. It offers chapter and verse to correct any misapprehension among health authorities that the community care reforms may mean that they would have no continuing responsibility for services for people with learning disabilities (Department of Health, 1991), and suggests that where the boundary between different agencies is set will depend more on the relative skills and experience of each agency locally than on artificial definitions of what tasks might be health or social care. It offers the experience of the Special Development Team in South East Thames Regional Health Authority (McGill and Mansell, Chapter 9), where the same type of highly staffed and organised houses are provided in some places by local authority social services departments and in others by health authorities, depending on the stage of service development reached locally.

Although the Report is clear that community-based residential and day care services are the option preferred by members of the Project Group, the guidance to health and social services authorities commissioning services for their local populations recognises that some will continue to need to use poorer quality services while they develop the local infrastructure and expertise needed:

> "Commissioners with no experience of local community-based services for people with challenging behaviour should begin developing these to gain information about local need and the expertise to improve services; continued use of poor quality

services (usually large institutions or residential homes) to provide long-term residential and day care should only continue to give a breathing-space for local service development. Service development should be planned on an iterative, incremental basis so that plans can be adapted in response to individual needs and as local expertise and confidence grows." (Section 5.3)

This is also the place where the Report focuses on staffing, saying that if the opportunities provided by community-based models of care are to be realised in practice, commissioners should have clear strategies for ensuring that providers have adequate numbers of suitably trained staff over the longer term, avoiding the perverse incentive for individual providers to rely on 'poaching' staff.

EMPIRICISM AND 'VALUE FOR MONEY'

Having recognised that one motive for commissioners to purchase poorer quality services was their lower cost, the Project Group had to produce a Report which addressed the problem of resources. It approached the issue partly by looking at resources as a question of priorities, partly by taking into account a wider range of costs and partly by focusing on 'value for money' as the yardstick by which service development choices should be made.

The Report points out that the services represented on the Project Group were all being developed within the existing resource framework available to their host agencies and suggests that resources are therefore as much a question of priorities as of the amount of money available.

Turning to costs the Report says that commissioners should take care to identify all the current expenditure. The Report says that although adequate services for people with challenging behaviour will probably take more resources than currently allocated (since there is no logical basis to existing resource levels), there are probably more resources in use than is apparent at first. It gives the example of some agencies which spend substantial amounts of contingency reserves held at agency level on this group, while failing for want of money to develop the local capacity to serve.

Commissioners are also advised to take account of the hidden costs of failure to develop local services (see Figure 1, reproduced from the Report),

Figure 1 The hidden cost of failing to develop local services

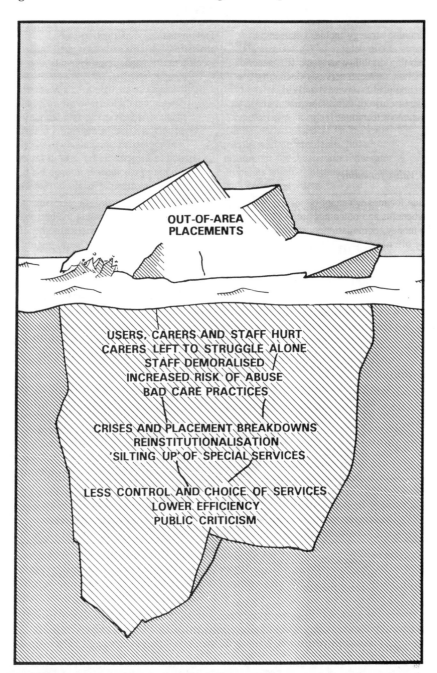

such as the costs of handling crises and placement breakdowns, and the financial and other costs borne by carers (Qureshi, Chapter 5). They are advised to avoid increasing the burden on carers by reducing levels of service. The Report calls for increasingly individualised costs to remove the confounding effect of averaging across clients and settings. In the short-term, the Report suggests commissioners should certainly look to redirect resources from relatively expensive out-of-area placements to local service development, although it also acknowledges that a very small number of individuals will be very expensive to serve wherever they live and it would be naive to expect cost savings as a matter of course

The Report also focuses on 'value for money', pointing out that value for money cannot be judged solely on the basis of costs but requires an assessment of the benefits and outcomes produced:

> "Commissioners should have equal regard for the value of services (the benefits they offer to the service user) as for their cost. They should attend to the general quality of life ... in addition to the specific treatment of challenging behaviour. At service system level, value for money needs to be demonstrated by the low number of placement breakdowns and of out-of-area placements."
> (Section 5.4)

Taken with the comments about models of care made elsewhere in the Report, this embodies the assumption that if all costs and benefits are taken into account community-based services are likely to prove the best choice. For example, in relation to residential care the Report says:

> "Members of the Committee are themselves persuaded that the best model of residential care is likely to be the supported ordinary housing model. The available research evidence shows consistently poor quality of life in hospital (whether old or new campus-style hospitals); on other large-group models of care there is little quantitative research but since they share many of the resource and organisational characteristics of hospitals there are no grounds for believing they will achieve very different results...Of course some of the newer supported housing services are not yet much better: but the best do offer a quite different quality of life. The key to the difference between good and indifferent community services lies not in resources, but in the quality of management (especially first-line management)."
> (Section 4.1)

In this sense the Report adopts a confidently empiricist approach to the debate about models of care. This reflects something of a change in the debate over models of care, which was characterised in the 1970's and early 1980's by the question "are community services feasible"; with more widespread development and clear demonstrations of success in community services, there is now more pressure for institutional models to demonstrate what they really achieve.

In this last connection the Report calls for a critical appraisal by those purchasing services; referring to the example of the services represented on the Project Group, it says:

> "... a crucial difference between these services and some others is that management can evaluate whether what the service claims to do it really achieves. Since virtually all services claim to provide individualised care based on the latest assessment methods it is essential that service managers and purchasers can really discriminate between good and mediocre performance. This can be a particular problem for services providing long-term residential or day care, where a successful service looks like an ordinary home or occupation, when in fact it is a carefully designed and organised service dependent on a great deal of skill and management."   (Section 3.4)

COMPREHENSIVENESS

The fifth strand which runs through the Report is that individual components or parts of the whole service system often depend on the existence of many other components working well, and that good services for individuals require the integration of different aspects or parts of services into an effective whole.

At the broadest level, this is a point the Report makes in considering relationships between different agencies. It suggests joint commissioning as a possible way for health and social services to work together, but also calls for good working relationships between these and other agencies such as housing, education and the police.

At the service system level, the Report calls for the required range of service types (for example, for the provision of good quality work or education placements as well as support for life at home) as well as the different functional elements needed (for prevention of challenging behaviour, its identification, assessment and treatment). In relation to services for people with learning disability who have mental health needs, the Report commends the policy of ensuring equal access to generic mental health services, but acknowledges that there may be a need for some specialized mental health provision:

> "The appropriate role for hospital services, where these will have a continuing existence, lies in the kind of short-term, highly focused assessment and treatment offered by the Mental Impairment Evaluation and Treatment Service. This implies a small service offering very specifically and closely defined time-limited services...This was quite different from the traditional hospital model operating in some of the services the Committee visited...Lack of an effective working relationship between hospital and community services was evident, with some hospital staff blaming community services for long hospital stays in a situation where the hospital took no responsibility for creating a partnership with the local services. Although these kinds of service reported heavy demand, members of the Committee were concerned that this reflected an easy option for commissioners rather than the best value for money." (Section 4.3)

Finally, within the individual components of services the Report emphasises the planning and management needed to routinely deliver high quality service to people:

> "Good understanding of the reasons for an individual's challenging behaviour and of how this interacts with the everyday organisation of the service ... requires a greater degree of skill among staff and particularly good management (especially first-line management) to keep the service on track. Management is also crucial in ensuring that professional specialists and front-line staff work together; that specialist advice is practicable and sensible and that staff follow it.... In particular, managers need to distinguish the middle ground between pessimism about models of care ('you can't do anything with these people') and naive misinterpretations about normalisation ('only values matter - all structure is oppressive'); life for people with major disabilities in good services will often look quite ordinary, but this ordinariness will

be the product of a great deal of careful planning and management." (Section 3.4)

IMPLEMENTATION

The task facing those responsible for services for people who have learning disabilities and challenging behaviour is clear, if difficult. They have to build on the work they did to introduce new values into services, to turn those values into practice; to bring 'mainstream' community services up to the level of the models which inspired their development. They have to do this while continuing to make an orderly transition from institutional to community-based service models, and against a background of many other claims on their time and resources (whether generated directly by the needs of clients or due to administrative change and reorganisation).

A report alone, even if backed up through official circulars, is not likely to produce change on the required scale, primarily because management attention and commitment from all members of the local service-providing coalition will need to be sustained beyond the period surrounding publication to carry out the improvements required. Commitment is required from managers of different agencies, not all of whom come into the category of 'developers'; new services and new ways of working have to be introduced and then sustained throughout learning disability services and beyond, among those generic services which include people with learning disabilities among their clients; and this will require strategic planning, especially in relation to developing a skilled workforce, as well as the diversity and competition a mixed economy of welfare is supposed to bring.

If this is left to the formal review mechanisms which operate through Regional Health Authorities and the Social Services Inspectorate there is the risk that poor performance in this area will be `traded-off' against work on other issues, since these reviews necessarily focus on a very small number of major priorities. What is needed is a process of implementation which targets the operational managers responsible for commissioning local services and their counterparts in provider agencies: a process which can facilitate local action without obstructing the main priority-setting pathway (which is often likely to be preoccupied with other matters).

There is a parallel here with hospital closure, as in the well-documented example of Darenth Park. There, little progress was made in developing local replacement services while the formal relationships between the Regional and District Health Authorities were used; it was only when the Regional Health Authority developed new links directly with local operational managers that real progress began to be made (Korman and Glennerster, 1991, Mansell, 1988a). These included forums to work collaboratively and to bring people together to learn from each other and a central task force which acted in part as interpreters and facilitators of local action within the framework of a Regional project.

One example of this way of working was the use of a 'learning set' to enable local teams to develop staffed housing as their main form of residential care at a time when the prevailing climate had favoured institutional solutions (Mansell, 1988b, 1989). The teams, drawn from Health and Social Services (and sometimes the voluntary sector too), met every six to eight weeks over a period of 18 months to work through the practical problems of implementation. As well as effective dissemination of the best available knowledge and experience, they derived support and credibility from working together and they produced a rapid expansion in community-based services.

A similar model is needed here. A national initiative, embracing enough field authorities to make a significant impact in services, through which the experience of existing examples of good practice can be securely put into practice. Regional initiatives like that in the South East and national publications and networks promulgated by the Kings Fund have made a start, but these have mainly focused on an already committed, and largely professional rather than managerial, audience. The commitment required of senior managers can only be sustained by Government leadership.

REFERENCES

DEPARTMENT OF HEALTH (1991). Stephen Dorrell's Mencap Speech: Statement on services for people with learning disabilities - Tuesday 25 June 1991. London: Department of Health.

DEPARTMENT OF HEALTH (1993). Services for People with Learning Disabilities and Challenging Behaviour or Mental Health Needs: Report of a Project Group (Chairman: Prof J L Mansell). London: Department of Health.

DOCKRELL J, GASKELL G AND REHMAN H (1992). *A preliminary report of the evaluation of the Mental Impairment Evaluation and Treatment Service (MIETS).* Departmental Research Report 92-42. London School of Economics Department of Social Psychology.

DOCKRELL J, GASKELL G AND REHMAN H (1990). Challenging behaviours: problems, provisions and 'solutions'. IN A Dosen, A Van Gennep and G J Zwanikken (Eds) *Treatment of Mental Illness and Behavioural Disorder in the Mentally Retarded.* Leiden: Logon Publications.

EMERSON E, BARRETT S, BELL C, CUMMINGS R, HUGHES H, McCOOL C, TOOGOOD A AND MANSELL J (1987). The Special Development Team: Developing Services for People with Severe Learning Difficulties and Challenging Behaviours. University of Kent at Canterbury.

JOHNSON D (1990). Steps to a better service. *Health Service Journal,* 7 June 1990, 844-845.

JOHNSON D AND COOPER B (1991). The Special Projects Team, Sunderland. IN D Allen, R Banks and S Staite (Eds) *Meeting the Challenge: Some U.K. perspectives on comunity services for people with learning difficulties and challenging behaviour.* London: King's Fund.

KORMAN N AND GLENNERSTER H (1990). *Hospital Closure.* Milton Keynes: Open University Press.

MANSELL J (1988a). Training for service development. IN D Towell (Ed), *An Ordinary Life in Practice: Lessons from the experience of developing comprehensive community-based services for people with learning disabilities.* London: Kings Fund.

MANSELL J (1988b). *Staffed housing for people with mental handicaps: achieving widespread dissemination.* Bexhill: South East Thames Regional Health Authority.

MANSELL J (1989). Evaluation of training in the development of staffed housing for people with mental handicaps. *Mental Handicap Research, 2,* 137-151.

McGILL P, EMERSON E AND MANSELL J (in press). Individually designed residential provision for people with seriously challenging behaviours. IN E Emerson, P McGill and J Mansell (Eds) *Severe Learning Disabilities and Challenging Behaviour: Designing high quality services.* London: Chapman and Hall.

McGILL P, HAWKINS C AND HUGHES H (1991). The Special Development Team, South East Thames. IN D Allen, R Banks and S Staite (Eds), *Meeting the Challenge: Some U.K. perspectives on comunity services for people with learning difficulties and challenging behaviour.* London: King's Fund.

MURPHY G AND CLARE I (1991). MIETS: a service option for people with mild mental handicaps and challenging behaviour or psychiatric problems - 2. Assessment, treatment and outcome for service users and service effectiveness. *Mental Handicap Research, 4,* 180-206.

MURPHY G, HOLLAND A, FOWLER P AND REEP J (1991). MIETS: a service option for people with mild mental handicaps and challenging behaviour or psychiatric problems - 1. Philosophy, service and service users. *Mental Handicap Research, 4,* 41-66.

WELSH OFFICE (1991). Challenges and Responses: A report on services in support of adults with mental handicaps with exceptionally serious challenging behaviours, mental illnesses, or who offend. Cardiff: Welsh Office.

WILLIAMS C, HEWITT P AND BRATT A (1991). Responding to the needs of people with learning difficulties whose behaviour we perceive as challenging: the past, present and future - a perspective from Exeter Health Authority. IN J Harris (Ed) *Service Responses to People with Learning Difficulties and Challenging Behaviour.* Kidderminster: British Institute of Mental Handicap.

PART 7

RESEARCH TO PRACTICE?

CHAPTER 16

**FUTURE DIRECTIONS FOR RESEARCH
AND SERVICE DEVELOPMENT FOR
PEOPLE WITH LEARNING DISABILITIES
AND CHALLENGING BEHAVIOUR**

Chris Kiernan

INTRODUCTION

In relative terms the 1980s have seen a massive research investment in the investigation of challenging behaviour shown by people with learning disabilities. This research has undoubtedly helped to point the way in which policy, service organisation, clinical practice and research should develop. This Chapter will briefly review some of the main themes which have emerged, drawing largely on the work described in earlier Chapters, and will raise issues which might point the direction for future development.

The Epidemiology of challenging behaviour

A substantial investment has been made in assessing the prevalence of challenging behaviour shown by people with learning disabilities. The studies by Murphy and her colleagues (Chapter 1), Russell and Harris (Chapter 2), and Kiernan and Qureshi (Chapter 3), offer an extensive basis on which policy makers and service planners could act.

Studies of the true prevalence of challenging behaviour are hampered by a number of factors (Russell and Harris, Chapter 2). A true prevalence could only be established by screening a total population of people defined as having learning disabilities using psychometric measures and measures of adaptive behaviour. Such a study would identify people with mild and severe learning disabilities. Administrative prevalence studies of the type described in this volume cover only people with learning disabilities who are known to learning disability services. They thereby leave out of account the overwhelming proportion of people with mild learning disability (Richardson and Koller, 1985). However the one British study which has followed a population of people with learning disability from childhood, and which includes both severely and mildly disabled people, suggests that people with mild learning disability and challenging behaviour may be more likely than others to be known to services (Richardson, personal communication). Amongst this group were people who had been convicted of criminal offences. Gunn, Maden and Swinton (1991) have established that a minority of the convicted criminal population have learning disabilities (one per cent of men and two per cent of women). The possibility remains that an unknown number of people with mild learning disability are in prison on remand or show challenging behaviour which creates difficulties for them in their adaptation, but which does not attract the attention of the Police. Such people may well be involved with field social work services. They may or may not be better served by specialist learning disability services. Their current pattern of services, and where they receive them, could well be subjected to research.

The studies described in this volume suggest that around one in six people known to services for people with learning disabilities show challenging behaviour on the basis of the definitions adopted. As Russell and Harris (Chapter 2) point out challenging behaviour is difficult to define. This difficulty reflects, in part, the essentially social nature of the behaviour. In particular, aggressive and destructive behaviours occur in particular social settings and may be occasioned by those settings and maintained by them. This has been a widespread assumption that institutional settings, in particular, generate challenging behaviour. Conflicting evidence on this issue is provided by other studies in this volume. Felce and Lowe (Chapter 8) show that, despite significant improvement in skills and in quality of life, challenging behaviour did not diminish (p 202). McGill and Mansell (Chapter 9) quote similar data although they report a change in the pattern of challenging behaviour. We will return to this issue later.

The studies agree however that the prevalence of challenging behaviour is higher in the learning disabilities hospitals than in community settings. This finding has clear implications for the development of community provision as hospital populations are relocated. Similarly, there is broad agreement on the overall age profile of the population of people with challenging behaviour, although peak prevalence appears to be earlier in the self-injury group, between 15 and 20, than in the aggressive behaviour or general challenging behaviour populations (15 to 29 years and 20 to 29 years respectively).

The studies also suggest that self-injury is more characteristic of severely learning disabled people with additional physical or sensory disabilities. However, the overall picture indicates that, in terms of abilities, people showing challenging behaviours are a heterogenous population. This has clear implications for the development of a variety of life-styles and interventions for the groups concerned.

All of the studies also agree that significant challenging behaviour occurs in children with learning disabilities. Murphy and her colleagues (Chapter 1, p 15) found around 140 children and adolescents under the age of fifteen showing self-injury of sufficient intensity to cause tissue damage. Kiernan and Kiernan (1987) found that, on average, schools for pupils with severe learning difficulties identified 23 per cent of their pupils as showing challenging behaviour, of whom eight per cent presented serious management problems. This gives five children presenting serious management problems in the average school with 61 pupils on the school role. Russell and Harris found a higher frequency of aggression in the school than in the adult population. However, children whose actions resulted in severe injury were less likely than adults to be seen as presenting extreme management problems. Sloper and Turner (Chapter 4) illustrate the types of challenging behaviour reported by parents of children with Down's Syndrome.

These findings highlight two issues. Firstly, challenging behaviour is not simply an issue for adult services. Secondly, the Russell and Harris finding points out the likelihood that behaviours which are present, but not an extreme management problem, in children may become so as the child grows in size. Both issues suggest that early intervention and intervention during childhood may be crucial, a theme which we will discuss in more detail below.

Russell and Harris (Chapter 2) and Kiernan and Qureshi (Chapter 3) both identify a small core of people who presented extreme management problems. There were 18 people showing aggressive behaviour in a district with a population of 370,000 in the Russell and Harris study and 42 people showing serious challenging behaviour of any type in an "average" district of 22 thousand in Kiernan and Qureshi. The studies agree in finding a substantial proportion of these people in hospitals (13 of 18 and 17 of 42 respectively). This population is likely to represent the group which receive enhanced services in the community where these are developed (McGill and Mansell, Chapter 9, Emerson et al, Chapter 10, McGill and Bliss, Chapter 13). However, several contributors to this volume have questioned the wisdom of specifically targeting this group when the majority of people with challenging behaviour remain served by mainstream services with no additional support (see below).

The Constructionalist model

Current analyses of the most appropriate form of management and intervention are outlined by several contributors to this volume. They reflect a 'constructionalist' approach (Goldiamond, 1974) involving the development of skills, including communication skills, and analysis of factors occasioning challenging behaviours with appropriate behavioural interventions based on these analyses (Remington, Chapter 6). A critical component of intervention based on this approach is the enhancement of the quality of life of people with learning disabilities brought about by increased staff/client interaction and engagement in worthwhile activities within settings which can maximise competence.

Management and Intervention

Early intervention. Data from the prevalence studies indicate an increase in prevalence to a peak between 15 and 30 after which prevalence declines. Why this decline should occur remains unexplored. Certainly the relatively sparse data on chronicity, reviewed here by Murphy and her colleagues (Chapter 1), and the longitudinal studies described by Sloper and Turner (Chapter 4) and Quine (Chapter 12), suggest that, once established, challenging behaviours reflect patterns of interpersonal interactions which are likely to be long-lasting. Consequently, attention is beginning to once again focus on prevention of the development of severe challenging behaviour through early intervention.

Research and service development in the 1970s emphasised the potential of early intervention for the development of children with learning disability. These studies were motivated by possibility that intervention would lead to general developmental gain and were, in this respect, disappointing (Kiernan, 1985). None of the studies specifically explored the impact of early intervention on problem behaviour.

Contributors to this volume present a variety of reasons why early intervention should be re-visited as an approach which may reduce prevalence of challenging behaviour in later life. Oliver (Chapter 7) presents the theoretical case most fully arguing that, in the case of self-injury, mild behaviours, which may begin by being occasioned and influenced by relatively simple contingencies will escalate to major proportions as the child grows. This will be affected in very young children, in Oliver's model, by both social and biological factors. The problems in management and successful intervention once self-injurious behaviour has become well established are illustrated by difficulties found by Murphy and her colleagues (Chapter 1). They conclude that 'programmes need almost prohibitively high inputs of psychologists' time, are extremely stressful to run, and the programmes themselves are very fragile' (p 31).

This volume does not explore services for children. However, several important conclusions concerning such services emerge. Sloper and Turner (Chapter 4), Qureshi (Chapter 5), and Quine (Chapter 12), all report that the presence of challenging behaviour is related to high levels of maternal psychological distress. Qureshi found that the advice concerning challenging behaviour which the majority of parents had received was not felt by them to be helpful (61 per cent, p 103), that 26 per cent had not received any advice and that only 13 per cent had received advice which they considered useful. This was despite a strong wish for help and advice. On the other hand, Quine (Chapter 12) illustrates the positive impact of a successful intervention to resolve sleep problems on maternal behaviour (irritability, smacking, and loss of control), mother's attitudes, and their relationships with their child and with their partners. Given the link between parent-child attitudes and challenging behaviour described by Sloper and Turner it seems clear that interventions of the type described by Quine might well break a vicious cycle of challenging behaviour, poor mother/child relationships, and maintenance of challenging behaviour. Sloper and Turner also highlight the need for advice and support at particular times, specifically in the early identification of health problems and in dealing with illness related behaviour.

The most common form of early intervention in the UK is based on the Portage model. A recent survey conducted by Vicki Horner of the National Portage Association indicates that projects are active in at least 70 per cent of English Local Authorities (Kiernan, 1993). Portage, as a service, emphasises the skill-building component of the constructionalist model. Within the model it would be expected that this would lead to a likelihood that interventions would have an indirect, but important impact on challenging behaviour, especially where such behaviour is associated with a failure to develop communication skills (Remington, Chapter 6, Oliver, Chapter 7).

Portage projects were given special Department of Education funding between 1986 and 1991. This allowed the establishment of projects throughout the majority of English Authorities, parallel arrangements being made in Wales. There is now a concern that, given that home-based intervention is not a statutory requirement, the planned ending of the special funding will lead to these interventions being run down or wound up.

Emerson and his colleagues (Chapter 10) emphasise the importance of prevention and early intervention in the development of a strategy for services for people with challenging behaviours. Their survey identified 17 Community Support Teams, just over half of which served children, usually in addition to adults (p 236). We know nothing of the effectiveness of these teams in assisting parents or schools. Similarly, we have no information on the effectiveness of any services which may be provided by other agencies (for example Educational Psychology Departments) or out-reach programmes established by schools. Given the likely importance of early intervention, and intervention with children and young people of school age, investigation of the existence and effectiveness of such schemes becomes critical.

Biological factors. The constructional model suggests that effective intervention involves the development of the skills of people with learning disabilities and challenging behaviour and the use of behaviour analysis in order to identify factors which occasion challenging behaviour. The approach is purely 'behavioural', biological factors do not play a significant part beyond setting the parameters of the behavioural repertoire which the person displays. In other terms, sensory, physical, and intellectual disabilities, play a part in determining the historical development of current repertoires and affect the potential for future development.

Oliver's analysis of the combined effect of biological and social factors in the evolution of self-injurious behaviour (Chapter 7) is a model attempt to integrate in detail what have been essentially 'alternative' accounts of the 'causes' of challenging behaviour. The model could lay the basis for interventions based on behavioural analysis combined with rational pharmacological intervention, ie pharmacological interventions based on hypotheses concerning specific biological mechanisms.

To date, pharmacological interventions have largely been based on the power of drugs, in particular anxiolytics, hypnotics and anti-psychotics, to affect challenging behaviour through their non-specific effects. The extent of use of anti-psychotic drugs has been noted in several Chapters in this volume as a major method of 'treatment' (Murphy et al, Chapter 1, p 7, Russell and Harris, Chapter 2, p 45, Kiernan and Qureshi, Chapter 3, p 59-61). The analysis provided by Kiernan and Qureshi suggests that anti-psychotic drugs are typically prescribed for their potential ability to control socially disruptive challenging behaviour. However, successive reviews of research have failed to trace well controlled studies which illustrate their effectiveness whilst also stressing the damaging side-effects of these drugs in leading to extra-pyramidal symptoms (eg Aman and Singh, 1983).

These data, and the data described by Kiernan and Qureshi which suggest that prescription practices vary widely depending on settings and individual prescription practices, are alarming. It would be easy to slide into the extreme positions taken by the 'anti-drug lobby'. but this would clearly risk the rejection of treatments which could be of substantial value. There is a need for careful re-appraisal of drug prescriptions practices and a need for the funding of carefully controlled combined behavioural and pharmacological interventions, if possible based on models of the type which Oliver has outlined.

Restraint. There can be little disagreement, however, on the undesirability of the long-term use of restraining devices in the attempt to control self-injury (Murphy et al, Chapter 1). Similarly, the common use of physical restraint by staff raises questions concerning the degree to which staff have been trained in methods of avoiding its use and in effective but humane methods of control and restraint (Russell and Harris, Chapter 2, p 44, Kiernan and Qureshi, Chapter 3, p 59).

Service development. Implementations of the constructionalist approach described in this volume lead directly to the broad recommendations outlined by Mansell (Chapter 15). Felce and Lowe (Chapter 8) and McGill and Mansell (Chapter 9) show that significant improvements in the quality of life of people with learning disabilities and challenging behaviour can be brought about in ordinary housing with appropriate support.

Similarly, the MIETS service has been shown to have positive outcomes for its clients (Murphy, Holland et al, 1991, Murphy and Clare, 1991, Clare and Murphy, 1993).

These authors emphasise the need for the development of well planned, tightly managed provision for people with learning disability in order to improve skills and quality of life. Unfortunately, such planning and management is clearly lacking in many facilities. Repeatedly throughout this volume lack of planning, management and staff commitment have been described as factors leading to a failure to implement or maintain effective programmes (Murphy et al, Chapter 1, McGill and Mansell, Chapter 9, Emerson et al, Chapter 10, Clements, Chapter 14, Mansell, Chapter 15). In commenting on the organisational contexts which frame Community Support Teams, Emerson and his colleagues conclude that they tend to be 'characterised by scarcity of resources, including skilled human resources, inflexibility of team working, structure and management, poorly developed service review, and inadequate mechanisms for matching resources to human needs' (p 240). In discussing the lack of coherent systems to motivate staff, Clements (Chapter 14) suggests that 'in a complex, high stress area of work such deficiencies have a disastrous impact upon the quality of experience for user and provider alike' (p 325). Mansell (Chapter 15) quotes the covering letter to the Project Group Report as saying 'we are confident that there is now sufficient knowledge and practical experience to substantially improve services' (p 338). The Report sees weakness of management commitment as possibly a more important limiting factor in development of services than knowledge and experience of models of services.

A possible index of the failure of development of local service provision is provided by Khan, Cumella et al, (1993). They describe a group of 31 people admitted to a learning disability hospital within the previous five years which they refer to as 'new long-stay patients'. The majority of the group (19) were under the age of 30 and mildly to moderately learning disabled. Twenty nine per cent were diagnosed as having a psychiatric disorder and 84 per cent were assessed as being either a severe management problem in their current setting or a 'potential' management problem if moved to a less restrictive setting. Sixty five per cent of the group showed more than one challenging behaviour. Khan and his colleagues suggest that the new long-stay residents of hospitals will be those for whom suitable community-based accommodation is unavailable or where the provision which is available proves unsuitable (1993, p 172). Half of the people in the group were admitted directly from supported accommodation in the community. They conclude that 'Health Authorities should continue to purchase hospital accommodation for this group of patients, until it has been demonstrated that community based services in their area provide a suitable alternative' (1993, p 172).

The Project Group Report identifies three different approaches of senior managers to service development for the client group; Removal, Containment, and Development. Removers seek to place people in out-of-area residential placement often at high cost, Containers seek to contain people in low-cost settings, and Developers seek to address individual needs through local services which are therefore more expensive than ordinary community services.

Clearly these differing policies will have an impact on line managers, including front line managers and on staff. However, even within developmentally oriented services the attitudes skills and patterns of work of managers and front-line staff can clearly have substantial negative effects. What is missing in this volume is an analysis of the current skills, attitudes, and activities of the workforce. It would be important in bringing about change in services to be able to identify what skills staff currently have, what their attitudes are, and what in their current pattern of activities may be preventing them from implementing policies. In discussions with front-line managers of broadly developmentally oriented services for people with challenging behaviour Lally (personal communication) found that they identified a heavy administrative commitment as a significant barrier to their direct involvement in the day-to-day activities of their front-line staff (Mansell, Chapter 15, p 345). In addition, they commonly lacked skills in programme planning and behavioural interventions and therefore found it difficult to provide practice leadership.

The outcome of service interventions based on the organisational models described in this volume are now readily measurable at the level of overall impact on the lives of clients (Felce and Lowe, Chapter 8, McGill and Mansell, Chapter 9, Dockrell et al, Chapter 11). Disentangling the impact of specific interventions, whether broader ecological interventions mixed with more specific interventions (Russell and Harris, Chapter 2) or specific interventions (Murphy et al, Chapter 1, Quine, Chapter 12) is more difficult. Quine's elegant analysis of the impact of interventions to solve sleep management problems represents one of the few clear cut instances of an intervention which was sufficiently powerful to override the influence of competing variables on behaviour. However, as Quine herself points out, the parents in her study were volunteers and, in addition, sleep problems occur in a defined, constant, context. How much effect the family variables described by Sloper and Turner (Chapter 4) might have in an unselected sample of parents is unclear.

For the majority of specific service interventions the impact of variables other than those manipulated is far less clearcut. The behaviour analytic approach recognises the complexity of the factors which influence any challenging behaviour. In addition, the findings from the epidemiological studies in this volume indicate that the majority of people with severe challenging behaviour show more than one such behaviour (Murphy et al, Chapter 1, p 13-14, 21, Russell and Harris, Chapter 2, p 44, Kiernan and Qureshi, Chapter 3, p 57). Disentangling the variables occasioning different challenging behaviour in an adult with long-established patterns of behaviour be extremely time-consuming. Moreover, once a programme has been developed maintaining programmes may be a constant task requiring considerable skilled input (Murphy et al, Chapter 1, p 31). Behaviour modification, with its widespread advocacy of 'bolt-on' contingencies to 'cure' challenging behaviour represented a simplistic, and potentially hazardous, solution (Remington, Chapter 6).

Behaviour analysis also focuses attention on the proposition that challenging behaviours are aspects of the individual's interaction with his or her total social and physical environment and, as such, that challenging behaviours may not 'disappear' from the individual's behavioural repertoire but require constant 'management'. This may explain the failure of the interventions described by Felce and Lowe (Chapter 8) and McGill and Mansell (Chapter 9). On the other hand these findings may reflect a relative failure to target challenging behaviour as the general management skills of staff improved.

The difficulties described in developing and maintaining effective behavioural interventions have to be placed in context. These difficulties relate, in particular, to interventions developed for individuals with well developed severe challenging behaviours. Research and practice utilising behaviour analysis is well established as an effective approach, even with such behaviours but, as we have seen, may be time consuming and difficult. With less severe challenging behaviours analysis and intervention is relatively less problematic. The data presented show that the majority of people with challenging behaviour do not present severe management problems. Interventions based on behaviour analysis should be provided for these individuals in order to improve their adaptation and quality of life and to, possibly, prevent their challenging behaviours from escalating to the point where management, and the lives of the individuals concerned, become more difficult.

Behaviour analysis is a rapidly developing field. Although British research has made some contribution there is an over-reliance on North American research and development. This results, mainly, from the reluctance of British research funders to encourage research concerned with controlled intervention studies based on single subject methodologies of the type described by Remington (Chapter 6). There is no doubt that this failure has a detrimental effect on the development of research and service development for people with challenging behaviour.

The relevant studies in this volume suggest that, at the time when the surveys were done, alarmingly few behavioural programmes were in place. Murphy and her colleagues (Chapter 1, p 7) identified 11 written psychological programmes in a population of 596 individuals. Russell and Harris (Chapter 2, p 45) found agreed written behaviour modification programmes for only three of 18 people presenting extreme management problems. Kiernan and Qureshi (Chapter 3, p 59) indicate higher reporting of written behaviour modification programmes (over 20 per cent). However the quality of these programmes was not assessed or their use monitored. Experience within the districts covered by the survey suggests that relatively few effective programmes are in place.

Training. The direct implication of these findings is that increased emphasis must be placed on the training and preparation of staff as well as on organisational factors. Here the contributors to this volume are in substantial agreement that staff skills are often woefully inadequate. In addition, from several viewpoints, it seems unlikely that this position will improve dramatically without national initiatives. Clements (Chapter 14, p 329) points out that we still need to identify 'competences needed by staff and managers to deliver particular kinds of services' and to 'promote models of training likely to deliver the competences required'. He argues that training needs to be linked closely to actual work with clients (cf Quine, Chapter 12) and that the type of short course training in one-off blocks typically offered to staff, although probably completely ineffective, is 'irresistible in terms of the reinforcement contingencies operating on all those involved' (p 327).

One factor which plays a part in determining the current pattern of training is cost. In practice many staff in adult services receive no paid training because Social Service training budgets are too meagre or are prioritised in other directions. McGill and Bliss (Chapter 13) note that recruitment of Social Services personnel to the full-time Manchester Diploma Course is difficult because of the costs of secondment. Recruitment from Health Authorities is currently easier but a part-time version of the course is being developed because of unmet need.

The courses described by McGill and Bliss also represent two of possibly only four such courses in the UK. There has been no national initiative to encourage field agencies to set up and run parallel courses. This means that there is only a trickle of qualified students entering services. The need for people trained in the use of behaviour analysis who can also establish and maintain Teams of the type described by Emerson and his colleagues (Chapter 10) is quite clear. Both of the courses experience difficulties in recruiting placement supervisors who have appropriate competences, again underscoring a national problem.

McGill and Bliss (Chapter 13), Emerson and his colleagues (Chapter 10) and Mansell (Chapter 15), along with others in this volume, point to the dangers of seeing challenging behaviour as a focused issue which a few highly trained practitioners can address effectively. We have seen in this Chapter that prevalence studies of challenging behaviour typically identify around one in six people with learning disabilities who are in services. Concentration of resources on the relatively few people with severe challenging behaviour at the expense of others in need is a questionable approach. There is an urgent need to enhance the overall skills of the workforce so that the challenging behaviours of all people with learning disabilities can be appropriately managed. In this context Mansell (Chapter 15, p 345) emphasises the need for broader strategic planning 'especially in relation to developing a skilled workforce'.

CONCLUSION

This Chapter has not attempted a detailed summary of all of the important points concerning policy, service planning and clinical practice which have been raised in the book as a whole. What it has tried to do is, to a degree, complement Mansell's chapter by drawing out further some of the strengths and weaknesses of the translation of research into practice. It indicates some of the successes of research, in particular in clarifying issues concerning the population of clients and in presenting well-researched models of analysis and intervention. These studies should help to reinforce examples of effective practice developed by field agencies. What seems to be clear from this volume is that there is a great deal known about how to develop good services and, within them, effective programmes. Mansell's call for Government leadership in order to ensure that good practice becomes universal can be extended to cover research which could ensure that good practice becomes excellent.

REFERENCES

AMAN M AND SINGH N (1983). Pharmacological intervention. IN J L Matson J A Mulick (Eds) *Handbook of Mental Retardation*. New York: Pergamon.

CLARE I C H AND MURPHY G H (1993). MIETS (Mental Impairment Evaluation and Treatment Service): A service option for people with mild mental handicaps and challenging behaviour and/or psychiatric problems. III: Follow-up of the first six clients to be discharged: Diverse measures of the effectiveness of the service. *Mental Handicap Research, 6,* 70-91.

GOLDIAMOND I (1974). Toward a constructional approach to social problems: Ethical and constitutional issues raised by behavior analysis. *Behaviorism, 2,* 1-84.

GUNN J, MADEN A AND SWINTON M (1991). *Mentally Disordered Prisoners.* London: Home Office.

KHAN A M, CUMELLA S, KRISHNAN V, IQBAL M, CORBETT J AND CLARKE D (1993). New long-stay patients in a mental handicap hospital. *Mental Handicap Research, 6,* 165-173.

KIERNAN C C (1985). Behaviour modification IN A M Clarke, A D B Clarke and J M Berg (Eds) *Mental Deficiency: The changing outlook* (4th Edition). London: Methuen.

KIERNAN C C (1993). Portage Survey 1992: Preliminary analysis, January 1993. Unpublished note.

KIERNAN C C AND KIERNAN D (1987). Challenging behaviour in schools for children with severe learning difficulties. Paper presented at the TASH Conference, Chicago.

MURPHY G AND CLARE I C H (1991). MIETS (Mental Impairment Evaluation and Treatment Service): II psychological assessment and treatment, outcome for clients, and service effectiveness. *Mental Handicap Research, 4,* 180-206.

MURPHY G, HOLLAND A, FOWLER P AND REEP J (1991). MIETS (Mental Impairment Evaluation and Treatment Service): a service option for people with mild mental handicaps and challenging behaviour or psychiatric problems. - I. Philosophy, service and service users. *Mental Handicap Research, 4,* 41-66.

RICHARDSON S A AND KOLLER H (1985). Epidemiology. IN A M Clarke, A D B Clarke and J M Berg (Eds) *Mental Deficiency: The changing outlook* (4th Edition). London: Methuen.

INDEX

Age, and challenging behaviour,..6, 11, 43, 56, 62, 91-92
Age, parental,..82, 95-96
Aggressive behaviour,..14, 21, 38-50, 59-62
Alternative care,..94-101
Aversives,..30, 128, 140-141, 146-151

Behaviour analysis,......................................124-129, 136-145, 150-153
Behaviour modification,....................111-112, 121-122, 126, 136-139, 143-144
152-153, 157, 193
Biological factors,..153-159, 162

Case management,...235-236
Challenging behaviour,.....54-64, 192-193, 195-196, 197-198, 202, 210-211, 216,
218, 223-224
Challenging behaviour, definition,................................4, 40, 54, 61, 248
Children,..2, 5, 42, 43, 54, 70-84, 236
Chronicity,...14, 21-22, 43, 199-200, 248
Communication skills,........................13-14, 49, 56, 82, 161-164, 166, 194, 215
Costs, to families,...93, 100-101
Costs, of services,..261-265
Crisis intervention,..44, 238-239

Dangerous behaviour,...40, 248-250
Down's syndrome,...70-84

Engagement,..195-196, 202, 217-218, 254-255
Epidemiology,..2-31, 61-62, 91, 159-160
Evaluation,........................45-50, 213-216, 220-224, 257-260, 281-295

Families,..70-84, 90-112
Fathers,...71, 74, 81, 82, 83

Health,...77-79, 84, 168, 170

Interaction, staff-client,...216-219, 221, 253-256
Intervention,......................23-31, 44-50, 59, 61-62, 120-131, 169, 171, 277-281
Intervention, early,................29-31, 76, 83-84, 168-169, 170-171, 232, 237, 239

Management,.........................63, 199-200, 224, 225, 236, 317, 324-325, 337-338
Maternal adjustment,...79, 80, 292-295
Mild learning disability,...4, 246-269

Ordinary housing,..192-203, 213-214

Parents, advice to,...83-84, 101-110, 278-280, 283
Pharmacological treatment,...........6, 7, 20, 22, 23, 59-61, 64, 120-121, 130, 136,
238, 275
Physical restraint,...44, 63
Policy,..............................62-64, 83-84, 110-112, 120, 130-131, 172-177
200-203, 224-225, 239-240, 267-269, 299-300, 317-318, 322-344, 338-346
Prevalence,.........................2-8, 39-45, 54-62, 70-80, 192, 195-196, 202, 250-251
Prevention,..168, 170, 232, 237
Protective devices,...6-8, 10-27
Psychiatric diagnosis,...10, 245-269

Quality of life,...46, 49, 197-199, 260-263

Research,...130-131, 172-176, 225, 318, 325-326, 328
Respite care,...82, 99-101

Self injury,..2-31, 57-59, 99-100, 135-178
Sleep,...73, 79, 100, 274-300
Stress, parental,..90, 93, 97-101
Stress, staff,...46, 48-50
Support teams,..193, 209-226, 230-240, 334

Temper tantrums,...14, 57, 58, 196
Training, staff,......................63, 174-176, 214, 275-300, 306-318, 326-328, 329